BR
1608
,C6
D36
1991

Lilies Amongst Thorns

by

Danyun

Translated by Brother Dennis

CCU Library
8787 W. Alameda Ave.
Lakewood, CO 80226

Sovereign World

Sovereign World Ltd
PO Box 777
Tonbridge
Kent TN11 9XT
England

Copyright © 1991 Brother Dennis

All rights reserved. No part of this publication may be reproduced, stored in a retrieval system, or transmitted in any form or by any means, electronic, mechanical, photocopying, recording or otherwise, without the prior permission of the publisher.

ISBN 1 85240 095 1

CCU Library
8787 W. Alameda Ave.
Lakewood, CO 80226

Typeset by CRB Typesetting Services, Ely, Cambs.

Contents

Foreword

Lilies Amongst Thorns gives the great contrast of the cruelty and persecution of leadership in China and displays tremendous love, compassion and endurance among believers.

I've had the opportunity to visit with one of the pastors, who is described so much in the book, at a hotel several years ago. I know these stories to be true and real because they came out of his own mouth. While visiting with him I asked him and his wife if they would pray for me. I felt so humbled because of their love and compassion for those who persecute them and for their tremendous zeal to see China come to Christ.

This is a book that tells the facts. The facts hurt us and call us to our knees. Let's pray daily for the suffering Body in China and for great revival to break through in the hearts of the Chinese people.

Marilyn Hickey

Author's Preface

Beloved Reader:

As you are living in a democratic, free country relishing real freedom; as you are sitting in your comfortable churches worshipping God; as you are in your warm homes cherishing family happiness, do you realize that the Christians in China are today still confronting extreme brutal persecution? For several decades, many authorities have continually persecuted the children of God. They have fabricated all sorts of accusations of crimes, have arrested God's children and used torture in an effort to force them to confess. They have misused punishment and have implemented all sorts of diabolical methods. The Christians have encountered shocking humiliation.

These brothers and sisters fervently love the Lord. Not only have they endured this extremely tragic persecution, but they have even shone forth brilliantly for the Lord in that pitch-black hell on earth. They pay no attention to dangers and pain, and are willing to pay any price. They do not even consider their lives so that with all their strength they may save lost souls. The Spirit of the Lord helps them as signs and miracles follow. The love of the Lord captivates one heart after another. One by one wicked sinners repent and are born again. Prisons holding thousands of prisoners are set aflame by the Gospel. These prisons are turned into places of worship where the cross is preached.

These are remarkable incidents in the history of the Church. They are the splendour of the way of the cross, the songs of victory on the Gospel battlefield. Hallelujah! Who are these people? Are they messengers from heaven? Are they apostles? Are they prophets?

They are unlearned ordinary people, commonplace house-wives and daughters of common village farmers. Among these people, some have already been taken by the Lord and ceased their labours. Some are still active today, labouring in this great harvest field for the Lord. Some who have been sentenced to life imprisonment are still in prison labouring with all their might to save others. They have no hope of ever leaving prison, but their hope is that at the Lord's return they will be caught up to be with him.

Who are these? They are lilies amongst thorns, the cedars of Lebanon. They are heavenly people of whom the world is not worthy. They are the soldiers of Jesus Christ, the faithful children of God. The true testimonies recorded in this book are just a few examples among the hundreds of thousands of occurrences of persecution in China. Through these heroic and moving testimonies the reader can come to know the rampant power of Satan's darkness today. The deceptive mask of 'civilized behaviour' has been removed. The reader will be challenged to awaken quickly and know that persecution of the Church is the way of the cross, even as it says in the book of the prophets, '*This is the way, walk ye in it.*' (Isaiah 30:21)

We hope that all who read this book will pray fervently for the church in China and intercede for those who are faithful in suffering. We give this book into the hands of our Father God and ask His blessing on every reader.

Amen.

Author: Danyun
November, 1991

PART ONE

The Cedar of Lebanon

The Cedar of Lebanon

'When the Lord's disciples leave the earth they only sleep,
Though their friends are grieved they are comforted,
For Jesus died to redeem the sins of mankind.
When the Lord returns we will meet again.
It is only temporary separation, not eternal.
Soon the saints will meet again.
Today they are in Father's home praising the Lord's grace,
Waiting for the Lord's return to meet again!'

It was the night of October 17, 1989 at a certain village in China's Zhejiang Province. More than 1,000 brothers and sisters sorrowfully sang this song, *'Waiting for the Lord's return to meet again.'* As the band began to play the funeral music, the body of an old brother was slowly lowered into the casket as the sound of the cannon echoed. The booms of the cannon mingled with the noise of the brothers and sisters' crying and weeping. This resounded throughout the mountain valley.

One brother stood up, and with tears he told how this old servant of God, throughout his life, had faithfully and gloriously served the Lord. His name was Miao Zizhong, born in 1916. The Lord took him home in October 1989 at the age of 73. As a young person he had greatly opposed the Lord and despised the church of God. He constantly, without provocation, hurled insults at those who believed in the Lord.

In the spring of 1948, Zizhong contracted a fatal disease and even the large hospital declared they were incapable of helping him. As death drew near, a relative came and urged him to believe in Jesus. He accepted the illumination of the Holy Spirit, turned to the Lord, confessed his sin, and repented. Complete healing came to his body. Seven weeks after believing in the Lord, a pastor sent him to a certain area to preach the Gospel. From that time he began to serve the Lord fervently and suffered much for the Lord and the message of the cross.

In the winter of 1954, Zizhong was summoned to go before the rural government where he was sternly criticized and 'struggled against' by the cadres and people's militia. The cadre said, 'Belief in Jesus is the poison of imperialism and a tool of foreign intervention. Our nation only believes in Marxism. You are not permitted to believe in Jesus. If you continue to believe, this is counter-revolutionary ...' Having said that he commanded Zizhong to abandon his faith and write a statement saying he would leave the Church.

Zizhong very calmly answered, 'Jesus is the Saviour of my life. I would be ungrateful to deny him and as such I would go to hell. I cannot do this.' Upon hearing that the cadres began to gnash their teeth and with their fists they started beating Zizhong viciously. Zizhong prayed fervently asking the Lord for His help. The evil men used every method, but in the end were unable to coerce Zizhong into submission. Therefore they accused him of being anti-Marxist and opposed to 'the great leader.' Declaring him a 'counter-revolutionary,' they put him under public surveillance.

Soon the government fabricated charges of 'collaborating with overseas counter-revolutionary organizations' and had him arrested. He was sentenced to five years imprisonment at the end of 1954 and sent to Heilongjiang Province, the coldest part of China, for reform through labour. After some time, due to the fact that Zizhong not only persevered in his belief in Jesus, but even preached to the people in prison, his sentence was increased by ten years. He then began an extremely miserable and painful period of 15 years suffering in labour reform camp.

The second year after he arrived in Heilongjiang, he went through a great trauma. Previously his wife had been faithful and loving. Now that he had been sentenced to 15 years' imprisonment in which he would suffer starvation and exposure to extreme cold, what hope was there that he would ever come home alive? Therefore she wrote a letter to Zizhong requesting a divorce.

The evening that Zizhong saw that letter, he was so shocked he could not believe what his eyes were reading. When he realized it was truly his wife's request for a divorce, he was so furious he fainted. As he considered his condition he realized there was no one close to him. He was in a heartless prison and was facing ground covered with ice and snow, the prison guard's leather-thonged whip and endless 'struggle' sessions. Back home he had no parents, nor a single brother or sister . His only hope was the prayers of his wife and her words of comfort expressed in her letters. But this day she heartlessly severed their relationship. He lost the one person on earth who was close to him.

He felt so forlorn, so unfortunate. Taking no notice of the cold, he opened the cell door and ran to a grove where he fell on his knees on the snow covered ground and with loud sobs, wept before the Lord. He was unable to suppress his grief and tears flowed like a fountain. Suddenly he heard a very clear, personal and tender small voice from heaven saying, 'You must be patient that you may fulfill God's will and you will obtain the promise.' He then immediately thought of Psalm 73:25, *'Whom have I in heaven but thee? And there is none upon earth that I desire beside thee.'* He received comfort and strength and, as he poured out his heart to the Lord, he sang:

> *My family has deserted me, my friends ridicule me,*
> *Lord, My heart loves you.*
> *I patiently and humbly accept the reproach,*
> *Lord, My heart loves you.*
> *Lord, My heart loves you,*
> *My heart loves you now and forever,*
> *Let the oceans dry up and the stones be crushed,*
> *Lord, My heart loves you.*

He returned to his cell and immediately wrote a letter to his wife agreeing to the divorce.

There were a total of 1,300 prisoners in this labour reform

camp, but very few believed in the Lord. Therefore Zizhong, as a Christian, was constantly under observation. All around him people sent by the Public Security Bureau (PSB) were watching him daily. Once, as he was secretly preaching the Gospel they discovered him. Several prison wardens tied him up. They forced him to kneel on a small wooden stool that was only as wide as four fingers. The people swarmed around him and one by one they smacked his ears, spat on him and mocked him saying, 'Where is your Saviour? Tell him to come to take vengeance on us!' Zizhong knelt on the stool and put up with this for several hours. Due to the cords, his wrists became swollen and his legs turned numb. Everything suddenly turned black and he fell from the stool unconscious.

On several occasions they used a fire grate from the oven and had him hang it from his neck. This fire grate was made of cast iron and weighed more than 40 pounds. The prison warden then put a sign on it saying 'Miao Zizhong, the leader of counter-revolutionary superstition.' He was then forced to parade with this. After that they put handcuffs and feet stocks on him and put him in solitary confinement for several months.

During one winter, the weather was much colder than normal. Throughout Heilongjiang the temperature fell to $-45°$ Celsius. Many old and weak people froze to death. Later a plague swept through the labour reform camp. It spread quickly and the temperatures of the patients soared to $42°$ C. As a result, their eyes bulged out and their hands and feet went into convulsions as they died. It was a horrifying scene. Within a few days, of the 1,300 prisoners in the labour camp, 1,050 had died. The authorities dug a huge ditch nearby. They used trucks to move the dead bodies to this ditch and threw them into it in a mass burial.

Zizhong was also infected by this horrible disease and was examined by the doctor who shook his head saying, 'Here is another one.' Then he had some people take Zizhong to a room specially reserved for dead bodies from where they were taken for burial. Zizhong, lying among many dead bodies, though barely alive, was alert in his spirit. He prayed in his heart, 'Lord, I ask you to save me. Don't allow me to die here whereby your Name will be reproached. Heal me and allow me to return home in peace. I will serve you all the days of my life and do the work of an evangelist.'

Then an angel dressed in a white robe whose face showed forth glory came and stood in front of Zizhong. On his back was a medicine box in the form of a cross and tenderly he said, 'Is your name Zizhong? Do not fear, only believe.' Then he stretched out his right hand and taking hold of Zizhong's left hand led him out of that building. He was taken to a room that was very beautiful, of pure white beyond description. The angel had Zizhong sit upon a white chair and then he took a stethoscope from his breast. He took a white tube and put it in his mouth. The angel blew on it and all of a sudden he felt a cool sensation and became very comfortable.

When he came to, his sickness had left him. He immediately knelt among the dead bodies and loudly praised the Lord. He again dedicated himself and turned his whole life over to the Lord. He quickly ran away from the dead, running and singing 'Hallelujah.' He went to the doctor to ask for food. When the doctor saw him entering he was so shocked he broke into a cold sweat and stumbled backwards.

He cried out, 'You ..., you ..., you .... Are ... you ... a ... ghost?'

Zizhong laughed and said, 'Don't be afraid. I am Miao Zizhong. My God has already healed me and saved me from death. He has sent me to proclaim the way of salvation to you. Therefore you must believe in Jesus.'

Upon hearing that, the doctor immediately, very calmly knelt down saying, 'Your God is true. Jesus is alive. I now believe and ask Jesus to receive me.'

Hallelujah! Time and time again the Lord brought Zizhong from the fringe of death. In this desolate land of snow and ice enduring much tribulation and suffering he miraculously survived those 15 long years. Very few people who were taken to the labour reform camps in Heilongjiang came back alive.

At this time we would like to relate a true incident: Not too far from this particular labour reform camp there were more than 70 old servants of God who were also part of labour reform punishment. All of you can imagine the hunger, pain and persecution they went through.

One morning, the authorities of the labour reform farm led this group of more than 70 people to another place to work. To reach their destination they had to cross a river that was frozen over with ice. Those in charge ordered the group to cross. Who would ever have thought that when they reached the middle of the river, the ice would crack due to the weight of so many people? As a result, these faithful servants of God all fell into the icy water and most of them drowned. Even though they pulled out the survivors onto the river bank, their wet clothes soon became ice, and they all froze to death, except for one.

There was another important reason why Zizhong survived his term in Heilongjiang. He took advantage of every opportunity, mostly late at night when others were sleeping, to go out to the grove to pray. As a result, he received great strength, was able to overcome death and remain victorious in all adverse conditions.

In 1969 he completed his 15-year sentence in the labour reform prison and returned home. During those long years there were many difficulties and bitter experiences. He could share many testimonies of blood and tears in which he experienced God's covering and protection! As he was sitting on the train bound for home, his heart was racing faster than the train and it had already flown to his home village. He could visualize himself standing in the midst of the brothers and sisters sharing beautiful testimonies about the Lord. But his suffering had not ceased for there were still many tribulations and testings awaiting him.

When Zizhong returned to the countryside and entered a certain village, the Great Cultural Revolution was at its height. Many government officials and cadres were paraded in the street, 'struggled against' and attacked. How much more did the Christians face extreme testings and agony.

As soon as Zizhong returned home, he was immediately taken to the commune for questioning: 'After 15 years of labour reform, has your religious belief changed?'

Zizhong very solemnly answered, 'These 15 years of labour reform have not changed my belief; moreover my relationship with Jesus has been strengthened and my belief is stronger than ever.'

So, soon after leaving the prison, having served such a long term, Zizhong had to face merciless beatings again in which they used both their fists and truncheons.

In the summer of 1970, he was detained by the commune to enter a 're-education class.' They had also detained in this 'class' large numbers of hooligans, thieves, pimps, gamblers, etc. This group of extremely crude, degenerate people were accustomed to showing off their toughness and self-confidence. But in this place they were as a cock who had been defeated in a cock fight, heads bowed down and totally dejected. Zizhong had to remain among these people for 73 days. However he was not dispirited by them at all. In spite of the intervention and beatings he received from these evil men, he continually sang and prayed. More than once as he lifted up his rice bowl to give thanks, they stole the rice bowl from his hand and struck his head with a fierce blow.

They brought a very famous Buddhist monk to this place to be 'struggled against.' He daily felt dejected and constantly sighed to the extent that he even considered suicide. One day, they were taken out to be paraded in public.

Upon returning he said to Zizhong, 'I saw as they paraded you through the streets, you lifted up your head high. Have you forgotten where you are?'

Zizhong laughed and said, 'I am a disciple of Jesus. Wherever I am, this Jesus who rose from the dead, who is real and alive is with me. He causes me to have unlimited joy and peace. How about you? Since you are a disciple of Buddha, is it possible that Buddha doesn't come to bring you comfort?'

The monk had nothing to say.

One afternoon, it was extremely hot. There was hardly any movement in the leaves on the trees. It was so hot people had a hard time breathing normally. Zizhong and a group of criminals were tightly bound by several thugs and taken to a place called 'Dongao' where they were 'struggled against.' They built a high platform and many spectators gathered. These evil men forced Zizhong onto the platform. One by one the cadres brought accusations against Zizhong for the 'hideous crimes' he had committed. Then they demanded that Zizhong deny Jesus before the crowd and renounce his belief. Moreover they said, 'Today if you continue to believe in Jesus, we will beat you to death.'

Zizhong stood up before the crowd, and with an intense fiery gaze looked at all the people below the platform. Then with a ringing voice he said, 'Fellow countrymen, because of belief in Jesus I have already spent 15 years in the Heilongjiang labour reform prison where I was 'struggled against' and beaten several times. Yet my belief is stronger than ever. Why is that? Because the Lord Jesus whom I believe in is the true and living God. He is the Son of God, the Creator of heaven and earth. He was born for us, because of our sins He was crucified on the cross. Therefore all of you should repent, leave your idols, cease from violence and believe in Jesus that you may obtain eternal life.'

Upon hearing this, the crowd of ruffians pounced on Zizhong like an angry lion. Nineteen people began beating him with their fists. Some struck his head while others attacked all parts of his body. Others used their shoes, violently kicking him in the abdomen, waist and chest. The people below the platform only heard the voice of Zizhong loudly saying, 'Lord, forgive them. Lord, I commit my soul unto you.' Slowly Zizhong collapsed onto the ground. Yet he did not die, for there was still much tribulation for him to experience and much work to do. Though he was seriously injured, he recovered after several months.

Zizhong's father was born in a mountain village. Hence, Zizhong had many relatives there. They realised Zizhong was all alone where he lived and faced constant reproach. Therefore they used every method available to change his residence registration so that he could return to his original village. As the storm clouds became very black, Zizhong escaped the tiger's cave to enter the wolves' den. Within a few days of moving back to this mountain village, he was seized and taken in 'to study.' Early one morning, the village cadres proclaimed to all the villagers in the public square the history of Zizhong's 'counter-revolutionary' activities. Then they announced, 'At 8:00 a.m. in Dingyu village there is going to be a major struggle session. We desire all the members of the commune to be there.'

Many years previous to this the churches in this area were established. The brothers and sisters endured much persecution. In spite of this they continued to love the Lord fervently. When they realized this old brother who had already suffered so much tribulation was to be castigated again, they all began to intercede fervently for him with tears. Then they went early to the field where the 'struggle session' was to be held. In front of the platform, there gathered a huge crowd of those who believed in the Lord.

The village cadres tied up Zizhong and carrying their rifles, brought him up onto the platform. As he looked out from the platform he saw the brothers and sisters. One servant of God standing in the front nodding his head with compassionate eyes full of comfort conveyed encouragement and hope. As their eyes met, it was as if a hot current flowed through Zizhong's whole body. He immediately sensed a surge of physical strength and inner joy. A smile came upon his face.

A thug pushed Zizhong to the front, and lifting his right hand, shouted the slogan, 'Down with the counter-revolutionary Zizhong!'

'Resolutely come against religious superstition!'

However, only a few people standing below the platform followed him in these slogans. The procedure was the same as the last 'struggle session' he had to go through. First one of the thugs stood up and viciously attacked the church. He declared that Zizhong had put on the cloak of religion to carry out counter-revolutionary crimes. After that they ordered Zizhong to confess his crimes and deny Jesus.

The brothers and sisters below the platform then noticed that Zizhong's face was shining with glory, like that of an angel. He nonchalantly opened his mouth saying, 'bring out a knife and cut out my heart. You will then know what is in it.'

Saying that, he loudly began to sing this song: *'Be faithful! Be faithful! Proclaim this everywhere.'* The brothers and sisters hearing this were all so moved they began to weep. Immediately they all opened their mouths and sang with him:

> *Be faithful to what has been committed to you. Be faithful to your glorious Lord. Be faithful! Be faithful! Though*

everyone refuses to follow, in spite of facing difficulties, stand close to the side of the Lord. Allow the Lord to always see you faithful.'

When the group of ruffians realized the situation, they were so afraid that they did not know what to do. Several people immediately came forward and pushed Zizhong off the platform and took him to the headquarters of the rural government committee. The brothers and sisters, thinking the affair had ended, returned to their homes.

In the afternoon, these brutes first pressed their knees into Zizhong's back. They used a very thin nylon cord to tie him up. Then they took him out into the streets to have him publicly 'struggled against.' Many middle and primary school students followed Zizhong shouting loudly, 'Down with class enemies of all descriptions' (the Chinese phrase literally means 'strike down the cow demons and snake gods');

'Resolutely fight against the counter-revolutionary Miao Zizhong!'

'Down with the reactionaries!'

'Long live the Communist Party!'

Zizhong straightened his chest and walked forward. He knew he was not walking alone, for the Lord was with him. After several paces, the ruffians asked him, 'Do you still believe in Jesus?'

Zizhong answered resolutely, 'I believe and will believe to the end!' Before he had finished someone hit him on the head with a small iron hammer and a large lump immediately emerged.

After a few more steps, they asked again, 'Are you still going to believe?'

With a very loud voice he answered, 'I believe. Even if you beat me to death I will believe.'

The thugs hit him again with the hammer and there was another large lump on his head. As he walked they struck him often. Many more lumps developed on his head. After walking half to one kilometer, they had beaten him on the head so many times that it swelled to the size of a gourd. His eyes had sunk into his swollen face.

He was paraded past the door of a shop where there was a large pile of stones. The ruffians, using their knives, forced him forward so that he fell over, hitting the stones. Since his hands were bound very tightly, he could not support his body. As a result, three ribs were broken by the uneven edges. The thugs again lifted up Zizhong. Then his face turned extremely pale and he started gasping for air as blood started to flow from his mouth. He could barely stand. But these thugs did not release him and continued to beat him as he walked. As the crowd of people passed a public lavatory, the thugs prepared to throw him into a cesspool deeper than the height of a man. However, seeing a huge crowd looking on, they decided against it.

Yet they were not going to give up. They threw Zizhong's hat into the cesspool, and using a bamboo pole, soaked it thoroughly with human waste. They then retrieved it and set it on his head. The night soil ran down his head, onto his face and neck until it soaked his shirt. Then one of the thugs, using two pieces of bamboo, picked up a lump of dog excrement and stuffed it into Zizhong's mouth. He shut his mouth tight, but they smeared his mouth and lips with the smelly dog waste. Zizhong opened his mouth and began to spit it out, but all that came out was several mouthfuls of fresh blood.

Oh, what cruel inhumanity! Beloved brothers and sisters, do you realize that in the world today these tragedies are still happening? These thugs also took Zizhong to a large tree where they hung him up very high. Then they threw stones at him, cursing him at the same time. Zizhong soon passed out. Seeing that the sun was soon to set, the thugs then brought him down from the tree, threw him to one side and left him.

As the sun was setting its rays shone on Zizhong who was lying on the ground. As the light shone on his face, it showed one who was strong, unwilling to compromise and very courageous. He was such a beloved brother!

The sky soon turned black as night arrived. The brethren heard what had happened that day, and ran to where he was. They took Zizhong, who had been unconscious for a long time, to the home of a brother. They placed him on a soft comfortable bed. Many brothers and sisters stood around the bed weeping, asking the Lord to save His faithful old servant.

Zizhong eventually regained consciousness. He was unable to open his eyes, but he heard the sound of the brothers and sisters crying.

Opening his mouth with effort he said, 'My beloved brothers and sisters, do not weep for me. But weep for our rebellious nation, for our unbelieving countrymen, for our sinful leaders.' Upon hearing these words they were so moved they were unable to control the tears and each one began to cry even more loudly.

Miao Zizhong not only had a life full of testings and pain. His life was also full of fear and reverence toward the Lord. From the time they took him to the labour reform prison in the north until he returned to his village, where he suffered so much, up to his death, he would rise early each morning to intercede with weeping for the country, the people and the Church. Every morning after the time of prayer, he would put on his reading glasses and, under a small kerosene lamp, read the Bible. He would often not go to bed and even skipped meals to study the Bible. He put much effort in studying the Word, and so, became very familiar with the Bible. You could ask him the location of any verse in the Bible and he would tell you. However, he was not satisfied and very often humbly requested that the brethren teach him.

Each time he received a revelation from the Bible, he would jump up and dance with great joy. He remained single after his wife divorced him. For years he lived a hard life in which he constantly travelled for the work of the Lord. He experienced much bitterness in this life. Even so his life was full of joy. In every home he stayed there was always the sound of singing. As he got older his voice was stronger than most young people. Often he would sing, cry and laugh until tears flowed. One servant of God was a 'clan brother' who was very close to him. The two of them often met together to share from midnight through until morning. They loved to sing this song:

'When I was drowning in sin, all around were winds of sorrow and rains of grief; when fierce wolves were howling through the night; when my heart was stricken with fear until my strength was depleted; when the desolate mountains and lonely valleys were covered with thorns; when I

desired to go to that place where all would cease: What great love that searched and found me! What precious blood that cleansed me! What vast grace that led me back into the flock! What vast grace that led me back to the flock!'

The two of them would sing and sing until they were moved to tears.

Throughout his life Zizhong put great emphasis on the Lord's day. This day was a very holy day to him. From the time he received God's grace and salvation until his death, except for the 15 years he spent in the labour-reform prison in the north, during his 42 years of serving the Lord there were only four Sundays in which he did not attend church meetings.

During the last 18 years of his life, his situation slightly improved and he could devote more time and energy attending to the ministry of evangelism. He was totally submissive to the leading of the Holy Spirit and to the church and was totally faithful in his work. Wherever the Lord sent him he went. He never refused to go even to the most distant and inaccessible places.

For many years he travelled throughout the Wencheng mountain district and with tears urged the people to repent. Many times he faced dangers as he traversed steep, narrow mountain trails through snowstorms in order to visit the brothers and sisters. Therefore throughout the whole of the Wencheng mountain district the Gospel went forth and he established many churches. To obtain these goals he shed many tears and paid a great price!

He was a disciplined man and was careful about all his words and actions. He hated sin and in every manner was an example to the believers. His lifestyle was very simple. He never wanted a life of leisure or pleasure. He ate simple food (sweet potatoes and vegetables) and dressed in common clothes. He lived in a very small black house. Yet he felt what he already had could be considered too 'luxurious.' He was content therefore, with what he had.

He had a great love for the brothers and sisters and took a great interest in their families, spiritual life and livelihood. He continually exhorted them with tears, was concerned about them and led them. Before Zizhong died, he was bedridden for 80 days. Every day many brothers and sisters came from many places to visit him. Though he did not have any children, in reality he had more children than anyone else. Therefore he felt fulfilled and joyful.

On October 18, 1989 in the morning, more than 1,000 brothers and sisters buried this old 'brother and father in the Lord' on the mountain. As they lowered the casket into the grave, they all sang: 'Waiting for the Lord's return to meet again!' The sound of weeping and singing resounded throughout the valley. Faithful servant of God, may you rest in your Lord!

PART TWO

The Heavenly Man

Preface

A Bible Given by a Messenger of the Lord

Brother Yun was saved at the age of 16. His mother was a Christian; she came to the Lord at a very young age. During the Cultural Revolution, missionaries were persecuted and forced to leave the country, so many sheep were left without a shepherd. It was at this difficult time Yun's mother left the Lord.

When he was 16, his father became very ill. The doctor said there was no hope for him. One night, Yun's mother heard a very gentle voice saying, 'Jesus loves you.' She was awakened by the Lord. So she got up and knelt down to pray. Once again she repented of her sins and rededicated herself to the Lord. Quite miraculously, the next day, Yun's father was healed. Aware that it was Jesus who healed his father, Yun too accepted the Lord. He also decided in his heart to serve Jesus.

His mother then told him that all the teachings of Jesus were recorded in the Bible. From that day on, Yun longed to see a Bible. He asked the believers in Jesus what a Bible looked like. But none of them had ever seen a Bible before.

So one day, Yun walked more than 30 miles to visit a man who used to be a preacher.

As soon as he arrived, Yun told him the purpose of his visit. Seeing he was young the man did not dare show him the Bible.

He said, 'The Bible is the Word of God; it is the book of heaven. No man can have a Bible. But if you really want one, you can ask God for it.'

He also told Yun to fast and pray. Yun did not know what fasting was. The preacher explained to him, 'Fasting is to go without food. When the fullness of time has come, the Lord will give you a Bible.'

Yun returned home and fasted and prayed for two months. But he did not really know how to pray. Every time he prayed he would say, 'Lord, give me a Bible. Amen.' Two months passed. Nothing happened. Yun still had not received a Bible. So he went to see the preacher again.

The preacher said, 'When you ask the Lord for a Bible, you don't just kneel down and pray. You have to weep before the Lord as well. The more earnest you are, the sooner you'll get your Bible.'

This time he ate only one meal a day and prayed and wept before the Lord. Several months passed. One day early in the morning, while Yun was sleeping, he saw an old man in his dream.

The old man asked him, 'Brother Yun, do you have anything to eat?'

Yun answered, 'No.'

The old man then handed him a bun. When Yun stretched out his hand to take it, it turned into a Bible. Yun knelt down and wept saying, 'Blessed be the Name of the Lord! He heard my prayers and has given me a Bible.'

Then Yun awoke. His weeping had awakened his parents also. When they saw him crying like that, they thought he was crazy. Yun told them about his dream, but they were all the more convinced that he had gone insane. At that moment, the door suddenly opened and two men walked in. They did not know Yun at all, but they were led by the Holy Spirit to deliver a Bible to him.

From that day Yun would memorize one chapter of the Bible every day. One day while Yun was reading the book of Acts, the Lord appeared to him in a vision. He told Yun three times to go and preach the Gospel. The Lord even told Yun the exact place where he was to serve Him. It was several years later that the following incidents took place.

Chapter 1

When They Persecute You in This City, Flee to Another

(Matthew 10:23)

It was 1984. Night was descending on Heping town, which borders Henan and Hubei Provinces. It was so dark, that stretching out your hand, you could not see your fingers. Freezing cold wind from Siberia whipped up stacks of hay that fell onto two men walking in the night. Several dogs emerged from the village lanes and barked frenziedly at them.

As the men walked they wrapped their ragged coats tightly around them and quickly stepped down the path leaving the village towards a large fish pond. One of them was Brother Ming from 'F' city who was over 30 years old and the other was Brother Yun from 'G' county who was in his twenties.

Both were ignorant, unlearned and insignificant men who were chosen by the Lord. They went from village to village and from town to town. Daily, tears streamed down their faces as they pleaded with people to repent and believe in Jesus. They encouraged the brothers and sisters to 'watch and pray and fervently love the Lord, for the day of the Lord is near.' They were full of grace and the power of the Lord and signs and wonders followed them. Wherever they went, many people repented and believed in the Lord. Lukewarm churches were revived and the churches in the southern part of Henan Province were established.

Just as the churches were experiencing revival, a great persecution broke out. The authorities, under the pretext of persecuting the 'Yellers Sect,' falsely charged many godly, precious brethren with being 'counter-revolutionaries of the Yellers Sect.' Many were arrested, suppressed, harmed and given severe sentences. The brethren fled their homes to avoid being arrested and to continue the Lord's work. Among the many who were being sought were two key people, Brother Ming and Brother Yun. They evaded arrest by the Public Security Bureau (police), and never ceased to do the work the Lord had given them.

On that day, they had gone to Heping Town on the border of Hubei Province. They had planned to visit the brothers and sisters, little knowing that the situation there was especially tense. Just that morning, Brother Enshen had been sentenced and the church was facing great persecution. The brothers and sisters, therefore, were fearful and no believer dared to receive Ming and Yun into their homes that night. It was already dark and the two brothers were unable to find a place to stay. There were many people's militia patrolling the streets. Therefore they had to leave. They decided to spend the night at a fish pond outside town.

As the night grew on, the wind blew more fiercely. It became colder and colder and the two men knelt on the embankment of the fish pond, their teeth chattering. They could only hug each other tightly and cry out to the Lord, 'Lord, dispel the dark cloud over China, change this environment, have mercy on our nation and save our people ....'

Brother Yun was inspired to sing this song:

> *That the Lord would allow me to live, to only love my Lord,*
> *To use all my heart, strength and talents, to only love my Lord,*
> *Regardless of what happens, to only love my Lord,*
> *In all my actions and words, to only love my Lord.*
>
> *In times of humility to learn from the Lord, to only love my Lord,*
> *In times of need to be joyous, to only love my Lord,*
> *Whether I face hunger or am full, to only love my Lord.*
> *I am His in life or death, to only love my Lord.*

For the Lord gave His life for me,
My depth of sin has been pardoned,
I have dedicated my life to Him,
To only love My Lord.

After about four in the morning, the two men were unable to stand the freezing cold. Suddenly, Brother Yun saw a vision. He saw that in this county everywhere Christians were being persecuted, arrested and many of the brethren had been chained and thrown into prison. Brother Yun said to Brother Ming: 'Let us leave here quickly.' They continued their journey in the dark, not even waiting for the dawn.

Chapter 2

Great Things He Must Suffer for My Name's Sake

(Acts 9:16)

After Ming and Yun left Heping town, they went to county 'A' in Henan Province. As they went they wept and sang Acts 20:22–24:

> 'And see, now I go bound in the spirit to Jerusalem, not knowing the things that will happen to me there, except that the Holy Spirit testifies in every city, saying that chains and tribulations await me. But none of these things move me; nor do I count my life dear to myself, so that I may finish my race with joy, and the ministry which I received from the Lord Jesus, to testify to the Gospel of the grace of God.'

The situation in 'A' county was also very tense. Along the roads, in the villages, everywhere one could see posters against God, signs attacking the church and wanted posters naming the brethren the government wanted to arrest. The brothers and sisters here were different from those in Heping town. They truly loved the Lord and God's servants and were willing to risk death by receiving those brothers and sisters who were wanted by the police.

The co-workers in 'A' county convened a meeting on December 15 to encourage one another to stand steadfast and be victorious in these adverse circumstances. Ming and Yun, together with Brother Jian, took turns to preach in this meeting. Brother Yun stood up. He was about 25 years old, of medium build and for the sake of the Lord travelled and laboured all the year long. He was skinny as a rod. His face, usually bright with a smile, was unusually sombre. Under his bushy eyebrows were a pair of large eyes that conveyed warmth and intense strength.

The brothers and sisters began the meeting with a song:

To be a martyr for the Lord

1. *From the time the early church appeared on the day of Pentecost,*
   The followers of the Lord all willingly sacrificed themselves.
   Tens of thousands have sacrificed their lives that the Gospel might prosper.
   As such they have obtained the crown of life.

2. *Those apostles who loved the Lord to the end,*
   Willingly followed the Lord down the path of suffering.
   John was exiled to the lonely isle of Patmos.
   Stephen was crushed to death with stones by the crowd.

3. *Matthew was cut to death in Persia by the people.*
   Mark died as his two legs were pulled apart by horses.
   Doctor Luke was cruelly hanged.
   Peter, Philip and Simon were crucified on a cross.

4. *Bartholomew was skinned alive by the heathen,*
   Thomas died in India as five horses pulled apart his body,
   The apostle James was beheaded by King Herod,
   Little James was cut up by a sharp saw.

5. *James the brother of the Lord was stoned to death,*
   Judas was bound to a pillar and died by arrows,
   Matthias had his head cut off in Jerusalem.
   Paul was a martyr under Emperor Nero.

6. *I am willing to take up the cross and go forward,*
   To follow the apostles down the road of sacrifice.
   That tens of thousands of precious souls can be saved,
   I am willing to leave all and be a martyr for the Lord.

Chorus:
To be a martyr for the Lord, to be a martyr for the Lord,
I am willing to die gloriously for the Lord.

They sang with all their might and the whole meeting place was shaken. One could only hear the sound of weeping. Yun was full of the power of the Holy Spirit and preached with great authority. On the morning of the third day, Brother Jian prophesied that, 'Within three days, there will be some among us who will suffer for the Lord and be bound.'

That evening it began to snow heavily. Soon a thick blanket of white covered the mountain. Nearby one could hear the sound of branches breaking under the weight of the snow. Some of the older homes in the village were also unable to withstand the heavy layer of snow and collapsed. Outside, it was unbearably cold and drops of water quickly turned into ice.

Inside the meeting place, a fervent fire was burning in the hearts of the brothers and sisters as the sound of intercession and praise ascended into heaven.

The meeting did not end until midnight and everyone left, going to the homes of different believers to rest. Brother Yun and several other brethren had not gone very far, when a group of people approached them. There were more than ten men with torches in their hands. As they rushed toward Brother Yun they cried with a loud voice, 'What are you all doing?' The brethren immediately sensed something was wrong, so they turned and ran. But one of them caught hold of Yun and used the electric (cattle) rod on him. His whole body was being electrocuted and he felt as if he had been stung by a scorpion or as if a thousand arrows had pierced his heart. He fell over, unable to move in the snow.

This group of people were from the rural Public Security (police) substation. Without a word, they tied up Yun very tightly. Suddenly, an intimate voice from above said to Yun, 'I know.' (See Revelation 2:9) Immediately all the pain and fear left him.

With a harsh voice someone shouted, 'Where are you from? 'What is your name?

'What are you doing here?

'How many were with you?

'Where are they now? Answer quickly, otherwise you will be beaten to death.'

Yun was very tense. He was not concerned about his own safety, but about Brothers Ming, Jian and many other co-workers. How could he warn them about trouble? He immediately thought of David when he feigned insanity. He called out very loudly:

'I am ... a ... **heavenly ... man**, live in **gospel ... village**. My name is **true ... new ... creation**. My father is **full of grace**. My mother is **faith ... hope ... love**.'

The police began to kick him, and said angrily, 'What kind of nonsense is this? We asked you where you came from and where are those who were with you!'

Yun answered loudly, 'They are all in the village back there.'

'Move, take us to them. If you are not telling the truth we will skin you alive,' the PSB threatened.

Yun then led the police back to the village, shouting as he went, '*I am a heavenly man*. The PSB has apprehended me.' He shouted at the top of his voice hoping the brethren would hear. A group of more than ten local brothers and sisters heard the commotion, and came out to see.

The PSB immediately asked them, 'What are you doing here?'

One sister said, 'Watching a movie.'

As soon as Yun heard that, he immediately thought of 1 Corinthians 4:9 and said silently to the Lord, 'Lord, I ask you to help me so I can act out a very good play for the world and angels to see!' Yun walked slowly, dragging his feet.

The PSB asked Yun, 'Which house is it? Quickly lead us there!'

Yun deliberately acted like he was confused and, feigning surprise, said, 'It is not this village, it is that village.'

His answer infuriated the police so much so that they used their fists, feet, electric rods, wooden truncheons and gun handles to viciously beat Yun. If it were not for the protection of the Lord, without a doubt Yun would have been beaten to death. When the brothers and sisters following Yun saw how cruelly he was being beaten, they all began to weep quietly.

Yun, fearful that they would be implicated, shouted out, 'I am a **heavenly man**, and do not recognize any of you. How could you possibly know me?'

Yun was taken to the police station. Brother Jian and three other brethren were also arrested and taken there. Several old mothers who were believers came, some on crutches, despite the weather to bring blankets, rice and vegetables. When the police asked them who these items were for, they replied, 'For the heavenly people.'

Yun heard this from inside his cell and tears welled up in his eyes. The love of the brothers and sisters gave him such warmth. In northern 'A' county, the temperature seldom fell below −15° Celsius. Yun's feet were numb with cold and his whole body shook all over. The handcuffs made it worse, for the more he shook the tighter the handcuffs felt. Yun likened himself to an eagle that stretched out its wings but was suddenly put in an iron cage. He continually called, 'Jesus' and sang choruses.

Yun noticed that in his cell there was a large drum so he immediately lifted up his handcuffed hands and began to beat on it. He sang Psalm 150 to the beat of the drum,

> *'Praise you the Lord, in the firmament of his power praise Him ... For his mighty acts praise Him ... use drums and cymbals to praise Him ....'*

He stood up and danced. His hands slowly regained feeling and his whole body felt warm. The guards were not amused. However, as they were all sleeping in their warm quilts, no one bothered to get up to stop this 'crazy man.'

The next morning, Yun, Jian and three other brethren were taken to the courtyard of the police station. The snow was piled high on the ground. The police unlocked their handcuffs and said to them, 'Today we have been generous with you and have removed your handcuffs. You must sweep away the snow in this courtyard. As for this "heavenly man," not only will we not loose his handcuffs, we will severely punish him.'

At that the man ordered Yun to kneel. But Yun said, 'I will not kneel before you, I will only kneel before my Lord, my God.'

Then the man said mockingly, 'I am your Lord. Only kneel before me and I will immediately release you.'

Yun said angrily, 'In the name of the Lord I say, you are not my Lord. My Lord is in heaven and I am a **heavenly man**.'

The man then switched on the electric rod and, with a sneer said, 'If you are a heavenly man, you will not fear the electric rod. Come, put your hands on the electric rod.'

He was forced by several other police to stretch out his hands towards the electric rod. As the power flowed through his body he immediately called out, 'Lord, save me!' The electric rod stopped working and he was able to hold on tightly to it with his hands staring at the one who declared he was the 'Lord.' He was so dumbfounded he broke into a cold sweat and, throwing down the electric rod, ran away.

That day, the five brethren were put into a stuffy vehicle and taken to the detention centre of the Public Security Bureau of 'A' county. As Yun and Jian were being taken to a certain prison cell, they realized that without a doubt many brothers and sisters would be here, too, as a result of this persecution. Yun, therefore, shouted, 'I am a **heavenly man**. A **heavenly man** will not become a Judas. A **heavenly man** must be strong and bold.'

A brother was brought in and asked by the PSB officials if he was a heavenly man. He denied it, saying, 'I am not a heavenly man, I am an earthly man.' The PSB official said, 'OK, since you are an earthly man, you will be locked up with a heavenly man.'

When he entered Yun's cell, Yun looked him in the eyes and said, 'We should tell Satan NO! NO! NO!' As he said this he stood up and while repeating 'NO' he wrote over and over on the wall 'NO! NO! NO!' until his fingers bled and the characters 'NO! NO! NO! appeared on the wall in blood. That brother was so ashamed he bowed his head and wept with sorrow.

The brothers and sisters had brought blankets, clothes and socks for Yun. But what he actually received was only a ragged quilt with the words 'Heavenly Man' written on the top. Still, Yun gave thanks to the Lord. They also brought him a new pair of boots, but the man in charge of guarding him seized them.

Life in prison was very difficult. For each meal the prisoners ate smelly, mouldy sweet potato paste mixed with some roots. Once a week they were allowed one small 'mantou' (steamed bread). A few days after entering prison it was Yun's turn to eat a mantou. Upon receiving it, with both hands he lifted up this mantou of two ounces, knelt down and thanked the Lord.

As he was giving thanks, a fellow prisoner snatched the mantou from his hand and hid it in his shirt. Yun continued to kneel on the ground with his hands lifted up. The monitor of that cell, noticing the mantou in his hand had disappeared, immediately began to question each prisoner in the cell. Everyone said they did not know where it went.

The monitor reported it to the prison police who searched each prisoner. As a result, they found the culprit. The prison police ordered him to kneel on the ground and then urged the other prisoners to beat him viciously. Most of these prisoners were hooligans and ruffians, full of hatred. They greatly enjoyed being allowed to beat up someone. They immediately began to strike and kick that prisoner with their fists and feet until blood started flowing from his nose, eyes and mouth. Like a small chicken they lifted him up and put his head in a bucket of urine until there was no more movement and he fell over dead on the floor.

Seeing that he was dead, Yun felt a surge of guilt and started sobbing uncontrollably. Brother Jian felt equally so distressed that he could hardly swallow his mantou. That evening they spent the whole night crying and praying. The next morning, the prison guard incited the prisoners to beat Yun. This became a daily routine for several days.

His body was already very weak. How could he survive the severe beatings of these ruffians? They knocked Yun onto the ground and they stamped on his chest and stomach. Yun began to spit out blood. He was barely alive. Brother Jian held Yun, sobbing uncontrollably.

Among them was a young prisoner whose mother was a Christian, but he had not yet believed in the Lord. Yet having spent several days with Yun in the same cell he felt strongly that Yun was not a mental case at all, but an outstanding person. He saw the manner in which Yun was beaten up. His feet were bare and had turned purple with cold. Blood constantly flowed from his mouth and his body frequently convulsed. He could not but weep tears of compassion for Yun and really felt for him. He was so moved by Yun's plight he even used his own ragged overcoat to cover Yun.

The Bible says, *'Blessed are the merciful, for they shall obtain mercy.'* (Matthew 5:7). The next day, they brought this young man out of the cell and allowed him to cook in the kitchen. Not long after, they released him from prison and he eventually became a Christian.

The PSB from 'A' county interrogated Yun several times. Despite severe beatings they were not able to extract any information from Yun. So, they sought help from the PSB offices of the surrounding counties, cities and districts, asking them to send people to identify him. They sent in pictures of wanted men, but Yun was not among any of them.

On January 25 the PSB officials of 'B' city came with photographs. When Yun entered the interrogation room, the supervisor of 'B' city PSB immediately recognized him. He laughed loudly, 'You put on a good act pretending to be insane. You think you are a very clever man, but there is no way you can elude me.'

Yun was denied breakfast. Before taking him to 'B' city, the police beat him up again. His eyes were blackened and his face was so swollen that he was unrecognizable. They crossed his hands and handcuffed them so tight the metal cut deeply into his flesh. Yun thought that he would certainly die and asked the Lord to receive his spirit. Instead, they transferred him to 'B' city Public Security Bureau.

Chapter 3

He Fasted Forty Days and Nights
(Matthew 4:2)

He that believes on me ... will do greater things than these.
(John 14:12)

On January 25 (the 23rd day of the 12th month of the Chinese lunar calendar), it was freezing as a blizzard moved down from the north. In the police truck, Yun was in so much pain he could hardly bear it. His clothes were soaked with blood. The handcuffs cut into both hands and if he moved even slightly the pain was as if 'ten thousand arrows pierced the heart'.

Yun thought, 'I have already spent several days in 'A' county. I wonder how they will deal with me at the PSB of 'B' city?' As he was thinking, the Word of the Lord came to him with great impact:

> *'Be still, and know that I am God ... The LORD of hosts is with us; the God of Jacob is our refuge.'*   Psalm 46:10–11

The fear and doubt in Yun's heart immediately left him. He received a fresh impartation of strength from the Lord.

As the truck passed through the streets of 'B' city, everywhere one could see red and green banners that read: 'Celebrate the arrest of the counter-revolutionary Yun by the Public Security Bureau!'

'The apprehension of the counter-revolutionary Yun is good news for the people of 'B' city!'

'Be resolute in striking down the Christian counter-revolutionary leader Yun!'

'Resolutely support the people's government of 'B' city in

the arrest and prosecution of the counter-revolutionary Yun who has clothed himself in the cloak of religion!'

These banners could be seen everywhere inside and outside the gates of the Public Security Bureau and within the detention centre. The news of Yun's arrest spread quickly and many PSB officials rushed from everywhere to see him. When they beheld a short, skinny man with an unimposing face covered with blood, and dressed in ragged clothes, his hair dishevelled and feet bare, they could not help but burst out in laughter.

One cadre said with great conceit, 'We have a net covering the heavens that is without any holes. Even if you had three heads and six arms, don't ever think you can escape the long arm of our law! Today you had better admit defeat. Your co-workers so-and-so and so-and-so have already fallen into our hands. Your church is now finished and you are all totally defeated!'

Upon hearing these arrogant words, indignation swelled in Yun's heart. But, not wanting to play into their hands, he simply smiled and said, 'The Gospel has been proclaimed everywhere under heaven and the truth has entered the hearts of tens of thousands.'

Yun's trial began almost immediately. The judge said condescendingly to Yun, 'Yun, you've gone through enough for today. You should realize how severe your crimes are. But the policy of the Party is that of leniency towards those who confess, and severe punishment to those who resist.

'Today, the government is giving you a way out. All you have to do is to report honestly in detail to the government about all your activities during the past several years, exactly how you opposed the leadership of the Party and the details of your organization. After which you will be set free and allowed to return to your home, family and mother and be with them during the lunar New Year.'

Yun answered hesitatingly, 'Look, I have been beaten in this manner and for several days have not eaten. I have no strength to speak. Moreover what you want to know has been going on for many years. I cannot recall the details right off. I request that you give me several days to think about this. Then I will tell you about it.'

The judge felt that Yun's words made sense and said, 'All right. I will allow you time to consider. But how many days will you need?'

Yun answered, 'The day that I have thought this through I will notify you.'

Yun was sent to the detention section of the prison. To enter this section they had to pass through four iron gates before they arrived at the Number Two prison ward. Surrounding this ward was a tall brick wall with an electric fence on the top. On top of the wall were four guardhouses at each corner. In the guardhouses prison police were on duty round the clock. It was truly a high security prison with a terrifying atmosphere.

On entering this prison one felt as if one was entering a den of devils. Yun realized that he would face great testing in this place. He determined that for the sake of the Gospel, for the many souls there, and in order that he might be completely victorious during this time of imprisonment, he would enter a time of fasting and prayer in which he would neither eat nor drink.

However, he faced great temptation from the time he began to pray and fast. They usually gave the prisoners only small portions of coarse rancid food. But that day was a major holiday. Therefore, as an expression of 'the humanitarian face of the great revolution,' and following the customs of the local populace, the authorities showed 'kindness' to the prisoners.

That evening, each person was allowed to have one small mantou and a bowl of soup with celery and pork. Upon receiving this food, these starving prisoners who were on the verge of passing out, devoured it like hungry lions. They gobbled it down and literally licked the bowl clean.

Yun had pretended to be a 'lunatic' for several days now and had since taken very little food. During that whole day he had not had one grain of rice and was so ravenous his stomach began to growl. Looking at the 'gourmet feast' before him, how could he not at least partake of a little? Satan greatly tempted him. For a while, in Yun's spirit a battle took place and he was in great pain. Thank the Lord, he remembered how Jesus was victorious. Then, trusting in the power of the Holy Spirit, he was able to overcome the devil's temptations. This was an important beginning and the key to victory for the 74 day fast that he was now to begin.

Yun gave his portion of food to the monitor of that cell and he in turn shared it with the other prisoners. Even though each inmate received only a very small amount, still they were extremely glad. As a result of Yun's gesture, the other prisoners began to develop a good attitude towards him. They all asked Yun to sing a song for them. He very happily sang this song:

1. *The northern wind blows, the southern breeze arises;*
   In everything God's will is done.
   The northern wind is strong and cold, but it will not last
   *   long;*
   Soon the southern breeze will arise.
   Be patient and wait, be patient and wait;
   The Lord has a time for everything.
   When the time has come, when the time has come,
   Abundant grace will be available to you.

2. *You who are sorrowful, don't sigh any longer;*
   The Lord will undertake for you.
   If the Heavenly Father does not permit,
   Who can do anything against you?
   Be patient and wait, be patient and wait;
   The Lord has a time for everything.
   When the time has come, when the time has come;
   Abundant grace will be available to you.

It was as if the prisoners understood, and yet they did not really understand. But they all believed in fate, therefore they had great interest in this song. Yun used this opportunity to speak to them from Psalm 90:10 and Hebrews 9:27: '*And as it is appointed unto men once to die, but after this the judgment,*' explaining what 'fate' was. Having spoken for over half an hour, Yun's head and chest became extremely painful.

He said to them, 'My head and chest hurt badly. Forgive me for I cannot speak any more. Starting from today, I cannot take any food. I will divide my rations among all of you. But you must not tell the leaders about this. If you tell them you cannot share my food.'

The prisoners were naturally willing to cooperate. Moreover, just before and after the lunar holiday the rations were a lot better than for the rest of the year.

On the 27th day of the 12th month (January 29, 1984) Yun was again taken out for interrogation. The presiding judge asked Yun, 'During these few days have you considered your answer? If you have, today give an account of everything so that you can return home for the lunar New Year holiday.'

Yun answered calmly, 'I have done so many things that I am unable to put them in order in such a short time. I would not like to make a report to you about matters that I myself am not able to clarify, lest during the New Year holiday my affairs cause you unhappiness.' Again, the judge felt it made sense. Without saying a word, he motioned to the prison police to take him away.

Thank the Lord! Back in prison, Yun reflected on overcomers and how they overcame. He thought of how Jesus died, of Joseph in prison, of Daniel in the lion's den, of the three courageous men in the fiery furnace. He also thought about Stephen who was stoned to death, Paul who was a prisoner on several occasions and of Peter in Acts 12. He recalled how in the past on many occasions the Lord had delivered him from evil. He continued to think on these things and knew he was as peaceful and safe as a baby nursing at its mother's bosom.

The Lord gave him the key to victory: 'Do not fear, only believe. Do not look at circumstances, do not look at yourself and do not look to men. Look only to the Lord, pray much and you will certainly see the Lord's glory.' Thereafter, he lay down and daily rested in the Lord. He continually meditated in his heart and used words of understanding to sing. He often sang Psalms 23, 34, 146, and Romans 8:35–39.

Time passed quickly and soon it was the New Year. On the 10th day after the lunar New Year (February 11), they interrogated Yun once again. This time they had to carry him to the interrogation room. The PSB officials saw Yun's eyes tightly closed as he lay on the floor motionless. They asked him several questions, but he did not even open his mouth. They thought he was pretending and started whipping him with their leather whip.

The prisoner who carried Yun in said, 'The day this man entered prison he said his head and chest were very painful. For more than ten days he has not eaten anything.' There was nothing the PSB officials could do but to have that man carry Yun back to the cell.

From January 25 to March 2, Yun had fasted and gone without water. For two days, he was carried out several times to face interrogation. Each time he did not say a word, but closed his eyes tightly and paid no attention at all. The PSB used every method imaginable including torture, but could not get him to open his mouth.

Although Yun was as thin as a stick, within his spirit he realized that his communion with God intensified greatly. As his fast entered the 38th and 39th day, there was suddenly an intense battle in his heart. Satan said to him, 'Yun, Jesus fasted only 40 days. Can the student be greater than the teacher? How can the servant be greater than his Lord? How could you surpass 40 days?'

Yun was tormented in his heart and the road before him seemed so black. A fearful feeling of discouragement and hopelessness came upon him to the degree that he even considered suicide. However, he knew that the sin of suicide was the same as murder. He did not know what to do, but to call on the Lord. 'Lord, what should I do? I ask you to take my soul!'

Suddenly, the light of the Holy Spirit shone and the Word of the Lord came upon him with great power, 'My son, *I know your works: behold, I have set before you an open door, and no man can shut it: for you have a little strength, and have kept my word, and have not denied my name.*' (Revelation 3:8) Hallelujah! The darkness fled and Satan was defeated. Then Yun's heart was filled with light, filled with power and filled with joy.

He could not restrain himself and began to sing gently to the Lord, '*While I live I will praise the LORD: I will sing praises unto my God while I have my being ...*' (Psalm 146:2–10) He said very tenderly to the Lord, 'My beloved, yes, while I have breath I will live for you.'

As he wept, sang and communed with the Lord, His word suddenly came to him, '*Verily, verily, I say unto you, He that believes on me, the works that I do shall he do also; and greater*

works than these shall he do; because I go unto my Father.'
(John 14:12) This verse, which he had previously not particularly noticed, came to him powerfully that day. He claimed
this verse daily and was able to fast for 74 days.

On the 41st day of fasting he saw a phenomenal vision: An
extremely powerful gale from the northeast and northwest
blew directly on Yun's house. It lifted up the whole house and
ripped off its thatched roof. Then there appeared countless
numbers of hornets, scorpions, centipedes and poisonous
snakes which filled the sky and covered the earth and flew
towards Yun. He was terrified and did not know what to do.
Suddenly, he saw a harlot beckoning him saying, 'Come
quickly and follow me!'

Just as Yun was about to follow the harlot, he saw his mother
standing in front of him. However, there was a glow about her
face. In a very stern manner she said to him, 'My child, quickly
kneel down.' Yun did so and his mother gave him a large loaf of
bread and lovingly said, 'Son, quickly eat this bread.' As Yun
opened his mouth to eat it, the swarm of hornets, scorpions,
centipedes and poisonous snakes attacked Yun and began to
sting and bite him. Yun screamed, 'Lord, save me!'

The vision ceased. Yun opened his eyes and turned to Li,
who was lying beside him, 'Tomorrow I suppose I will be
interrogated again.' This Li was the prisoner who always
carried him to the interrogation room. He was originally sent
by the PSB to watch and observe Yun. But being locked up
with Yun day and night, he ended up accepting Jesus as Lord
and became Yun's brother and friend.

As he was speaking, Yun went again into a trance. He
entered a small, white, and beautiful spotless room. In an
instant this small room turned into a vast limitless expanse.
There he saw much white paper. A man dressed in white came
to Yun and said to him, 'You must leave your fingerprint on
this paper.' Following the instructions of the man, he stretched
out his hand and pressed his fingers onto a stack of paper. He
did this on one sheet after another, but strangely there was no
ink mark. The prints on the paper were all red.

He came out of the trance and began to ponder the significance of the second vision. But he could not understand it. He

said to Brother Li, 'Tomorrow I will be tried and you must fervently intercede for me and ask the Lord to have mercy on me and to protect His servant.'

The next morning at nine, the prison bell sounded and the guard shouted, 'Bring out Yun.' The interrogating PSB officials, seeing that Yun adamantly closed his eyes and refused to answer their questions, brought out ropes, whips, electric rods and other instruments of torture. They then began to hit him on the head and face.

'We will beat you to death,' they said. 'You were always saying that the government-supported Three Self Patriotic Church is a harlot. Why is it that now you are pretending to be deaf and dumb?'

After some time the judge said, 'Today we are giving you your last opportunity. If you promise to attend the Three Self Patriotic Church, we will not only cease from investigating your previous activities, but we will even allow you to have the official position of chairman of the Church. Now you must tell us, do you agree to this?'

Suddenly, the vision that Yun saw the previous evening again appeared: hornets, scorpions, centipedes and poisonous snakes all attacked him and began to bite and sting. Then the harlot tempted him to follow her down a road. Hallelujah, praise the Lord. Though Yun's body had endured extremely cruel and inhumane torture, in his spirit he trusted in the Lord's promise and was strengthened and made alive. He paid no attention to this temptation from the authorities.

Brother Li was unable to hold back the tears. In his heart he cried out to the Lord saying, 'Lord, I cannot bear the pain of your servant. I ask you to have mercy on your servant! Protect your servant!' Yun also prayed quietly asking for the Lord's protection. Their hearts were in one accord and a powerful surge of love began to emanate from them. This love flowed toward those authorities, throughout the prison, and was able to overcome all the obstacles.

At that time, the court doctor, a short fat man dressed in white, came sauntering in. He told everyone, 'So is it true that this man cannot speak? Look, I will get him to speak!' As the prison policemen stood on one side, the doctor held up Yun's hands and with a scornful look and sneer said, 'So you really can't speak? OK, today I'm going to give you an injection to heal you of your mute condition!'

The doctor then had four prison officers hold down Yun's hands. Then from a box he took out a size six large needle. With a fiendish laugh, he stuck the needle under the nail of Yun's left thumb. An intense pain shot through his whole body and Yun was unable to keep from screaming. He immediately remembered the vision the previous evening in which he had his fingerprints taken.

Next, the doctor took out one needle after another poking them under the nails of each finger on both his left and right hands. After the fourth needle, Yun fainted. His face soon turned yellow, perspiration dripped from his head and blood oozed out from his fingernails. The PSB men then kicked Yun repeatedly until he was down on the floor, and scornfully said, 'Take your stubborn mind and go meet your God!'

Li carried Yun back to the prison. Upon entering the cell he fell on his face and cried aloud. The other prisoners, seeing this deplorable situation, all began to weep tears of pity.

Beloved reader, today in the decade of the nineties, all around the world people are advocating civilized behaviour. Have you ever realized just how many Christians are facing ruthless and inhumane persecution right under this banner of 'civilized behaviour'?

After several days, the PSB officials thought up a 'great strategy.' Several armed PSB men came to take Yun, who was barely alive, to the hospital for examination. The doctors said there was nothing wrong with Yun, only that he was suffering from acute dehydration.

The doctors took out several bottles of saline water and suspended them from a pole ready to infuse the solution into him. One of the PSB men stood at one side snapping pictures with a camera. Their intention was to let the people see how 'our Party, our country and government has a great humanitarian heart!'

They searched for Yun's artery for a long time, but were unable to find it. So they carelessly inserted the tube and infused the saline solution into his muscles. Yun soon began to swell from the upper arm to his shoulder. The pain was so intense that he again passed out.

Not satisfied with their schemes, the PSB men put on their thinking caps and eventually came up with yet another 'great strategy' to deal with Yun! They told the other prisoners in Yun's cell, 'Yun is a counter-revolutionary political prisoner. He knows that his crimes are serious. Therefore he has pretended to be sick and has refused to eat to resist the government. The doctors have examined him and found that he has no sickness. Your cell has been influenced by him which has brought bad luck to you, and yours is the most backward cell in the prison. Therefore you must separate yourselves from this counter-revolutionary and everyone must unite and struggle against him. Whoever does the best to this end will be greatly rewarded and their sentence will be reduced.'

Except for Brother Li, the rest of the prisoners, while having great respect for Yun, still had not accepted Jesus into their life. Incited by the PSB officials, the evil streak in all of them surfaced and they became obsessed with assailing Yun. These men were degenerate criminals. Now they waited daily to do to Yun what was second nature to them. Regardless of how they humiliated and beat him, nobody would take action against them. It was much worse to fall into the hands of these men than to fall into the hands of the PSB!

They moved Yun's bedding to the urinal next to the wall. (Note: there is a place to urinate within each cell. To defecate one must wait until certain times when the prisoners are allowed to relieve themselves at a toilet outside the cell block). When these prisoners urinated, many of them would deliberately do it on Yun's head. He was too weak to protest and could only endure silently. One day when they were allowed to go outside to relieve themselves, they took Yun to the toilet and forced him to have a bowel movement. Poor Yun had not so much as eaten a single grain of rice for two months. How could he possibly do this?

Then a tall and burly prison officer walked by, holding an electric rod in his hand. Seeing what was going on, he said with a sinister laugh, 'I will take care of him.' He switched on the electric rod and prodded Yun's thigh. A shock ran through Yun's body as if he had been bitten by snakes and insects.

Seeing that Yun did not move, the officer lifted him up as if he were a rag doll, then threw him on the ground. He did this several times. (By that time, Yun was merely skin and bones. He weighed less than 30 kilograms, so it was very easy for the officer to throw him around). He kicked Yun and said mockingly, 'Get up and start crawling for me.' He meant to play with him like he would a dog. By then several hundred prisoners stood around laughing.

Suddenly, from among the prisoners a young man in his twenties came forward. He was the brother of Yun's wife. He had broken the law, been arrested and placed in the cell next to Yun's. He threw himself on Yun and sobbed uncontrollably.

The prison officer, who was behaving like a wolf immediately hit him with the electric rod and with a fierce voice cursed him, 'Who are you and how dare you come here to hold him and cry?'

The young man said, 'I am his brother-in-law.'

'Get out, otherwise I will electrocute you with the electric rod,' the officer said in a loud, threatening voice. There was nothing he could do but obey.

The following account took place in the second month of the lunar calendar. It was a dark, cloudy day as the cold north winds of early spring blew from the northern plains. After a time of being allowed out in the prison yard, the prisoners all returned to their cells. Yun was thrown into the toilet wearing a frayed shirt under a shabby padded jacket with only a shawl covering the lower part of his body. This was the shawl that was given to him by God's servant Brother Ming the night they were arrested. At that time Brother Ming had said earnestly, 'The weather is freezing cold, you must put on this shawl.' Yun had kept it ever since. All his other clothes, including his trousers, were taken from him. But because the padded jacket was so shabby it was not stolen.

Yun lay on the floor all alone, forsaken without a friend. Who would come to comfort his sorrowful heart? Who would have pity on him? He was despised and in their eyes he was less than a dog. He wanted to cry out, but there was no sound. He wanted to weep, but the tears had already dried up.

He could barely move his lips and in a sorrowful voice sang:

> '*Unto thee I lift up mine eyes, O thou that dwellest in the heavens. Behold, as the eyes of servants look unto the hand of their masters, and as the eyes of a maiden unto the hand of her mistress; so our eyes wait upon the LORD our God, until that He have mercy upon us. Have mercy upon us, O LORD, have mercy upon us: for we are exceedingly filled with contempt. Our soul is exceedingly filled with the scorning of those that are at ease, and with the contempt of the proud.*'
> Psalm 123:1–4

Toward evening, Yun was taken to his cell. The prisoners continued to urinate on him. Weeping, he said to the Lord, 'Lord, I ask you to forgive them.'

Yun had a porcelain tea cup tied to his waist. A sister from 'A' county had given it to him when she visited him. The figure of a cross was on this cup and to Yun it was a precious treasure. Now, these criminals, who had lost all sense of decency, snatched the cup from him and threw it in the urinal. Very sorrowfully he struggled to get up and with utmost difficulty crawled into the urinal to retrieve the cup. He then held it to his bosom and cried silently. He held it as if it were a long lost friend and for a long time did not let go of it.

Soon the wrath of God came upon these prisoners. One by one their bodies were covered with boils that itched to the point of being unbearable, and they were unable to sleep day or night. The Almighty God protected his son, for Yun was not infected at all and he did not have a single abscess on his body. The prisoners thought this to be very strange and made him sleep in their midst. They took the blanket of the monitor of the cell (he was the cruellest and had the worst case of boils) and covered Yun with it. Even so God protected him and he did not have a single boil.

Before these things happened, Brother Li had been moved to another cell, and another prisoner surnamed Yu took his place as Yun's cell mate. Yu saw all that happened and quickly changed his attitude. He replaced Li in serving him. The Lord especially blessed this man and later he became an outstanding Christian.

The PSB officials thought that without a doubt Yun would die, but they were unable to force him to say a single word. If he were to die, how would they give account to their superiors? They had to think of another plan. They sent several nurses to the prison in an attempt to force open Yun's mouth and tried to force some rice into his mouth. One reason was so that after Yun died, they could show pictures of this when they made their report. In addition, they wanted to use this as propaganda to show to the people their 'great revolutionary humanitarianism.' However, they were unable to force one grain of rice or one drop of water into Yun's mouth, because he would spit it out.

In desperation, the PSB allowed his wife and mother to visit him in the hope that he would say something. His family had not been allowed to visit him since his arrest.

From January 25 through April 7, 1984, for the sake of the church, for the many souls in prison and that he might be victorious in his imprisonment, Yun had already fasted for 74 days and nights without drinking any water. Beloved reader, in the 6,000 years of human history, have you heard of anyone who did not eat or drink anything for 74 days and yet lived? But such a man has appeared in this generation. Moreover he is just an ordinary, unlearned person, an ordinary preacher. This is the mighty work of God, an amazing miracle.

During the extraordinary 74 days, it is impossible to relate the humiliation, reproach and outrageous beatings he had to put up with. These sufferings included the use of the electric rod and other instruments of torture on him, and having all his fingers pierced with large needles. Had it not been for the protection of the Lord, not just one 'Yun,' but 1,000 'Yuns' would have died from the torture long ago.

On April 7, early in the morning, Yun saw a vision: Many brothers and sisters were kneeling outside the prison wall with their hands lifted in prayer. He also saw himself resting on his mother's bosom and his wife, younger sister and the brothers and sisters were holding on to him weeping. Then he saw a young boy of about seven or eight years old sitting on the handlebars of his bicycle and saying to him, 'Uncle, let me sing a song for you!' He began to sing John 14:6, *'Jesus said, I am the way, the truth, and the life: no man comes unto the Father, but by me.'* As Yun rode the bicycle he listened to the boy singing and received great strength.

Later, he saw another vision, actually the previous vision repeated: countless numbers of hornets, scorpions and poisonous snakes again attacking. At 8:00 a.m., the PSB officials told Yu to carry Yun to the interrogation room. His mother and wife had arrived earlier. But the PSB did not want him to see them right away. They wanted to try again to use torture to make him speak. Thus, as soon as he walked into the interrogation room, the PSB men immediately used their whips and electric rods on him, just as he had seen in the vision. Yun passed out.

As he was lying unconscious, his body felt very warm and comfortable. He felt as if refreshing drops of warm liquid were falling onto his face. Yun slowly gained consciousness. Just as he had seen in his vision early that morning, he found himself lying in his mother's bosom and her warm tears were falling onto his face like beads. His wife Lingling, older sister, younger sister and several brothers and sisters in the Lord, a total of eight people, were all around him.

They could hardly recognize him. His face was gaunt, his skin stretched tightly over his cheek bones. His body was like a stick. As a result, his eyes appeared rather large, his lips protruded and hung open. He was unable to close his mouth so that two rows of yellow teeth could be seen. His hair fell onto his face and his beard had grown unkempt. His face was covered with dried blood and his clothes were absolutely filthy. They could not help but wail loudly. Lingling was so shocked she almost fainted. To see this awful scene would bring tears to the most hard-hearted, callous person.

Then Yun felt great power surge through him. He had already prepared to speak this day. As he began to speak, his elder sister quickly covered his mouth with her hand. She knew that he had refused to confess and had not spoken for 74 days. If he talked now he would receive severe punishment. But with supernatural strength Yun pushed her hand away and declared loudly, *'Put not your trust in princes, nor in the son of man, in whom there is no help.* (Psalm 146:3) *It is better to trust in the*

LORD *than to put confidence in princes.* (Psalm 118:9) *Fear not.'*

Then he held tightly onto Brother A-Hong's hand and said, 'Brother, wealth cannot corrupt us, threats cannot make us succumb, poverty will not move us, trust in Jesus Christ and be strong. The Heavenly Father already told me that you would come to visit me today.'

Upon hearing this, nobody was able to control themselves any longer, and they all began to cry sorrowfully. Then Yun, with a heartrending cry said, 'Mother, your son is hungry! Mother, your son is thirsty! The autumn has passed and winter has come. It is freezing. Why have you not given your son inner garments? Mother, your son is hungry! Your son is thirsty!'

One of the sisters sped to the store at the gate of the prison and bought some food. His mother, eyes brimming with tears, said to him, 'It is not that mother has an uncaring heart. I tried many times to send things, but there was no way to deliver them to you!'

Yun cried out, 'Mother, your son is hungry and thirsty not for earthly bread and water, but for the souls of men! If only you can preach the Gospel and save souls, then that is the only food I need!'

'Mother, I have already fasted for 74 days and the Lord told me that I would see you today, but it is possible that I may yet be beaten to death. Mother, today have you brought with you the flesh and blood of the Lamb?'

By that time, the sister who ran out to buy food returned with a box of crackers, several cans of food and a bottle of grape juice. Lifting up a cracker, Yun blessed it and gave it to his mother, Lingling, A-Hong and the rest of the brothers and sisters.

Very solemnly he said, 'This is the Lord's body that was broken for us. Every time we do this it is in remembrance of the Lord.' (See 1 Corinthians 11:24) Everyone, with heads bowed, received communion.

Yun then poured out some grape juice. After blessing it he took a sip and then gave it to the rest of them saying, 'This is the blood of the Lord that was shed for us. I believe this is possibly the last time I will be able to take communion with you.

Mother, Lingling, brothers and sisters, I will see you again in the kingdom of heaven.'

His words pierced the hearts of his mother, Lingling and everybody in the room. His older sister embraced him sorrowfully and said, 'Yun, how can you possibly leave behind your old mother, your young wife and die? Moreover, Lingling has been pregnant for nearly five months. How can you be so cruel?'

His mother cried out, 'Son, you cannot possibly die! Your brother yesterday knelt in our home the whole day crying and praying. There is no difficulty that cannot be solved. Son, you cannot possibly die!'

The above incident took place in the interrogation room with PSB officials looking on. God used His mighty hand to protect this extremely solemn and moving communion service. After the meeting ended, it was as if the PSB officials awoke from a dream. One of them pounded his fist on the table, and screeched, 'What are you all doing here? That's enough! Quickly get out of here! Come someone, carry Yun back to the cell!'

How could his mother let someone take her son away? How could Lingling possibly leave her beloved husband? How could his older sister, younger sister and the brothers and sisters in the Lord just stand there and watch while their beloved was taken away? Yun's mother and wife clung tightly on to him and the rest of the people held fast to his hands. Several prison officers tried to break them up by kicking and punching them and finally yanked Yun from their grip. They then dragged him through the iron gate which clanged shut.

Beating her bosom, Yun's mother cried out, 'Son, remember mother's words. Be strong and continue to go on living!' From the other side of the gate Yun's voice rang out, 'Return and preach the Gospel and save men. Tell all the churches to pray for me and fast ....' His voice faded into the distance.

Yun's mother, Lingling, A-Hong and the rest of them were all in tears but were forced to leave the interrogation room of the prison. They walked through the main street of the crowded city, wailing out loud. The people in the market, bewildered, surrounded them and demanded to know what had happened.

Chapter 4

The Righteous Shall Flourish Like the Palm Tree

(Psalm 92:12)

When Yun returned to the number two prison cell, the monitor of his cell started kicking him and said contemptuously, 'How about it now? Are you still going to pretend to be deaf? Do you plan to go without food any more?' The rest of the prisoners also used many words to humiliate him.

Then Yun was mightily moved by the Spirit of the Lord. He stood up and addressed everyone: 'Friends in adversity, today I want to say a few words to you. You must listen attentively.' Hearing him speak they were greatly shocked. This man who had fasted for 74 days was now speaking with such dignity and authority. Everybody could not help but have great respect for him.

He continued, 'God has sent me here for your sakes. As soon as I entered prison I told you about the Gospel of the cross of Jesus. Moreover, you have seen with your own eyes how I have not taken one grain of rice nor one drop of water for 74 days. I would like to ask you: Over several thousand years of history, who has seen anyone do this for 74 days and live?

'Today, I stand alive in your midst. Is this not sufficient proof that my Lord is true and alive? Will you continue to be stiff-necked and resist Jesus Christ? When judgment comes how will you be able to escape the wrath of that judgment?

'Today, the Lord has mercy on you and offers you forgiveness. He has called me to tell you the message of repentance and forgiveness of sins. Therefore each of you should kneel before Jesus Christ, confess your sins and repent, so that you can escape the judgment and death that will come upon you, be saved and enter that eternally joyful kingdom of heaven!'

Those few words were dropped on them like an atom bomb. This group of more than ten exceedingly wicked men who had committed all types of crimes fell before the Lord. The first one to kneel was the monitor of the cell. Then one after another, all of them knelt down. Each was touched by the Holy Spirit and the sins they had committed passed before their very eyes as if they were seeing a movie, scene after scene. They all began to cry out loud.

Outside the cell the prison guard heard the commotion and rushed inside. He stood rooted to the ground at the scene before him. He did not move for a long time. Seizing the opportunity, Yun baptized these 15 men. After this they took advantage of the times when they were allowed to leave their cells, to go to the other cells. The Gospel was therefore preached throughout the prison and many prisoners repented and believed in the Lord.

Hallelujah! All the prisoners in number two cell became children of God. Enemies became Yun's spiritual brethren. This place that had been 'hell on earth' turned into the Church of God. Yun was like a palm tree that had been cut, stripped of its bark, yes a palm tree that endured much pain. But now it was producing abundant fruit that could be seen everywhere. In addition to this the churches outside the prison walls started to experience revival.

This was especially true of the churches in 'B' county. As a result of the arrest of Yun and several brethren and their subsequent persecution, many grew cold in their spirit. As news of the suffering that Yun endured in prison and his prayer and fasting of 74 days spread everywhere it brought great strength. Everywhere it shook the fearful, lukewarm and sleeping spirits of the brothers and sisters. Prayer meetings mushroomed and many believers began to fast and pray fervently for the ministry of the Gospel and for the brothers and sisters who were in prison. The Gospel greatly prospered as new converts were added daily.

A sister whose husband was not yet a believer lived in a certain village. Their only son developed a terminal illness. The husband agreed to call the brothers and sisters over for prayer. That evening as more than ten brothers and sisters came, they knelt down and were unable to refrain from weeping as they prayed for Brother Yun who was suffering in prison.

The husband of this sister heard everyone praying and weeping for Yun in this manner and said, 'If my child is healed, not only will I believe in Jesus, but I will arrange to visit this man through contacts in my family.' God did hear the prayers of these believers, and the son of this man was delivered from the hand of the devil. He was exceedingly glad and two days later he went to the PSB to visit a relative who was an armed policeman of cadre status.

He told the cadre, 'Yun is my nephew, please take special care of him.'

He also said, 'In prison he did not eat nor drink for 74 days. He is an extraordinary man whose God is true and alive. Whatever you do, don't offend him.'

The cadre was shocked to hear him say this because he was Yun's chief persecutor. He knew Yun's case very well. The fact that he had not starved to death in 74 days was well known by every person in the PSB. From that time on, the cadre stopped persecuting Yun and was extremely nice to him.

Before long, Yun was promoted monitor of number two cell. One day, the supervisor of the warden's office came to take him to the administration office. They told him, 'We know that you have a good heart. Today we have a job for you. There is a murderer locked up in cell number nine who has tried to commit suicide daily. Today we are transferring him to your cell so that you can watch over him. Don't allow him to kill himself until the day of his execution when he must be handed over to us in a state of good health. If you are careless and allow him to commit suicide, you will be totally responsible.'

Yun sensed that he was not only being given a man's body to take care of, he was being given a precious soul as well. Therefore he committed himself to this task with determination. Returning to the cell he discussed the matter with the brethren there and they were all willing to help.

This man was only 22 years old and named Huang. He had not only murdered someone, but he had raped, robbed and committed other crimes. His father, who had a very high position was ashamed to visit his criminal son. But he sent him a shirt on which he had written these words on the back side. 'Beloved son, I am now unable to see you, but I will see you at the mass meeting (meaning the day of his execution)!' When Huang read it he was heartbroken. So every day he looked for an opportunity to kill himself.

In number nine cell Huang was mistreated by the other prisoners. They ate most of his food, leaving just a little for him. Then they would deliberately pour the food all over him. His clothes were always covered with food stains.

Everyday they would tie his hands behind his back and lock his feet with metal rings clamped so tight they cut into his flesh and he bled. But he was not afraid of pain and not only did he continue to move around the cell, he would jump up and down until the bones of his ankles could be seen. His cellmates were afraid he would kill himself and that they would be held responsible. Still, they continued to beat and humiliate him. One day when they were not looking, he rammed his head against the wall. He did not die but left a dent in the wall.

That afternoon, Huang was taken out by several policemen and transferred to number two cell. When he entered this cell, he could feel the atmosphere was totally different from that in number nine cell. Here, the 'brethren in adversity' looked at him with a sympathetic, friendly smile as if they were welcoming a friend.

Yun, in a gentle voice like that of a loving mother urged him to have a seat, and to remain still and not move around lest the feet-cuffs caused his feet more pain. Yun brought out some hot water, and after cooling it, washed the wounds on Huang's feet.

Soon it was time for the midday meal. Each of the brethren ate a little less rice and they gave Huang half a bowl more than his ration. They fed him one mouthful at a time. The meal that evening happened to be the one in which they were allowed to eat a mantou (steamed bread). Only once a week were they given a two-ounce mantou. Yun told all the brethren to eat their mantou, but to leave a bowl of vegetable soup for Huang. Then he broke off one-fourth of his mantou and kept the remainder in his shirt pocket.

The next morning, breakfast consisted of a noodle soup in which a few strands of noodles were boiled in water. It was extremely watery. Looking into the bowl you could see the reflection of your eyelids very clearly. The authorities must have thought that the previous night's meal was too extravagant, and therefore they decided to reduce the rations for that day's meals.

The brethren agreed that each of them share a little of their soup with Huang. Yun fed him some rice and then with his back towards Huang broke up the remainder of last night's mantou, put it Huang's bowl and continued to feed him. At that moment, Huang's hard heart melted. He suddenly fell on his knees and began to sob aloud. It was probably the first time he had ever cried as an adult.

Weeping, he said, 'My brother, I am a murderer whom everyone hates. Even my father, mother, older and younger sister and fiancee don't want me. Why do you love me in this manner? There is no way I can repay you now, but after I die and turn into a ghost I will find some way to repay your goodness towards me!'

Then Yun was filled with the love of the Lord and turning to Huang, said tearfully, 'You should thank Jesus, for we believe in Him. If we didn't believe in Him we would have treated you the same way as the prisoners in cell nine. Today we love you because of the love of Jesus Christ. Also, after you die not only can you not repay us, but your soul will enter eternal hell and punishment. Therefore you should repent and believe in Jesus for He is the only One able to save your soul.'

Huang immediately and very sincerely said to the Lord, 'Thank you Jesus, for loving a sinner like me.'

Yun comforted him. As he fed him he told about the birth, death, resurrection, ascension, and the second coming of Christ and explained salvation.

He told him, 'Earthly kingdoms have laws, how much more is there a law in heaven? Here on earth there are prisons, how much more must there be an eternal prison (hell) in the next life?'

Huang listened as the light of the Holy Spirit slowly shone in his black heart. He could not control himself and knelt before the Lord and cried out to Him with repentance and confession of sins.

His story unfolded. After he graduated from middle school, Huang worked as a technician in a power plant in 'B' city. His parents were both Party secretaries in two large work units. His family enjoyed a superior lifestyle and both his parents especially loved him. Huang was engaged at this time and his fiancee loved him very much. Still he did not seem to appreciate any of these things. His closest friends were a group of degenerates in society. They 'lived it up,' got drunk, got into fights in which they injured people. They even put some dynamite together to blow up several people.

It was for this crime that the PSB arrested them. But because of the influence of his parents, this serious crime was dealt with leniently and he was only given a two-year term of labour re-education. He was to have been released on May 1, 1983. Who would have thought that on the night before his release, he ran into a friend who had also been sentenced to labour re-education.

As the two of them began to talk all kinds of negative things came out. They talked about their future and how they both felt so empty, insignificant and hopeless. Later they started drinking to kill their boredom, but the more they drank the more morose they became. As a result they made a pact.

'If we cannot live together, then tonight we will both die together,' they decided.

These two degenerate men then went to the warehouse and stole two metal truncheons and more than ten pounds of dynamite. Then they swore to heaven that if one of them was killed by the other, the one who was still alive must take the body of his dead partner to a power transformer where he would set off the dynamite. The living one would embrace his dead comrade and in that way that night both of them would die together.

Each of them then began to viciously strike the other with the metal truncheon. Huang was the stronger of the two. During the third round he fatally struck his friend and cracked his skull open, spilling out his brains. As Huang was carrying the body of his friend, he was discovered by a cadre from the labour camp, who immediately fired a warning shot. Realizing that he would not be able to follow through with the original plan, he dumped the dead body and escaped from the camp.

He went to another district, changed his mind and decided not to kill himself. He decided to travel to every major city in the nation, visit all the well-known attractions and enjoy all the pleasures of life. Then only would he return home and end it all.

He purchased a flashy sharp knife and used it to rob countless numbers of travellers and sexually violate many young girls. He travelled to all the cities, famous mountains and places. But giving in to sin and lust still could not satisfy him. In fact, he felt even more pain, torment and hopelessness. He climbed many famous mountains where they told him his fortune and he worshipped Buddhist idols. But this brought him no peace.

In desperation he bought a box of safety razors and unbuttoning the collar of his shirt hung the razors all around his neck. Then using his knife he went to the drugstore and stole two bottles of sleeping pills. After that he boarded a train to return to his home, where he planned to commit suicide. However his plan was foiled. As soon as he got off the train, PSB officials apprehended him.

But that day in prison, Huang surrendered to the Lord and He saved Him. He then allowed Yun to remove the razor blades hidden under the collar of his shirt.. He had a great hunger for the Word of the Lord and constantly asked Brother Yun to teach him the Bible. He also loved to sing choruses. Yun taught him to sing 'I love Jesus.' He sang out constantly:

> '*I love Jesus, I love Jesus,*
> *All of my life I love Jesus;*
> *Love Him in the sunshine hour,*
> *Love Him when the storm clouds lower,*
> *Every day along my way,*
> *Yes, I love Jesus.*'

Generally, control over the prisoners was very strict. Anyone caught making a noise would be severely punished. At the bottom of the cell door there was a small hole just large enough for a man to put his head in. The police would stick the heads of those who violated the regulations in that hole and then kick them or use the butts of their rifles to beat them. Most prisoners kept quiet out of fear. Who would dare to talk or sing carelessly? Though the brothers in cell two usually sang most of the time, they did so in a soft voice, or they waited until there was no guard at the door before they sang louder.

Though prisoner Huang had received the Lord's grace, he was still a prisoner on death row. He had no fear of death. Day and night he sang at the top of his voice, 'I love Jesus ....' It was strange, for none of the guards paid any attention. The courage of the brothers greatly increased. This prison cell was filled with singing, the prayers of the saints and meetings every day.

Huang had a great desire for the Lord's cross and he earnestly implored Yun, 'Brother, please draw a cross on the wall for me. If it is discovered by the prison police, I will take full responsibility.' Yun could not bear to disappoint this new believer who was soon to die. Whenever they were allowed outside he would look everywhere for broken glass or iron nails so that he could etch a cross on the stone wall of the cell for Huang.

This wall was made of concrete and was extremely hard. With great effort, Yun spent his spare time working hard until a tall, large cross was eventually etched on the wall. Under the cross he drew a picture of the world and over that these characters were written horizontally, 'God so loved the world.'

The brethren, especially Huang, shouted out for joy. He was so happy that he began to cry. He also asked Yun to chisel out a grave right below the cross, with a grave stone in front and to write on it the words, 'The grave of Huang who has received grace.'

The more Yun etched, the more strength he had. Eventually the cell door and the four walls of the cell were covered with, '*The prodigal has returned*,' '*In tribulation trust in the Lord*' John 3:16, Romans 3:23–24 and other Bible verses. Praise the Lord! The Lord said: '*I have given you the key of David and I am he that opens and no man can shut and shuts and no man can open.*' (Revelation 3:8) It was true. Though they did all these

The Heavenly Man

things, not one guard discovered it and from that time on nobody ever came into the cell to investigate.

The cross and Bible verses remain in this cell to this day. Every prisoner sent to that cell can read them and many have repented and believed in Jesus. The brethren in cell number two used the pins on the prison emblems they had to wear as needles. They pulled out the threads from their towels one by one. Each one embroidered a very dainty cross on the upper left side of his prison uniform. They embroidered a red cross on Huang's garment. Soon everyone had a cross on his chest and they were all so inspired that they knelt down and wept.

Chapter 5

To Walk in the Midst of the Fire

(Daniel 3:25)

The day that Yun ended 74 days of fasting was the day he saw his wife and mother. He was certain then there was no way he could escape a more severe and harsh judgment. Therefore in his heart he had already prepared for death. But who would have known that the Lord would have mercy on him and protect him for another two months until the Gospel prospered throughout the whole prison? Only then was he taken back for his trial.

The PSB were well prepared for this interrogation. During the previous months, they had gone to the various districts and villages where Yun had carried on his activities. They launched a wide and thorough investigation and found much 'evidence of crimes.' When Yun was brought forth for the trial, he felt very weak. Though this time he would speak, the interrogation by the PSB would certainly be daunting. He asked the brethren in prison to earnestly pray for him while he asked the Lord to give him sufficient strength and faith to stand victorious during the trial.

The judge was over 30 years old, a short man with a dark face and treacherous eyes. He had an extremely violent disposition. As soon as Yun was brought in, he stared at him with great fury. Next to him was a tall man of about 50. His hair was white, he had a smiling face and he appeared rather gentle.

The trial began and the judge said to Yun, 'The government has been forgiving towards you and considering that your body is not strong we have given you several months to rest.

Therefore we have not called for you in the past two months. Now your strength has returned and you have had sufficient time to consider. Today you will have an opportunity to 'Receive forgiveness through being honest and receive merit to redeem your crimes'. You must lower your head and confess your crimes.'

Next, the judge asked Yun the following questions:

(1) Who is your contact in 'A' county. How often did you go there?

(2) What kind of counter-revolutionary propaganda did you spread throughout 'B' city? How did you incite the believers against the religious policy of the Party?

(3) What were your activities in 'G' county?

Pounded with so many questions, Yun's only answer was that he did not know. This infuriated the judge who struck the bench with great force. Then, gnashing his teeth, he said, 'Let's see how you defend yourself today. Someone bring forth the machine!'

A PSB official brought out a tape recorder and turned the knob. A powerful voice of someone preaching accompanied by the sound of weeping said, 'Brethren, don't be deceived by the harlot ... don't be fooled by the false appearance of the harlot ... be like Phinehas who took a javelin in his hand (see Numbers 25:6–18) ... Don't be a Judas and betray the Lord and friends.

'You should be willing to be a martyr for the Lord ... rise up, be faithful and brave in proclaiming the truth.' From the recorder came the voice of many people weeping. After that the speaker sang this song:

> *'Be bold and courageous, be bold and courageous,*
> *For the Lord is with you, be bold and courageous.*
> *Though there are thousands of demons, though there are*
>   *tens of thousands of enemies,*
> *Trust in the Saviour, do not be afraid,*
> *Be bold and courageous.'*

Immediately that brother, in a sorrowful and moving voice that seemed to shake heaven and earth, prayed:

'Lord, remove the dark clouds from the heavens above our country, bind the powers of darkness, cast out the evil spirits that control. We ask you to change the despotic government of our nation, set free all the brothers and sisters who are in prison and raise up Esthers and Daniels for this generation ....'

After that was heard the voice of another two brethren leading in prayer.

As Yun heard himself preaching, singing and praying in a meeting in 'B' city two years before, his heart was greatly inspired by the mighty power from his own preaching and prayers. All of a sudden, he put on the full armour of Christ, and the sword of the Holy Spirit was in his hand. He stood in the courthouse with the demeanor of a general of the Kingdom of Heaven.

With a 'click', the tape recorder stopped. The judge said confidently to him, 'You have heard it clearly! Your preaching, prayer, in fact the songs you sang, are all clearly and brazenly opposed to our Party, and have disgraced our government stating that the church of our government is a harlot. Now you must confess, is this your voice? Who was the other co-worker with you? Who were the two men who prayed after you?'

Yun answered, 'The voices on this tape are not too clear and I can't recall whether it is my preaching and prayer. Please play it once more so I can hear it again.'

The judge was so furious his eyes bulged out, and he again struck the bench. He approached Yun, pointing his finger in his face, he cursed him, 'You obstinate scoundrel, the evidence against you is like a mountain. You would dare to talk back to me? I now command you to kneel down and repeat this prayer once again that I can hear it!'

In the courtroom, several armed policemen with electric rods screamed at Yun, 'Kneel down! Kneel down!'

But the power of the Lord came upon Yun and he remained strong and courageous. Without any fear at all, and in an inspiring voice he said, 'What power do you have to command a servant of God to kneel before you? This type of interrogation is totally unreasonable. Now in the name of Jesus of

Nazareth, I command you to kneel down. I will lay hands on you and ask the Lord to forgive your sins. Kneel down! All of you kneel down!'

At this the judge turned purple with rage, his ears burned red, his mouth contorted with anger and his eyes blazed with fire. For a long time he was beside himself and he continually pounded the bench shouting in a grotesque voice, 'Treason! Treason! How dare a counter-revolutionary political prisoner command the judge of the Public Security Bureau to kneel down! You ... you ... you ... you are audacious in the extreme! You ... you ... you are not human!'

Yes, beloved reader, Brother Yun is truly not an ordinary man, as he stated on the evening that he was arrested, 'I am a heavenly man.' Yes, only those with heavenly talents will have this heavenly courage! Because Brother Yun lifted up Christ, and was strong and bold as a lion, the plans of the PSB came to absolutely nothing. Hallelujah, glory to the name of the Lord!

In dealing with Yun, the PSB connived, schemed and used every method possible including the most barbarous methods of torture, but in the end they were unable to make him say a single word to incriminate himself. Moreover, their cheap tricks were made evident to all. Therefore they sent this 'case' to the prosecutor of 'B' county and the People's Court of that area. After several days, the prosecutor of 'B' county brought Yun forth for judgment. Who would have guessed that the judge was none other than Yun's cousin, the son of his uncle? Yun knew that this was yet another trick of the devil!

The judge said to Yun, 'According to the materials sent to us from the PSB of 'B' city in relation to your appeal, you have reviled our Party's policy as the programme of darkness, the Devil's domination and the kingdom of Satan. Moreover you have attacked the Party's religious policy and have instigated believers in opposition to the leadership of the Party and the People's Government. Accordingly this is sufficient to sentence you to ten years, life imprisonment and the death penalty.

'Today you can personally tell me the truth whether these things are true. Also you must tell me the names of the others (meaning the names of other co-workers) and the scope of their activities by which you can obtain merit and redeem yourself.

In this way, only if you do this, can I find a way to lighten your punishment.'

Yun answered without hesitation, 'Although you are my relative, you must do your work and I will be consistent in my faith. I must be true to my Lord. All that you have just said is not factual. As for the affairs of others, I have no knowledge.'

His cousin could do nothing and in the end he could only say, 'You must listen to my admonition, otherwise you will certainly live to regret it!'

Officials from the People's Court of 'B' county began to judge Yun's case. Two policemen brought Yun into the main hall of the Court. On the way there Yun was full of joy. As he arrived at the courtroom, he saw many empty seats and he did not know which was for the defendant, which for the prosecution or judge and, without thinking, he sat on the large round chair of the judge.

The judge said angrily, 'Hey, after all who is judging who? What a nerve you have to sit on the justice's bench. Quickly get down!'

Yun stood up and said lightheartedly, 'If you insist I'll get down. You should have told me before.' As he did that he thought to himself, 'One day with the Lord on His throne I will judge you people, and I will judge angels!'

The trial began. In the courtroom were the PSB officials, the prosecutor, the officials of the United Front Department and officials of other such organs, making a total of 40 to 50 people. Behind the bench sat the judge, jury, chief prosecutor and the secretary, altogether about eight or nine people. On the bench was a reference Bible and many other spiritual books.

The judge said haughtily, 'Yun, is this loot yours?'

Hearing the word 'loot,' Yun was greatly indignant and in a very righteous manner he said, 'This is not loot, rather these are sanctified unto the Lord.'

The judge hesitated, not knowing what to say. 'Regardless of what you call them, are they yours?'

Yun replied, 'Bring them to me so that I can have a look.'

A PSB official brought the reference Bible and gave it to Yun. Yun opened it and saw his name written inside. He said, 'It is mine.' He then took a copy of *Streams in the Desert*. With great hunger and thirst he began to look through it, as if he had found a long lost friend. He opened to the devotion for August 14 and his eyes stopped at the verse on the top of the page, *'You could have no power at all against me, except it were given you from above.'* (John 19:11)

Yun seeing the Word the Lord gave him that day, knew the time had come. He must submit to the will of God and go down the path that He had determined for him. Therefore without any fear he said to the judge, 'These are mine.'

They then played the recording of his preaching. Hearing it gave strength to Yun and he confessed, 'That is me.' After that they continued to ask about Yun's co-workers and other people, but he said he did not know anything.

After a recess of 30 minutes, the court reconvened for sentencing. According to the original plan of the PSB, Yun was to be immediately executed. However, the Lord still had much work for him to do. Therefore, to everyone's surprise, he was sentenced to only four years in prison. When he returned to the cell, the brethren were beside themselves with joy at the turn of events. They all bowed their heads and worshipped God. On the evening of August 16, the brethren baptized Huang and another two men.

The latter had been sent to the cell after the original 15 were baptized. One of them had been sentenced to life in prison. He was in his twenties, and was the head of a gang of ruffians. Before his arrest he participated in robbery, gang violence, and other serious crimes, which were too many to be mentioned (Chinese saying: *'Bamboo would be exhausted before crimes could all be recorded'*). The filthy things he did would make the listener embarrassed. According to the laws of the nation, this man should have been executed. But because his relative was a high-ranking official, the death sentence was commuted to life imprisonment.

The other was a young man a little over 20 who was sentenced to 20 years in prison. He had a wife and parents at home. He had a very evil nature and was so suave he deceived many women. He had seduced many unmarried girls to commit adultery with him. More serious than that, he had sneaked into a women's dormitory in a certain middle school (high school) with another man and they had raped several young girl students.

When he was apprehended by the PSB, they beat him half dead. When he was first put in cell number two, he had no clothes and his body was covered with scars. Brother Yun had compassion on him and helped him to get some clothes. Therefore he was touched, and later repented and believed in the Lord. This extremely evil man had found new life in this place.

After the baptism service, the brethren sang this song:

'*I have a glorious home over there in heaven,* (3 times)
that I will always think of.
Jesus Christ can save me and he can save you, (2 times)
only come and believe Him.

Chorus:
Lord, Lord, Don't forsake me, (3 times)
Remember me always.'

One group after another began to sing. The sound of singing echoed throughout the crammed prison cells. With tears in his eyes Huang said, 'Brother, can the members of my family be saved? Will my mother be with me in the future?'

Yun said, 'You must fervently pray for your father and mother. They will then certainly believe in the Lord and in the future they can be together with you.'

That evening Huang spent the entire night praying for his parents. On the morning of the second day, Huang said to Yun, 'Beloved brother, there is one thing that I want you to help me with. I would like to write a last letter to my parents. Would you figure a way to give it to them?'

Yun said, 'All right, I will certainly think of a way. But where will we get paper and a pen?'

Huang said, 'I have a way.'

Then he turned and faced the guard standing outside the door and shouted, 'I want to appeal. Please bring paper and a pen to me.' Shortly, the guard brought a ball point pen and two sheets of paper.

Now you may ask how could a person who has both hands handcuffed behind his back write with a pen? Praise the Lord, after he repented Yun said to the guard, 'Huang will not try to kill himself anymore, so please loosen his handcuffs!' Although both his hands were still tied behind his back, he could stretch one hand to the right almost to his mouth. When he sat on the floor he could put the paper on his right hand side, and leaning over wrote his last letter while weeping.

However, after writing only two lines, the pen ran out of ink. Immediately and without hesitation he bowed his head and bit the forefinger of his right hand and used this bleeding finger to write a moving 'blood letter.' (As the Chinese saying goes, '*As a man approaches death, his words are virtuous; as a bird approaches death, the cry is sorrowful*'.) This last letter was thus written:

'Beloved father and mother; your son has not honoured you. Your son knows you love him. After I am gone, do not be sorrowful. Your son now tells you tremendous news – your son is not dead for he has obtained eternal life. In prison your son met a wonderful person, that is the greatly respected Brother Yun. He has saved my life, has led me to believe in Jesus. Moreover he has been concerned about me in so many ways and has loved me with everything he has. He fed me daily. Beloved father and mother, I will soon go to the kingdom of heaven. In that place I will pray for you. You must believe in Jesus and allow Brother Yun an opportunity to preach the Gospel to you. At the same time he will tell you about the other matters concerning me. I pray that you obtain eternal life and that I will see you in heaven!'

That evening the atmosphere in prison was especially tense. Every five minutes the patrolling guard walked past their cell door. Every 30 minutes the guard would enter the cell and check on each prisoner. The prisoners knew that every time this occurred it meant a prisoner would be executed the next day. Weeping, the brethren washed Huang's feet. But Huang's heart was full of an amazing peace and calm and he left the brothers with a smile on his face.

All evening Huang sang, *'I love Jesus'* and *'I have a glorious home on that side.'* On August 13, the third day after Huang received water baptism, a light shower fell outside. Early in the morning, the prison gate opened with a clang. A fully armed prison guard stood at the entrance and said loudly, 'Bring forth Yun.'

Then he said, 'Bring forth Huang.'

Brother Huang said to everyone, 'I will see you again in heaven.' He was then taken away. As he approached the execution ground he was prepared to die. As he walked he kept turning his head back to look at Brother Yun, thinking that Brother Yun would also be taken out to accompany him.

There was a gunshot. Though his body lay dead because of sin, Huang's soul had ascended to rest in the Great Shepherd Jesus. As it is recorded, *'This is a faithful saying, and worthy of all acceptance, that Christ Jesus came into the world to save sinners.* (1 Timothy 1:15)

Yun was bound from head to foot and bundled into an open truck. He was taken out to be publicly paraded and struggled against. Yun was unable to contain the joy as it bubbled up, so he sang about Jesus and spoke about Jesus. This made the chief of police extremely furious. He commanded his subordinates to tie Yun up even more tightly.

This did not deter him. He praised the Lord even louder. The chief of police aimed the electric rod on his neck. Gnashing his teeth he threatened Yun, 'I warn you, if you dare to sing in this manner while you are being paraded, when you return I will skin you alive.'

There were eight or nine people who were in the prison truck who were to be part of this public display. Among them was a young woman prisoner just over 20 years old by the name of Xiaojuan. She was bound with the same rope as Yun and stood in the front.

The prison truck slowly went into the street and as the intensity of the rain increased Yun called out loudly saying, 'Lord, how I thirst after your rains of grace! Greatly pour out your rain of grace upon your servant!' He then began to sing;

'In this wicked and perverse generation,
All will change and the heaven and earth will be shaken,
The devil is busily working,
Many workers and believers have already disappeared.

Is there fear within your heart, is it full of doubt and
without direction?
Rise up, work hard and persevere for the Kingdom of
Heaven.
Rise up, Be courageous and faithful to your king.

Chorus:
Be faithful, be faithful, spread this message everywhere,
Be faithful to that which has been committed you, be
faithful to your glorious Lord,
Be faithful, be faithful, though the crowds don't follow.
Whatever you meet, remain close to the Lord's side,
Allow the Lord to always see you faithful.

The people along the roadside held umbrellas as they watched with great interest this 'show.' The believers were so moved that they all began to weep. Xiaojuan, who was tied up with Yun, was very embarrassed and hung her head because she was afraid people would recognize her since she was being 'struggled against' in her home district. But Yun kept singing and preaching, in fact he was so joyful that he wanted to jump up and down. Xiaojuan looked at him in amazement.

She said to Yun, 'Mister, today we are being openly paraded and struggled against. Why are you so joyful?'

'How could I not be happy? For I am counted worthy to be reproached for the name of Jesus!' Upon hearing that, Xiaojuan's face turned red. Yun continued singing loudly,

'Though the whole world is displeased with me; friends
forsake me,
My flesh and blood depart; in accusations, slander, persecu-
tion, rejection or beatings; I will even give my life and
spill my blood.
In all my life I only desire to please the Heavenly Father,
That wearing a crown I will enter the Kingdom of
Heaven.'

The prison truck drove to the rural area. Yun looked out and saw that it was approaching late autumn and the whole earth was like a sick old man. There was nothing green and no flowers were to be seen. Nothing was alive. Everywhere there was only desolate ground that looked so sorrowful. Looking around him, Yun thought about the condition of the church and could not control himself. He could not help but feel sad and as the tears began to flow he sobbed out this song:

> '*Lift up your eyes and look forward to the vast desolate harvest fields.*
> *The Lord's heart is broken daily; who is willing to go forth for the Lord?*
> *Tears fill my eyelids, blood is splattered over my bosom,*
> *As I lift up the banner of Christ and save the lost perishing sheep.*'

The rain poured down in torrents mixing with his tears. Upon hearing this moving song, Xiaojuan was no longer embarrassed but was greatly moved. She was greatly attracted by Yun's love for the Lord. She was unable to control herself and started to weep tears of repentance. Suddenly she turned and pulled out a handkerchief from her pocket. Then, standing on her toes she wiped away Yun's tears.

Yun was greatly touched, surprised and said tenderly to this little sister, 'Little sister, I am being struggled against for the sake of the Lord. Why are you here?'

Xiaojuan began to wail. She said, 'I also believe in Jesus, but my mother and I were not willing to endure. We got into a fight with our neighbour and my little sister pulled down the dress of the neighbour's young daughter. They were people with authority and so mother and I were arrested and put in prison.'

Yun's compassion was stirred and he said to her, 'The prodigal's return is more precious than gold. It is not too late to return. Sister, you need to know that the Holy Spirit is daily grieved for you and your mother. Return, Father is waiting for you!'

Yun's words were as powerful as a hammer and struck Xiaojuan's heart. She wept bitterly as she prayed, 'Lord, have mercy on me and forgive my sins.'

Yun also prayed earnestly for her and asked God to have mercy on her. Thank the Lord for she immediately received peace in her heart. Xiaojuan then turned to him, 'I heard about a Brother Yun who was imprisoned for the Lord and suffered much affliction. Do you know him? Where is he now?'

Laughing, Yun said, 'Are you interested in seeing this man?'

'How can I see him?'

'It is he that is speaking to you,' Yun responded.

When she heard that this man standing in front of her was the servant of God who had fasted for 74 days for the sake of the Lord, and as she considered Yun's bold and fearless attitude in the truck, she was so moved that she immediately held onto him. She looked at him with great amazement and said to herself repeatedly, 'Lord, I thank you! Lord, I praise you.'

The downpour did not relent. The late autumn rain and the cool winds beat down on the faces of the people until they shivered. All the military police had their raincoats tightly wrapped around them. They did not pay any attention to Yun. As a result of the unusually heavy rain, the large 'struggle session meeting' was cancelled. Yun and the other prisoners were taken back to the local police station.

That evening each prisoner was given pieces of steamed bread (mantou) to eat. The poor souls were so hungry they were on the verge of fainting. They gobbled up the food in two mouthfuls. Xiaojuan managed to obtain a whole mantou and she gave it to Yun.

'Brother Yun, the women prisoners usually eat somewhat better than you men, and I am not hungry today. Please take this mantou and eat it.'

Yun was very touched. But he knew that like himself, Xiaojuan had not eaten the whole day. How could he accept this one and only mantou?

Yun suddenly remembered the words of the Lord and realized the Lord wanted him to understand an important truth, *'It is more blessed to give than to receive.'* (Acts 20:35) He received the mantou, and after blessing it broke it in two and keeping the smaller piece gave the larger portion to Xiaojuan.

He said, 'The Lord told me it is better to give than to receive.

Therefore we both can receive this blessing.' After that with tears in their eyes the two of them ate the mantou. No wonder this mantou was especially fragrant and sweet.

Chapter 6

Through Fire and Through Water …
Out Into a Wealthy Place
(Psalm 66:12)

One day in October 1984, Yun was taken from the detention prison of 'B' city and sent to the Baoshan labour reform farm. This was located at the border of Henan and Hubei provinces. A range of mountains encircled it giving it a particular climate. Most of the year there was heavy fog and rain. There were many mosquitoes and poisonous snakes.

Most of the populace made their living by growing rice so this labour reform farm, with more than 1,000 prisoners, was surrounded with flooded rice paddies. During the four years Yun was in the labour reform camp, mist and water became his daily companions. Every time he stepped into the flooded rice paddies to work, leeches would crawl up his feet and thighs. There were so many that with one swipe he could catch a whole handful. To commemorate those years he wrote this song:

> In spring, summer, autumn and winter,
> snow follows the rain,
> Continual heavy fog and few clear days,
> Poison snakes, mosquitoes with leeches,
> Electric rods, ropes with leather whips.

The second day that Yun arrived at the labour reform farm with the other prisoners he had to dig a ditch. Then they carried the earth up a ladder to an upper slope. From the time of his arrest, he had encountered health ruining attacks and physical torment, so his body was very weak. As he struggled to carry one load of earth to the top of the ladder, he would become dizzy and faint. With the load of earth he tumbled down to the ground below.

It was a long time before he regained consciousness. Upon seeing what had happened, the brigade supervisor came over and asked Yun for which crime he had been sentenced. After reading his sentence, he nodded his head and said softly, 'Oh, so it was for believing in Jesus. One who believes in Jesus is not a bad person!'

Thank God, He had compassion on the weakness of His servant. From that time on the brigade supervisor was a bit more lenient towards Yun. Before long, those in the same cell with Yun sensed that he was no ordinary person. His words had a special power as he spoke with wisdom. He was full of love and compassion toward others and everyone gradually developed a great respect for him. Yun earned a reputation throughout the prison as the Christian who had fasted for 74 days.

There was a 70-year-old Catholic priest who was sentenced to ten years in prison for opposing the use of the Catholic Church as a political tool. He was taken to this labour reform farm the year before Yun arrived. Yun looked for ways to meet with him. At first the priest was wary of Yun and would not so much as greet him. But Yun prayed for him fervently, and loved him from the depth of his heart and served him. He gave him milk powder and some of the food that the brothers and sisters brought him. Eventually he came to know all about the torture that Yun had gone through in the prison and how he had fasted for 74 days. He could not help but respect him and from that time on his attitude towards Yun changed.

Yun gave him a Bible and some spiritual books and he was thrilled beyond description. He was a very learned person, and after studying the Bible and the spiritual books, he accepted the teachings of the Christian church. He became one of Yun's closest co-workers in the labour reform camp. He notified the Catholic believers outside prison to come and visit Yun. After both of them were released from prison, the priest visited Yun regularly and often invited him to the Catholic church to preach. Yun relied on the Holy Spirit and preached with great authority, so much so that he was well received by even the Catholic believers.

Yun touched the life of one other prisoner surnamed Zhou, who had been sent to a large Buddhist monastery when he was eight years old to receive training to be a monk. Hence, he had been a monk for several decades and not only did he have a thorough grasp of the Buddhist teachings but he was also a calligrapher. People were all the more amazed when they discovered that he was skilled in martial arts as well. His fingers could penetrate bricks and he could smash stones with his palms.

Once when he went to the market to purchase something, a pickpocket stole his money. He grabbed him and hit him only lightly but the thief died. This was reported to the PSB. Aware that Zhou had amazing abilities in martial arts several armed policemen were sent to capture him. Even if he could fly, how could he escape being captured by these well-trained police-men all armed with weapons? Zhou was eventually apprehended and beaten with the electric batons and rifle butts until he was barely alive. His left arm was broken.

While being held at a detention centre, he heard the Gospel of Jesus Christ and was attracted by what he heard. He began to doubt the teachings of the Buddhist religion of 'no colour, no taste, no feeling, no consciousness' and the 'five abstinences.' After he was sentenced he was sent to Yun's labour reform camp. Within a few days of his arrival at the camp, he met Yun. Yun explained to him in detail the superior way of salvation through Jesus and showed him the errors in the Buddhist religion and the sin of idol worship. Zhou immediately surren-dered all the 'yellow paper,' 'charms' and different types of amulets and burned them. He confessed his sins to the Lord, repented and turned to Jesus.

One was a Catholic priest, and the other an active disciple of Buddhism. But both were touched by the saving grace of Jesus Christ, and became Yun's brethren. You can imagine the great joy that was in Yun's heart.

Then there was another prisoner, a preacher in his thirties, who had fallen into sin, who also ended up in the labour reform camp. He, too, met Yun and through his love, exhortation, instruction, and prayers, obtained forgiveness of sins and a spiritual rebirth.

This brother was always at the forefront and willing to put up with hardship. He had a meek spirit, loved others as himself and was always smiling. Therefore, he earned the nickname, 'the laughing face.'

On December 25 of 1985, A-Hong and another brother came to visit Yun in prison. Yun was greatly touched by this. He said to the supervisor of the brigade, 'My two brothers here need to go to the lavatory and we ask you for permission.' The supervisor was very friendly towards Yun so he granted his request. Yun did this so that they could celebrate Christmas and worship the Lord in private together.

When the three of them entered the toilet, they remembered the birth of the Lord and visualized the Lord in the manger. Yun began to weep streams of tears and kneeling on the floor prayed, 'Lord, the situation is such that we can only worship you in such a place as this. You became a poor baby and were born in a freezing manger. Lord, we want to have a part in your manger, a part in your suffering and a part in your cross.'

While they were thus praying, someone came suddenly. It was a man named Ke, who was a relative of the supervisor of the labour reform camp. Ke was also the group leader of the prisoners. He was a very wicked man who continually reported the prisoners to the authorities and behaved like a tyrant.

When Ke discovered the three brothers praying in the toilet, he yelled at them, 'Yun, how dare you privately bring outsiders into the reform camp to conduct superstitious activities. I am going to report you to the superiors!'

Yun felt the power of the Holy Spirit well up in him and he said boldly, 'Ke, how dare you oppose our true God? In the holy Name of Jesus Christ of Nazareth, I command you to kneel down, surrender to the Lord and repent!' Hallelujah! His words were full of authority, and were more powerful than an emperor's edict. Ke found himself kneeling on the floor and, just like Saul on the road to Damascus, surrendered to the Lord.

Four years full of tribulation and suffering in the labour

reform camp soon ended. A hundred days before Yun's sentence was to end, the PSB went to Yun's house and conducted a thorough search. Several dozen PSB men surrounded the house and went through every drawer and cabinet in his home. As a result, Yun's Bible, spiritual books and notebook were all found. Of significance to them were the letters he had written to his family and the church while in prison and which were inspired by the Holy Spirit. In these letters, Yun had urged the brothers and sisters to be strong and bold and not fear the storms. He urged them not to attend the false church created by the government, because she is a harlot. On the back of one letter was a song describing life in prison:

> 'Living in a place of thorns, truly like a new grave,
>   One who enters with one devil turns into one with seven
>   devils, for chains cannot change a life.
> If one wants to change his life, he must repent and be born
>   again;
> The old man becomes a new one and daily he will sing
>   praises.'

There was another letter a brother had written to Yun in which he mentioned that a certain famous American evangelist had been invited by the Party leaders to visit China and to 'evangelise.' After they found these materials, the PSB immediately returned to the prison to search Yun's cell where they found his Bible, devotional and spiritual books.

Yun was bound and taken to the interrogation room. The supervisor of the PSB, the labour reform cadres and many PSB officials all glared at him.

The PSB chief pointed at him and said, 'You wretched prisoner, don't you fear anything?'

Yun replied calmly, 'Supervisor, I wish to report to you that from the time I was arrested until now I have obeyed the prison regulations, respected the leaders, worked diligently and I have not committed any crimes.'

The supervisor was so furious at his answer that he struck the bench and cursed Yun.

'You deceiving scoundrel. You have used so many tricks.

First when you were arrested in 'A' county you pretended to be insane and didn't say anything. Then while in detention in 'B' city you pretended to be sick and refused food. From that day until now you have resisted us. Who would have thought that when you were sent to the labour reform brigade you would commit all the more crimes?

'Firstly, you have conspired with foreigners. Several months before a certain American is to come to China, you already know about it. Moreover, the one who notified you about this is a wanted criminal in our country.

'Secondly, during your time in labour reform, you have won countless numbers of converts. If we were to allow you to remain locked up here a few more years, we are fearful you would take over control of the whole labour reform camp.' (Upon hearing this, Yun's joy was beyond measure and he praised the Lord).

'Thirdly, you have described the prison as a place of thorns, a new graveyard. You have ridiculed the Party's policy of labour reform saying that one with one devil turns into one with seven devils.

'Fourthly, you have opposed the religious policy of the Party, and regard the church that is supported by the Party as being a false church, a harlot. You! You! You have such nerve! We will show you a thing or two. Someone come and beat him up!'

At his command, several prison guards pounced on Yun and began to beat him mercilessly. It was as he had written in the song, 'electric batons, ropes and leather whips.' He was beaten until his flesh was cut open and wounds covered his body.

As a result, Yun was sentenced to solitary confinement for 100 days during which he was not allowed to see anyone. He was handcuffed and taken through four iron gates before reaching the solitary confinement cell. Inside, there was only one very dim light. The total area was about 12 square feet and the floor was very wet. It had been closed up all the year-round so the smell of mildew was exceptionally strong. It made one feel dizzy and nauseated. In this cell Yun never saw any sunlight. At first, he felt very lonely and the pain from the wounds caused by the whipping and the tight handcuffs made him feel all the more despondent.

One day, he heard the sound of a little bird chirping. He quickly jumped up to the iron gate. On the upper part of the gate was a small iron window that the guards used to observe the prisoners inside. But through a small crack in the latticed window he could actually see outside. He saw several small French parasol trees. On the branches were several small birds happily hopping about and spreading out their wings in play. They were so free!

Yun, with tears running down his face, asked of Him, 'Lord, when will I have freedom like these little birds?' Then the Word of the Lord came powerfully to him, *'For even hereunto were you called: because Christ also suffered for us, leaving us an example, that you should follow his steps.'* 1 Peter 2:21

He dropped to his knees and, lifting up his handcuffed hands, cried out, 'Lord, I am willing. I am willing to follow in your footsteps. Let your will be done in your servant!' Then his heart was consumed with the love, joy and peace of the Lord so that he was unable to refrain from singing out,

> *'Your love has bound my romantic wings, look down and listen to my tender song. Sweet love has moved me so deeply, I am willing to be a prisoner and don't want to fly away.'*

Yun had not read the Bible for days and there was such an intense hunger that he prayed fervently to the Lord for one. One night he had a dream in which he saw the handcuffs fall off his wrists and he was holding a Bible and reading it. The Catholic priest whom he had befriended in prison was standing on one side joyfully declaring, 'Jesus is victorious! Jesus is victorious!' Yun then awoke and, stretching out his hands, the handcuffs fell off.

The next day at 8:00 a.m., a section chief in the labour brigade pushed a Bible through the lattice window and said to him, 'Even though you have committed crimes, we still respect your faith. Come, here is your Bible. Take it!' Hallelujah, it was simply incredible! This section chief had always hated those who believed in the Lord. If he caught a prisoner reading the Bible he would snatch it away and rip it up. But God used him to bring a Bible to Yun.

Yun wept with joy. He held the Bible with reverence and turned to Revelation 22:20–21, '… *Even so, Come Lord Jesus.*' Then he studied the Bible day and night and in the short period of 90 days he not only read the entire Old and New Testaments, but also memorized all the scriptures from Hebrews to Revelation, a total of 55 chapters.

Chapter 7

All the House Feared God

(Acts 10:2)

God blessed Yun with a God fearing family. He had a loving mother and a virtuous wife. His mother was already in her seventies and throughout her life she faced tribulation, went through much labour and was faithful in service toward the Lord. She had love towards others. What's more, she continually fasted. Daily she wept and prayed for the church and the tens of thousands of lost souls.

Yun's wife, Lingling, was very young and came from a family that did not believe in the Lord. But when she met Yun and his family she came to know the Lord. When they were yet newly wed Yun had to leave home to evade arrest by the PSB for preaching. But she had sympathy for and understood her husband and prayed for him day and night. When Yun was finally arrested she was pregnant. She was very weak in health but all the responsibilities of the household fell on her.

At that time many brothers and sisters were also arrested and the church seemingly suffered a great setback. After Yun's arrest few brothers and sisters came to help her. And when Yun was sentenced as a counter-revolutionary political criminal, even her own brothers attacked her. All her relatives broke off ties with her.

Although she was several months into her pregnancy, she still had to go daily to the fields to work. One day she was very exhausted, and with great difficulty made it to the fields to pull out the weeds. She did this for several hours but the wheat field appeared so vast and so full of weeds she did not know how she could finish it. All of a sudden she became dizzy and fainted. She lacked the strength to stand and had simply collapsed.

After a while she came to. She realised that her family and friends had deserted her, her neighbours had ridiculed and reproached her, and her own brothers had dishonoured her. She felt so alone and brokenhearted as she lay in the wheat field. Then she looked up to heaven and began to sing Psalm 123, *'Unto you I lift up mine eyes, O you that dwell in the heavens.'* She sang until she burst into sobs.

It was some time before Brother Ming from 'F' city recruited some brothers and sisters to help Lingling with the farming. A-hong, who lived in a neighbouring village, also came to help. But the wife of Yun's brother together with the neighbours cursed and ridiculed her. Lingling daily washed her face with her tears and the time passed bitterly for her. Even so, the Lord's hand was upon her and she was strengthened in her heart by the scripture, *'We are troubled on every side, yet not distressed; perplexed, but not in despair; persecuted, but not forsaken; cast down, but not destroyed.'* (2 Corinthians 4:8–9)

Then Lingling received a letter from Yun that had been sneaked out from the prison. It gave her great comfort, for in the letter he had written this song,

> *'The body may grow older, relatives and friends may disperse, the road we go down may become more difficult, but you must obey the way of the Lord.'*

Her strength was renewed and she determined in her heart to be willing to bear the cross alongside her husband. Eventually the time came for Lingling to give birth. She was both happy and sad. She was rejoicing because she safely delivered a baby boy, but her heart pined for her husband who could not be there to share this precious moment. She thought, 'This child should be named by his father!'

That same evening Yun had a dream in which he saw Lingling holding a baby boy and walking up to him saying, 'Give this child a name!' Yun took hold of the child and said, 'His name shall be Isaac!' The next day when a relative came to tell Yun the good news he already had a name for his son.

Soon, the wheat fields were ready for harvesting. The brothers and sisters helped Yun's family to bring in part of the harvest. They left a small portion that had been reaped but had not been brought in from the field. That afternoon the weather suddenly changed and the blue sky was replaced by dark clouds. Thunder rumbled.

Lingling was still recovering from her pregnancy and was unable to get out of bed. Thus it fell on Yun's old mother to bring in this portion of grain. The old lady pulled the cart, shuffling on her tiny, bound feet, her gnarled hands trembling for lack of strength.

Then the inevitable happened. The cart overturned and landed in a ditch. Yun's mother suffered a broken arm and was severely injured in the thigh. Such were the tribulations that Lingling and her mother-in-law went through during Yun's imprisonment. Even so, the Lord watched over them and their hearts were always filled with heavenly peace.

Chapter 8

Go in to Possess the Land That the Lord Your God Gives You to Possess

(Joshua 1:11)

One day in 1987, the labour camp cadres told Yun he was to be transferred to 'B' city. His cell-mates thought that for sure he would be taken to the detention centre there to be severely punished. For the PSB had found much 'evidence' to use against Yun. Thus Yun was certain much more suffering was to come. However, he had determined in his heart not to hesitate at any sacrifice. He would be willing to give his life for the Lord and would even be glad to shed his blood.

The next morning a labour brigade truck from the PSB in 'B' city came to take him. There he faced PSB men in addition to several Party cadres, supervisors from the United Front Department of 'B' city, and the head of the Religious Affairs Department.

Gravely, the head of the PSB said, 'You should know that your problem is very serious. You should be severely punished. However because your stubborn head will not change even if we kill you, we have decided to allow you to return home. Moreover we want to proclaim to you;

1. **You have been stripped of all your political rights and there is no way you can remove 'the hat' of having been a political prisoner. You must come under the control and supervision of the local government.**
2. **You must report to the PSB once a month.**
3. **You must attend the Three-Self Church that is recognized and supported by the government.**

Yun answered, 'Respected leaders, since I have been stripped of all my political rights, how could I have the privilege of attending this great organization that is supported by the government? Is this not a contradiction in terms?'

The PSB chief was speechless with anger. 'Yun, you are so deceitful. We must sternly warn you that after you return home if you dare to incite the believers to oppose the religious policy of the Party, you will bear the consequences!'

Soon after Yun returned home, he was visited by the provincial PSB, and the district and county PSB officials. In the village where Yun lived a major mass meeting was held. This was attended by all the cadres and people's militia. During the meeting they played up the religious policy of the Party and 'how it was supported by the people.' They stated that previously Christianity was a tool used by foreign countries to invade China and it had poisoned the people.

They also warned, 'Only the Three-Self Church is recognized and supported by the government.'

They reiterated that all home meetings were illegal and all the cadres and people's militia had the authority to punish people who take part in such meetings.

At the end of the meeting the PSB announced:

1. **Yun is still a political prisoner and has been stripped of all his political rights.**
2. **The local authorities, cadres, people's militia and all the people have the authority to supervise his activities.**
3. **He must report once a month to the PSB.**
4. **He cannot leave his village on his own.**
5. **If any unknown person has contact with him, Yun must immediately be bound and taken to the police station for investigation.**

But how can man stop the work of the Lord? Soon after Yun returned home, the work of the Gospel in his village began to prosper greatly. Yun was full of the power of the Holy Spirit and many miracles and signs followed him.

Those neighbours who had ridiculed Lingling in the past now became believers in Jesus. They deeply regretted their persecution of Yun's family. Yun's brother and sister-in-law also repented. The fire of the Gospel spread throughout the whole village. It was just as Yun had said the night he was arrested, that he lived in Gospel Village! In the neighbouring villages the number of believers increased dramatically. The churches in 'B' county experienced a great revival. Hallelujah. Glory to the Lord's name!

Yun located the family of Brother Huang. When Huang's father and mother saw Yun they embraced him and cried out loud. 'We received the blood letter that you helped our son to write and we know how much you loved him when he was in prison. You are the saviour of our son and the saviour of our whole family. Even though our son is dead, from now on you will become our son.'

Yun said, 'Though your son's body is dead, his spirit is alive for he has gone to rest in Jesus. Similarly, the words he has written to you in the blood letter are not dead. His prayers are as much alive. Today the main reason I have come is to tell you the last wish of your son. He said you must believe in Jesus!'

Huang's parents knew it would be very difficult for them to do so, because they were high-ranking cadres. Yun spent several hours talking with them and eventually they stuffed several hundred dollars into his pocket. Yun pulled out the money and left it on the tea tray.

He said, 'I do not want your money, but your souls. Now in the holy Name of Jesus Christ of Nazareth I command you to kneel down and accept Jesus as your Saviour!'

His words poured out like a mighty torrent. Huang's parents immediately dropped onto their knees, and with tears confessed their sins to the Lord. From that day on, they became the disciples of the Lord.

As he left them and was walking down the road, Yun thought he heard many voices coming from all around saying, 'Come over here! Bring the torch of revival to us here!'

Yes, he had to take the abundant grace of the Lord, to bring the healing power of the resurrected Lord, to save millions of souls. He must go to each province, each district, every mountain, every island, and every race.

Yun went boldly forward for His Lord.

PART THREE

The Mother Who Gave Birth to Many Children in Prison

Chapter 1

For the Son of Man Came to Seek and to Save That Which Was Lost

(Luke 19:10)

I was previously one who persecuted Jesus. One day, mother became very sick and was in great pain. Then, she desperately wanted to believe in Jesus. But I objected vehemently and forbade her to become a Christian. To my sorrow, she succumbed to her illness and died. In the winter of 1979, I myself became sick and my three children fell ill, too, one after another. I had prayed to Buddhist gods, but I never found any peace. On the contrary, it caused me more sorrow. There was no way out but suicide.

As I drew near to the gates of hell, the Lord saved me through a neighbour and the Holy Spirit enlightened me. I confessed my sins, repented and the Lord healed me of all my diseases without the help of any medicine. My children were also healed and since that time they have always been healthy, full of life and loved by all.

My heart brimmed with joy and I constantly sang, prayed and hungered for the Word of God. Naturally, I shared the Gospel with my husband and prayed for him. As a result he was healed of high blood pressure. However, Satan used him to attack me. He forbade me to attend Christian meetings and to pray. Every evening I had to wait until he went to sleep before I could pray in the courtyard. If he found me praying, I would be harshly reprimanded. But I was not discouraged. Instead, I was always full of joy and I prayed fervently for the Lord to make a way for me to lead my husband to repentance.

Five months after I was saved, my husband was electrocuted while working at a factory. I was full of sorrow and despair. Then due to much persecution from my mother-in-law and the family, I went into shock and fell unconscious for about 30 minutes. The brothers and sisters came and prayed for me after hearing what happened. Thank God for his grace, for I regained consciousness, and immediately stood up, totally restored.

Life was very difficult after my husband's death. I had to care for not only my three children (at that time the oldest child was nine years and the youngest three), but also my mother-in-law. She tried to force me out of the house and used all kinds of ways to persecute me. She even cursed me daily. But my God always watched over me and took care of me so that I had the will to continue to live.

I had been married to my husband for many years and though he was gone, I still had some feelings for him. So I looked for a picture he had taken before he died and had it enlarged at the photo studio. Then I brought it home and wept daily whenever I looked at it. As a result, I lost my peace and joy and the devil caused me to have painful memories. This photo soon became a snare to me and I almost caused a disaster because of it.

One day, a servant of the Lord came to visit me. As soon as she entered my house, she fell over and died. Petrified, I did not know what to do and could only kneel before the Lord and cry for mercy.

'Lord, how can I bear this burden? Lord, have pity on this widow! I don't know where I have offended you. I ask you to show me my sin and have mercy on me!'

Then, I carried this sister to my bed. My oldest son ran a distance of 15 li (7.5 km.) to ask the brethren to come and pray.

Suddenly, the photo of my deceased husband flashed through my mind. Instantly, I felt led to put it away. A miracle took place. The dead sister came back to life. The Lord loved me, but He knew my heart, and He knew that I loved the world and vanity. He had wanted me to forsake all idols, look to him alone and serve Him singlemindedly. I ripped the photo and threw it into the fire. When the believers arrived, we all worshipped and praised the Lord together and sent God's servant on her way with rejoicing.

However Satan would not leave my family alone. Whenever the brothers and sisters came to visit me they would feel uneasy in their spirits. At that time I lived on the 4th floor.

One day, an old sister in her 70's came to visit me. As she knelt down to pray with my family, my young daughter cried out from her bed, 'My legs hurt!' I did not think anything about it and continued to pray. After some time she let out a piercing scream, 'Mother, my leg …!' She screamed and screamed, but soon she ceased screaming. She was dead!

My eight-year-old daughter jumped on the bed and embraced her dead sister. For no rhyme or reason she, too, died. Truly 'misfortunes never come singly.' Then the old sister who had come to pray with me immediately stood up and went to lift up my older daughter. Strangely, she also fell over on the floor and died. It was too much for me. I was scared to death and did not even know how to pray. I sobbed and prayed at the same time, crying 'God, please save us!'

The neighbours heard the sound of wailing from our house and immediately ran over. When they observed what had happened and found me praying unceasingly, they simply shook their heads and went home one by one. One of them reported the matter to my factory supervisor. Soon, a flat-bed cart arrived at my house to take the three deceased to the hospital.

The supervisor of the factory said, 'Chan, after all this are you still going to continue to believe in Jesus?'

'I not only believe, but I will believe to the end,' I replied. 'I must be a testimony to you so that you can believe in Jesus too.'

The supervisor retorted, 'Nonsense. Take the dead bodies to the hospital. Superstition cannot save you. You have been a victim of superstition.'

Then, the Spirit of the Lord came upon me. I stood up and declared boldly, 'We are not going to the hospital. Our Lord will certainly save us.'

Those words barely left my mouth when a second miracle took place. My daughters and the old sister simultaneously came to life again. The supervisor was astonished beyond words. He left in a huff.

The above incidents showed how God dealt with my life. He knew that I was weak and pitiful in spirit, and that I loved my children more than the Lord and the world more than the souls of men. Therefore He allowed these things to try me, purify me and cause me to truly know His love. My heart was brought into total submission to Him. I was being prepared for the suffering I was to face in the coming days so that I might shine for Him in prison and save others.

God used my home to minister to those in need. Nearly every day the brethren would bring with them those who needed prayer. The Word of the Lord tells us, *'If you cannot love your brother whom you can see, how can you love the Lord who you cannot see?'* (1 John 4:20) Therefore I was very willing to receive the brothers and sisters.

At that time, my three children and I were only given food rations for one person. Life was extremely hard, but the Lord blessed me with wonderful children. They were of one heart with me and daily we determined to eat only one meal, which was mostly very coarse food. The children would go uncomplainingly into the fields to look for wild vegetables to eat with the coarse steamed bread (mantou). When the brothers and sisters came to visit we would hide the mantou and purchase fine flour instead to make a meal for them.

By God's grace, He protected our health and we praised the Lord daily. Sometimes, as I went about my Father's business I became late for work. The factory deducted my wages and I had to face criticism. Yet, I was full of joy and peace.

Chapter 2

Whom Shall I Send? And Who Will Go For Us?

(Isaiah 6:8)

In 1982 God called me to go to a distant place to preach the Gospel. At that time, I did not have a Bible nor did I have the gift of preaching. I did not know where God wanted me to go. (He was actually calling me to enter prison and preach the Good News there.)

In March of the following year I went with five brothers and sisters to a certain place to baptize believers. When we returned home, a sister who had cancer came to my house for prayer. Brother Wu, Sister Lin and I fasted and prayed for three days. There was no improvement, in fact she became worse. She was barely breathing and it became apparent that there was no hope.

In despair, I cried and asked the Lord to take the soul of my child instead of her. God did not answer my prayers and as a result this sister died in my home.

Many brothers and sisters from the church soon came. They criticized me and told me I was ignorant, but I had peace in my heart. I was not discouraged, I did not complain and I was not afraid. Brother Wu and Sister Lin stayed by me. However, I knew this matter would result in severe consequences and I did not want to implicate them. So I firmly insisted that they leave quickly that I alone might bear total responsibility. But they refused to leave and chose to suffer with me. As a result, Sister Lin and I were taken to the local police station.

As soon as we arrived we were separated for questioning.

They interrogated me first and my interrogator asked in a harsh voice, 'Who was responsible for that woman's death?'

'I am,' I said.

'No, it wasn't you. It was a man!' (Actually my neighbours had already reported the other two to the Public Security Bureau).

'No, I alone prayed for her. Nobody else participated.'

'How did you cause her death?'

'I urged her to go to the hospital, but she absolutely refused. I only sang hymns and prayed to God,' I replied.

The officer exploded and slammed his fist on the table. 'You had better come clean. Otherwise you will suffer much!' As he was speaking he picked up an instrument of torture to scare me.

The Lord poured out His mercy on me, so that I was able to stand strong.

I insisted, 'Truly I was the one who prayed for her. Because her time on earth had ended, her spirit was taken to heaven.'

'What spirit, what heaven?'

I said, 'Yes, man truly has a spirit. We believe in Jesus not only that we may have health, but also that our souls might be saved. I entreat you to believe in Jesus also, for He has said: *"He that believes has eternal life and he who doesn't believe is condemned already."'* (John 6:47, 3:18)

'Shut up! Woman, you should fear for your own life,' the officer shouted. 'Your belief in Jesus has caused someone's death and you want me to believe too?'

I looked him in the eye and said, 'Sir, I have already preached the Gospel to you. If you don't believe and are judged in the future, I am not responsible.'

The officer was speechless with anger and, with a wave of his hand, signalled to the other guards to take me away.

It was Sister Lin's turn next.

'Tell the truth,' the officer commanded. 'Was it that man who killed the sick person? If you admit the facts, you can redeem yourself and your crime will be forgiven.'

Without hesitation, Sister Lin answered, 'No, no, this has nothing to do with Brother Wu and it has nothing to do with Sister Chan. I bear full responsibility, for I brought this sick person to Chan's house and I prayed for her daily in Chan's house.'

95

In spite of threats as well as enticements from her interrogator, Sister Lin stood firm and would not change her statement. She insisted, 'I bear full responsibility.'

Thus the PSB allowed me temporarily to return home and ordered me to pay ¥500 RMB to the deceased's family to cover the funeral expenses. But where would a poor widow like me find that kind of money? My children and I went all over borrowing money. Brother Wu and Sister Lin thought of many ways and eventually we were able to give ¥500 RMB to the family of the dead sister.

Brother Wu knew I had three small children and realized they would become his responsibility if I went to prison. He also knew that Sister Lin's husband and mother-in-law were not believers and her children were small. So he considered giving himself up to the authorities rather than leave the responsibility to others.

After praying earnestly the Lord gave him sufficient strength to leave his own family and without considering the consequences, Brother Wu turned himself in. The investigating officer immediately questioned him. He did not deny anything and bore all responsibility. He did his best to remove any suspicion of wrongdoing from myself and Sister Lin.

The PSB considered him the main culprit and duly arrested him. When I heard the news, I quickly purchased some presents and went to Brother Wu's house to comfort his wife and children. After returning home on March 2, 1983, I then went to the detention centre of the Public Security Bureau to look for Brother Wu. However how would the PSB allow people to freely see the prisoners?

I told the PSB official, 'This case is my responsibility. Why have you locked up Brother Wu? You must release him. I will take the blame.'

'This matter has nothing to do with me. He was brought here on the orders of those above me.'

'Well, can I give him a towel and some food?' I asked.

'No, it is impossible.'

I persisted and demanded, 'Comrade, allow me to do so! People in prison need towels!'

Finally, he gave in out of pity, and said, 'Give me the towel and I will give it to him.'

I saw him walk towards cell number one. I had heard others say that this was where people who have committed serious crimes are held. The prisoners there are severely punished daily. I felt very bad and called out Brother Wu's name loudly.

Then one of the guards reprimanded me, 'Where do you think you are that you can shout like this? Don't you know prison regulations?'

Seizing the opportunity, I said, 'Wu has committed no crime. Here, lock me up instead and set him free.'

They firmly propelled me out of the detention area without another word. The next day, I again took some daily necessities and a blanket to the prison. I called out Brother Wu's name loudly hoping he could hear. But once again I was driven out.

On March 15 Sister Lin was arrested. I had waited in my home for half a month, but they still had not come for me. I still had to work in the factory daily. Two weeks later, in the morning, my beloved children faced me and began to cry bitterly. I patted their heads and comforted them.

'My beloved children, don't cry. When you cry this way it breaks mother's heart. If mother goes to prison, the Heavenly Father will raise you. The brothers and sisters, uncles and aunties in the Church are your sisters, brothers, uncles and grandmothers. They will be concerned about you.' After consoling them I took them to work as usual.

At 9:00 o'clock, the supervisor of the factory called me into his office and told me he must take me to the police station. I knew, from that moment on, that for the sake of the Lord I would have to walk a very difficult road. As I walked past my children, I tried not to show my emotion. These three pitiful children had already lost their father at a young age. And now their mother had to leave them and they would become like orphans without anyone to depend on. How could I bear to look at their tear-stained faces?

When I arrived at the police station, the PSB were waiting for me.

'Do you know why we brought you here today?'

'I know why.'

'You are under arrest.' The PSB showed me the warrant for my arrest. It was 9:45 a.m.

I signed my name on the arrest warrant. The Lord had mercy on me and they allowed me to return home to pick up some clothes and put things in order. Then I wanted so badly to break down and cry, but the Lord gave me wonderful peace. Although I had found myself in such a situation, I would not shed a tear in the presence of others.

They bound me tightly and put me on the 'prisoners truck.' I was full of joy. The Word of the Lord came to me, *'For I am not ashamed of the Gospel of Christ: for it is the power of God unto salvation to every one that believeth; to the Jew first, and also to the Greek.'* (Romans 1:16) As the truck proceeded through the main street, many people lining both sides of the road stared at me. The Lord told me not to hang my head, but rather to look up with a smile at the crowds.

In my heart I said to myself, 'I have not broken any law, but am a prisoner for the sake of the Lord.' I did not feel any shame at all, in fact this was a great honour for me. At the same time the Lord reminded me of a poem written by Madam Curie, 'Your love has bound my romantic wings.'

When I arrived at the courtyard of the Public Security Bureau, I knelt down on the ground to pray. A man seeing me in this place continually praying came up to me with great anger. With one hand he grabbed me and pulled me up and with the other he untied me and dragged me into the prison. Sister Lin, who was in cell 24, saw me and cried out in tears, 'Why have you brought my sister here? This matter concerns only me and has nothing to do with her!'

Oh, such compassion! Even though she was in the same boat, she was still concerned about me and my three small children. She took the total responsibility of this 'crime' upon herself. I wanted to run to her, embrace her and cry. But there were compassionless prison bars separating us as the hard-hearted prison guard pushed me into cell number 20.

Thank the Lord, for in everything He watches over us. Although Brother Wu, Sister Lin and I were separated and placed in different cells, we were able to communicate with each other through a woman prisoner who had been sentenced to death. Sister Lin led her to the Lord not long after she began her prison term.

The inhumane persecution and cruel treatment meted out to Sister Lin in cell 24 would shock anyone. There is no guarantee it will never occur again, and it is certainly without precedent. After Sister Lin entered the prison, she saw the pitiful condition of the prisoners and had compassion for them. She loved them with the love of the Lord. Not only did she give them food brought in from outside the prison, but she would daily eat only a small amount of the food so that she could share the rest with those who were on the verge of starvation. She preached Jesus and in a very short time many repented and were saved.

After a time of observation, the women prisoners seeing how gracious, meek and gentle she was towards them, warmed to Sister Lin. She was also willing to suffer, so they chose her to be their monitor. One morning, Sister Lin went to the canteen as usual to bring a bucket of rice to the cell. She found some red toilet paper near the top of the bucket by the lid. Upon a closer look, she found some human faeces on it. Unfazed, she took the bucket of rice to the cell, scooped out the clean rice in the middle of the bucket for the others to eat and left the remainder of the contaminated rice on the side and bottom for herself.

As she was eating she thought of Isaiah 53:7–8, *'He is brought as a lamb to the slaughter, and as a sheep before her shearers is dumb, so he opened not his mouth. He was taken from prison and from judgment.'* She said to the Lord, 'Lord, you are the Son of God, yet you opened not your mouth and accepted reproach and humiliation, and willingly died on the cross. A student cannot be greater than the teacher. Lord I am willing to accept the reproach of the world.' She ate her meal with tears in her eyes. This went on for many days.

The husband of the sister who had died in Sister Chan's house was an evil man and was an enemy of the Gospel. When his wife was alive, he had persecuted her for her faith. Each time he found her praying he would either kick her or beat her with his fists. Once, he found his wife kneeling on the floor in prayer. He found a large stone weighing several dozen kilograms and placed it on her legs. After her death not only did he demand ¥500 RMB from me for the burial expenses, but he continually accused me and was determined not to give up until he had the three of us executed.

All through several sessions of interrogation, the three of us were consistent in our confessions. Each of us insisted on being responsible for the 'crime.' This caused the authorities great consternation. However, they finally discussed among themselves and said, 'Whenever we interrogate the prisoners, they always do their utmost to deny the charges against them and insist on having a lawyer come to argue their case. But who has ever heard of someone wanting to be 'charged with a crime' and asking for execution? Just what type of people are these Christians?'

The authorities permitted us to hire a lawyer, but we knew that it was God's will that we were in prison. Therefore we decided to forego this privilege. The authorities were greatly amazed. The family of the deceased had demanded that the authorities execute one of us, sentence another to life imprisonment, and the third to 20 years in prison. However, because the three of us insisted on being executed, they had to change their original plans. I was sentenced to six years, Brother Wu received seven years and Sister Lin, eight years. These sentences were totally in the hands of the Lord.

I was sentenced on July 23. But the amazing thing was that a few days before, I was allowed to return home for a few days to see my children. I entered our house, and saw my poor children, especially my six-year-old daughter who continually pleaded, 'Mother, you cannot go back to prison. I cannot leave you!' Then I lost all courage and great sorrow flooded my heart. Later, I realized that Satan used this time to attack my faith. But God truly loved me and sent His servant to use words from the Bible to comfort me and strengthen my faith.

The day before I was sentenced, God sent a sister to pray for me. I called the children together and very calmly comforted them and gave instructions to them as though I was leaving for just a short period or being sent on a job somewhere.

'Tomorrow Mother will leave you so tonight we will all pray together.'

So we all knelt on the floor and prayed with one heart. We thanked God and praised Him. I committed the children to the Lord, and after the children had gone to bed I prayed with the sister all night long.

I thank our Lord, for He truly loved my children and I. From the time I arrived home all my children would not stop crying and did not want me to return to prison. But now that they had been comforted in their spirits the Lord used my six-year-old to increase my faith. The next morning as I kissed the children goodbye I said, 'Mother must leave now, so you must listen to the Word of the Lord and be good children who love God.' My six-year-old daughter did not cry. Instead, her eyes shining, she comforted me with these words, 'Mother, you are going to prison for the Lord so do not worry!'

Hallelujah! I thank the Lord, for out of the mouth of babes the Lord has ordained strength. 'Thank the Lord, please come downstairs with me.' Everybody accompanied me to the door and saw me off. I was praising the Lord. I asked the Lord to give me the words to speak to the judge.

There was tight security in the courtroom when Brother Wu and Sister Lin were brought in. Because they had preached the Gospel in prison, they faced severe persecution. Brother Wu suffered a great deal. He had become as skinny as a stick and there was no colour in his face. His handcuffs had cut deeply into his wrists and his arms were red and swollen. The wounds on his body had become infected and pus was oozing out. I could not bear to look at him.

Before we entered the courtroom for the trial, we had discussed certain matters in notes passed to each other. Brother Wu had asked, 'Sister, on the day we are to be tried should we have a lawyer represent us?' Sister Lin replied, 'Of course we must. We have already found a lawyer who is the greatest and the most righteous of them all, that is our Lord Jesus!'

In the courtroom, Brother Wu looked at me, his eyes full of faith, which greatly encouraged me. The trial began and the three of us stood before the judge, each clamouring to be recognised as the 'chief culprit.'

I said, 'I am the leader.'

Brother Wu swiftly declared, 'It is not you, it is me.'

Then Sister Lin interjected, 'It is not either of you, it is me.'

The judge shook his head and heaved a sigh. 'I have been a judge for several decades and I have never seen such people.'

Then I became especially concerned, for Brother Wu had an

80-year-old mother, a young wife, and two small, weak children. Sister Lin had an unbelieving mother-in-law, husband and two young children. How could they bear this burden? But the Lord said, 'This is of Me.' He wanted the three of us to attend that 'university' so that we could learn how to save the souls of men.

Finally, the judge stood up and read the sentence. As I have mentioned before, Brother Wu and Sister Lin were sentenced to seven and eight years respectively. I was given six years. After reading the sentence, he took out a rope and I voluntarily put my hands behind my back and allowed them to tie me up. But they handcuffed me to Sister Lin instead. And they used a thin nylon cord to tie up Brother Wu tightly.

That day was Good Friday, the day our Lord suffered for us. My heart was full of joy and I said, 'Lord, you have chosen this day for us. We are certainly greatly blessed.'

As we were being taken back to the prison, the Holy Spirit prompted me and Sister Lin to walk quickly. So we jogged to the gate and when the guard was not looking we loosened Brother Wu's bonds. It was a rather long way from the courthouse to the prison. All along the journey many brothers and sisters from many provinces turned out to see us. They were all crying. When we were eventually pushed inside the formidable prison gates they all stood outside wailing loudly.

That evening, the Lord gave me a special vision. I saw a large character for the word 'Congratulations' written in the sky. An extremely bright, golden light was flashing. Joy began to bubble in my heart like living waters and I opened my mouth wide, lifted up both hands high and, praising the Lord, declared, 'Lord, You have provided for me this road of the cross. This is the sign that your love has come to me and this is a celebrated and joyful road. Hallelujah!'

On August 13, the authorities notified my family that they could bring me things. Brothers and sisters from many districts quickly came. Among them was God's servant, Brother Jian from 'F' city who brought many brothers and sisters as well as my children to visit me in prison. They were not afraid of the prison guards and came to see me personally. In the prison courtyard we exhorted and encouraged one another for about half an hour. Eventually, the guards sent them away and shut the large prison gate. Then I ran up the stairs to the first floor to look out at the brothers and sisters outside. The Holy Spirit urged me to speak briefly to them.

At that moment, it was nearly impossible for me to speak, but I looked at my children and exhorted them, 'You must love one another, be one in heart and mind, let absolutely nothing divide you and the God who is Three in One will be with you and protect you.' The brothers and sisters also understood that the message was for them, and they were greatly touched and began to weep loudly.

I said to my children, 'Be of one heart, for although Mother has left you, there are one thousand mothers and fathers who will take care of you.'

A prison guard pushed me down but Brother Jian and the other brethren stood outside the prison for a long time and refused to leave. Many prison guards were greatly moved by the scene and could only say, 'Only those who believe in Jesus have this kind of love!' That night I was taken out for a tongue lashing by the PSB head. But I kept quiet and did not say a word. My heart was full of joy, however.

Two days later, the authorities told me that I would be sent to a labour reform farm in another county. I had imagined that the three of us would ride the same prison truck to the labour farm. The authorities, however, had other plans and were determined to separate us. Sister Lin was sent to prison cell number five and Brother Wu was sent to another labour reform camp. I was bound tightly and pushed into the prison truck, my heart heavy with sorrow. Along the way, I saw an old man holding a tiny lamb that had just been weaned. The little lamb was bleating as though it was not willing to be taken from its mother.

'Lord, truly I am like this lamb, for as I was drinking milk I have had to leave my brothers and sisters. I ask you to protect my children!'

I remembered how Brother Wu, Sister Lin and I would communicate with each other with letters. The three of us had once written, 'I will see you again in heaven.' We believed the day of the Lord was very near and as each of us had such long prison sentences, we were fearful we would never have the opportunity to see each other face to face again. As I began sobbing sorrowfully, the captain of the guards responsible for transporting me snapped, 'What are you crying about? You should have thought about that before you committed the crime.'

I said, 'I have not committed a crime, for I am a prisoner for Jesus. Comrade, I urge you to quickly believe in Jesus for He can save me and you. If you believe, you will be more fervent than me.'

Then the Lord allowed me to preach the Gospel and my heart was restored. I felt at peace again. Soon we arrived at a labour reform farm where I was to spend five years doing arduous labour there. (I had already spent one year of my sentence in the detention prison.)

Chapter 3

I am Sending You To Them
(Acts 26:17)

All the prisoners at the labour reform farm were women, altogether 600 of them. Apart from me there was only one other woman prisoner who was a believer and she was in my cell. However, she was full of fear and had a timid spirit. All types of criminals could be found in this place – murderers, ruffians, prostitutes, kidnappers, thieves, corrupt people and so on. Some were sentenced to life, some to 20 years, 15 years, ten years and eight years. Their hearts were full of sin, darkness and hopelessness.

Whenever the inmates were taken out for exercise or for meals, and everywhere in the prison cells all you could hear was filthy, crude language, cursing and fighting. Quite often one could hear wailing and reports of people committing suicide. This was truly hell on earth, the most filthy, squalid place in the world. When I saw these poor souls, living without hope and facing eternal damnation, I was so burdened in my heart that I was unable to rest day or night.

I earnestly prayed to the Lord, 'Lord, you called me to go to a distant place to preach the Gospel. I know this is the place and I want to thank you. When I look at these poor, unfortunate people, how can I keep silent? Woe is me if I do not preach the Gospel! I ask you to help me!' But this was a prison, a place where one was not allowed to talk freely. We were forbidden to kneel down to pray. Only on Sunday when the rest of the women prisoners were allowed into the courtyard could I kneel facing the wall and pray. The only other time was at midnight when I could seek the Lord for quite a long time. The rest of the time although I prayed fervently and unceasingly, it was quiet prayer.

My inmates observed that I was different from the others. I did not fight or curse, but I was cheerful, gentle and cared about others. The love of Christ in me attracted many people to Him. I used every opportunity to preach the Gospel and many of them wept as they accepted Jesus. I would share with them during meal times or out of the cells. Sometimes we would talk in the bathroom or during the screening of movies or when we were allowed to watch television. I would lead them in prayer and, having scribbled Bible verses and songs in my notebook, I would rip these out to give to the new believers.

Their lives began to change and the whole prison was transformed. Not all the inmates accepted the Gospel, but even those who did not would seek me out whenever they had difficulties or learned about family problems in letters from home. After a time of comforting and counselling, their depression and fears left. The Lord daily added new converts to my ministry. In the first cell that I was in, 15 out of 20 prisoners repented, were born again and became my sisters.

Then when I was transferred to prison cell number two the circumstances were incredibly difficult. The guards were very strict in their supervision. Anyone found preaching the Gospel or praying would be severely dealt with. But the Lord knew my weakness and time after time I was able to stand up to the punishment. Later I was moved to cell number five.

This women's prison was built on a plain. Spread over several hundred acres there were four large buildings of four storeys each. In the main prison complex there were 30 cells on each floor. To the west and east of this were the factories where the prisoners worked. The block to the south, next to the main gate, housed the administrative offices and the living quarters for the cadres. The courtyard at the front and back was very spacious. In the middle of the courtyard was some sparse vegetation. It was late autumn and the flowers and leaves had long gone, leaving the countryside devoid of colour and life, awaiting a bleak winter. Surrounding the prison was a wall 3,000 meters long and seven meters high that separated it from the world. Topped by a high voltage electric fence it was enough to deter break-outs.

The prison was supposedly built over a graveyard. Not long after I arrived I heard rumours that during the night one could hear 'ghosts' crying. It made one's hair stand on end. There were several hundred prison guards, with a brigade supervisor, unit head, disciplinary supervisor and prison warden, all of whom were women. The head warden of the prison was about 50 years old. She had been in charge of labour reform for many years and had much experience. She was gentle, thorough in her job and put her whole heart into her work.

As for our unit head, she was respected by all and a 'good person' in the eyes of the world. She was of medium build with a long face and large eyes. Though she was over 40 years old, she still looked very young and attractive. She always wore a smile and did not look at all like an official. She was concerned about others and took an interest in the prisoners' daily lives and their health. Sometimes she would buy candy and leave it on the table for the inmates. They were so touched by her kindness that they felt too embarrassed to grab the candy.

Sadly, they did not know God. Moreover they did not realize that laws, prison and torture were unable to change hearts. During my years in prison I desired to preach the Gospel to them, but never had the opportunity. This caused me great regret. The disciplinary supervisor was the one who wielded authority. She was in her 40s, rather thin and short with large eyes set unevenly on a long, lean face. She was hot-tempered and extremely fierce and brutal. She was always in military attire and wore a police helmet. A natural at bullying, she loved to flaunt her position and authority with smug confidence. In her hand was an electric prod and if one was not careful she would either beat or curse them or shock them with it. Our sisters suffered much at her hands as she instigated most of the persecution.

Whenever the prisoners saw her coming they would all begin to work hard and avoid looking at her, for fear that she would use the instruments of torture to attack them. But as soon as she left the unsaved prisoners would curse her and mutter under their breath, 'tyrant'.

Shortly after we arrived, several sisters were brought into the prison for evangelistic activities. Among them was Sister

Sheng. She was also sent by God to the prison to preach the Gospel. Though her prison term was short, she led many to believe in the Lord.

One day, a very young sister whom Sister Sheng had led to the Lord met me as we were washing our clothes. Greatly moved and with tears in her eyes she asked me, 'Mother, I truly thirst after God's word. Can you find some way to get me a Bible?'

Rejoicing I told her, 'Daughter, put your heart at ease for God has provided.' I gave her a notepad in which I had copied many Scripture portions. She was so joyful that she began to dance.

Every afternoon at 3:30 the prisoners were allowed into the courtyard for an hour of free activities. Two days later, she again sought me out during the free time and, carefully placing the notepad under my clothes, she implored, 'Mother, I desperately need a Bible!' I eventually was able to get a New Testament for her. Upon receiving it she worked hard at copying the Bible.

How did she achieve this under the watchful eyes of the prison guards? During the day, everyone had to work ten hours of hard labour under constant surveillance, so it was not possible to do it then. But at night when all the other prisoners were sound asleep she hid under her blanket and, allowing a small amount of light in (the lights were never turned off at night), she would scribble furiously with all her might. But the long hours of hard manual labour often left her body extremely exhausted. As winter approached the thin blanket could not keep out the cold so her teeth would chatter as she copied. Undeterred, she took advantage of every opportunity to copy the Bible, driven by the other sisters' need for God's Word.

Line after line of beautiful calligraphy, scripture after scripture, precious words from the Bible flowed from her pen. She prepared one copy after another of the Bread of Life. Often, she was tempted to sleep, and she would find herself nodding off and her pen slipping out of her fingers. But each time she would see a picture of the sisters with their hands outstretched begging for a Bible. She would then wake up with a jolt and continue copying until the small hours of the morning.

The completed hand copied Bibles were then given to believers in the cells. The recipients knelt before the Lord in thanksgiving and lost no time in reading and studying. They would forego several minutes of their meal break while others rushed off to eat. And when they were allowed to walk about in the courtyard, many of the believers would rather stay in their cells to study the Bible. Sometimes they would even read when they went to the bathroom or late at night when it was quiet for study. They used every opportunity to earnestly pursue the Truth.

Chapter 4
Endure Afflictions,
Do the Work of an Evangelist
(2 Timothy 4:5)

In the latter part of 1983, after Sister Sheng joined us in prison, the number of prisoners increased until there were more than 4,000 inmates. Sister Sheng and I often fellowshipped together and she informed me that in every cell the sisters were fasting and praying for great revival in the prison that it might be turned into the Lord's church. Many of them wept before the Lord and their fervent prayers and tears ascended to heaven without ceasing.

It was impossible to count the many wonderful works the Lord did during that time. God's Spirit worked through each of His children as they boldly preached the Good News to all the prisoners without fear of detection. Many sinners who had committed every evil under the sun turned to the Lord, confessed their sins and repented. Many hearts were cleansed by Jesus' precious blood, including many prison officials.

By 1984 the revival in the prison had reached unimaginable proportions. The number of believers were like clusters of ripened fruit drooping from the branches of a large vine. So many were being born again that we lost count! The powers of hell had been defeated. This prison, that was once full of filth and shame, was now filled with the love and glory of the Lord. Darkness had been driven away by this light. No longer could we hear people wailing in despair, nor cursing, nor swearing, nor dirty jokes and foul language. Instead, shouts of 'hallelujah,' praises, gladness, rejoicing and praying could be heard.

Whenever the believers met, one would greet the other, 'Hallelujah, Praise the Lord!' And the response would be, 'Hallelujah, Amen!' Wherever you went, you could hear this one phrase, 'Hallelujah' to which many would chorus back the same.

When the prisoners had their break in the courtyard, the believers would gather in groups to pray, or to share what they received from Bible study. Others would share about things the Lord had spoken to them while another group might be learning choruses.

Oh, how could this be a prison? It was literally heaven on earth! This was especially true of one large prison production brigade on the fourth floor. More than half of the inmates there had accepted Jesus. In one cell 28 prisoners had turned to the Lord. They had meetings every day in which they prayed, sang and had Bible studies.

Beloved reader, I wish to remind you that this happened in an atheistic nation with a totalitarian government bent on persecuting the church and where many of God's servants have been killed. How then could the authorities allow so many believers in Jesus to turn the whole prison upside down?

As the revival spread, Satan reared his ugly head. He used a woman who had been sentenced to 20 years to come against the believers. In order to have her sentence reduced she would diligently report our activities to the authorities. Before long, persecution came like a flood. As it was, the sisters faced corporal punishment and beatings for the sake of the Lord most of the time. Actually, the Lord had already revealed to us what was to come. Therefore, we were prepared, had gathered all our Bibles and had very carefully hid them outside the prison block.

On the day of the great search security was very tight. Many Public Security agents and prison officials surrounded our cell block and conducted a 'search and find' operation through each cell. We had deliberately left some small Scripture portions on notepads for them to find, so that they would be content in finding them and not look for the many Bibles that we had already moved out of the cell. We had planned it in such a way that the notepads contained verses about repentance and

111

knowing God, such as John 3:16; Mark 1:15; Romans 3 and so on. Thus we could preach the salvation message to the cadres and the prison guards.

After the search, two of the sisters were taken to the basement to a totally sealed cell where prisoners were tortured. There was water on the floor, and it was dark, humid and dank. Yet day by day the sisters felt God's presence and were warmed by His light.

Several other believers were taken to the drain room to 'consider their ways.' The drain room had no walls and the cold blew into it, freezing their bones. It was October and the temperature was usually between Celsius 8° to −10° (46°–14°F). Though our bodies constantly shivered, inside we sensed indescribable warmth and sweetness.

God had a special job for the pair who were locked up in the basement cell. A young girl was also thrown into the dark, damp room with them. She had been arrested for being a hooligan and was sentenced to more than ten years. Even after entering prison, her evil nature did not change and she continued to curse people, and violently attacked them with her fists. Quite often she was somehow able to get to the administrative offices where she fought with the officials and threw things around. Therefore, the prison staff lost no time in locking her up in solitary confinement.

Hence, when the two sisters joined her in her fate, all the other believers were greatly concerned for them. They were afraid that she would beat up the sisters, so they earnestly prayed for them. As they entered the room, the young girl glared at them hatefully and cursed loudly, 'What are you two scoundrels doing here?'

The two Christians said gently, 'Since you are all by yourself, you must be very lonely. We have come to keep you company.'

She felt a strength emanating from the sisters. She was very touched and as she let her defences down, the believers used every opportunity to share the Gospel with her. A miracle happened. She was convicted by the Holy Spirit and, falling on the floor, she wept and confessed her sins, repented of them and was born again.

After 20 days' confinement in the basement room, all were allowed to return to their original cells. The young girl was a changed person. Many of her cellmates asked her, 'How come you do not hit and curse people anymore?'

With all humility and remorse she said, 'I must apologize to you, because I didn't know Jesus before, that is why I did those things to you. Please forgive me, for now I believe in the Lord and never again will I hit and curse others.' Those who were listening were astonished.

The section chief also knew about her conversion and called her in for questioning one day.

'I heard that you believe in Jesus. Who was it that caused you to believe?'

She answered with great joy, 'Yes, I have already become a Christian. It was Jesus who caused me to believe.'

'No, you have been deceived by those believers in Jesus!' the supervisor shouted.

She smiled, 'If I did not believe in Jesus, I would have caused you no end of trouble on being released from the basement cell after such a long time.'

The section chief was left speechless. She could only dismiss her with a wave of her hand. Thus the sister returned to her cell without further questioning.

One of the two sisters who was thrown into the basement cell with her fared worst. She was questioned eight times. But each time the Holy Spirit taught her to be like Jesus when He stood before Pilate. Therefore each time she kept her mouth closed and did not answer.

The section chief would roar at her, 'Speak, who led you to believe in Jesus? Where did the Bibles come from?'

She remained silent. The section chief was livid. 'Today if you don't speak, I will beat you to death!' She threatened, 'How dare a little criminal come before me eight times and not utter a word?'

Still she refused to answer and earnestly prayed for God to help her. Then the prison guard took an electric rod that was long and large, turned up the voltage, and hit her body with it. Normally, the rod only has to be turned on to the normal voltage and when placed on one's body it feels as if ten thousand sharp arrows have pierced the heart. It is extremely painful and people usually pass out. However, as this fearsome instrument of torture was used on this sister's body, it had no effect on her. She still stood upright.

The prison guard was astonished and she decided to test it out on a dog. The dog cried out in great pain, and began to froth at the mouth. It fainted. The guard turned the rod on the sister and again she was not hurt. Panic stricken, the guards sent her back to the basement cell.

All the way to the cell, that sister sang praises to God. As soon as she entered the cell she knelt down and with a heart full of thanksgiving loudly sang 'hallelujah' and gave thanks to the Lord.

'Lord, you truly have such great love! You have not forgotten your promise, for you said, *"God will not suffer you to be tempted above that you are able; but will with the temptation also make a way to escape, that you may be able to bear it."'* (1 Corinthians 10:13).

Another sister who was very young was imprisoned on the first floor. She continually copied Bibles and songs and someone reported her to the authorities. When she was taken in for interrogation, she denied everything and claimed ignorance. The guards threatened her, tempted her and beat her. But she had no fear at all. As a result, they handcuffed her and she had to eat all her meals and go to the bathroom with her hands bound. It was truly very difficult, especially as it was winter.

We slept on bunk beds and usually the older prisoners slept on the bottom bunks and the younger ones slept on the top bunks. As this sister was handcuffed, it was very difficult for her to climb to her bed. She tried with all her strength, but often did not succeed until she had tried several times. The handcuffs cut deep into her flesh and the pain was so great her whole body broke out in a cold sweat. Not all the inmates in her cell were Christians. The unbelievers mercilessly taunted and ridiculed her saying, 'You always say your Lord is true and living and is an omnipotent God. Have Him loose your handcuffs!' In this way they daily insulted and mocked her and her Lord.

One evening she wept before the Lord saying, 'Lord, it is only right that I should be bound and handcuffed for Your sake and I am willing to do so. Yet so that your Name will not be reproached any longer, and that many more may believe on You, I ask You to loose these handcuffs. Lord, as you caused the chains to fall off Peter, so cause these chains to fall off me! For you are not only Peter's God, Paul's God, you are also my God ....' When she had finished praying, her handcuffs fell to the ground.

The next day, when the guards brought her to the interrogation room they discovered that her handcuffs had come open so they asked her, 'What method did you use to open these handcuffs?'

'They opened of themselves and I don't know how they did so,' she answered.

The prison guards knew that these young girls who believed in Jesus were extraordinarily honest and there was no way they could open the handcuffs. They remembered the incident when the electric rod did not work. They were so frightened that they did not dare to question her any more. Due to these two miracles, many believed in Jesus.

After two months, the work of the Gospel in the prison, far from being suppressed, prospered all the more and there was an even greater revival. The fires of revival began to burn intensely throughout the prison and the numbers of believers dramatically increased. This women's prison became a totally new place. The majority of the prisoners repented and believed in the Lord.

The authorities, extremely alarmed, began to initiate stricter supervision of the inmates. We realized that there was a greater persecution to come and that they would increase the sentences of those they considered to be the leaders of the believers. The whole group of us fasted and earnestly prayed for this matter, asking God to increase our faith and strength.

One morning in November 1984, it became very dark and a piercing cold wind from the plains of the northwest began to howl through every cell of the prison. Soon it began to snow and every window was covered in white. It blew upon the plants in the courtyard that had already withered a long time previously.

On this day the prison guards had risen especially early.

Each had her helmet on and was in full police uniform with belts secured firmly. Each had an electric rod, truncheon or pistol in her hand and was marching around the main prison block. All the prisoners were especially tense and had no idea of what the day might bring. The sisters also sensed that something very unusual was about to happen, therefore they all fervently prayed that God would protect His children.

At 9:00 a.m., officials from the PSB, legal department and prosecution department from 'H' city and 'M' county all came to the prison. In the large courtyard they had set up several rows of tables. The heads of the PSB, prosecutor's department, legal department, team leaders, head secretaries and secretaries all sat there in an awe-inspiring array. Their eyes gleamed with hate as all the prisoners were brought out and made to sit on the ground. All the PSB officials had real bullets in their pistols and guards surrounding the courtyard held machine guns. They aimed their weapons at these totally unarmed women prisoners as if they were facing a formidable enemy. There was an uneasy silence in this field of several thousand people.

'The mass struggle session has now begun,' the loudspeaker blared out the chilling words of the chairman. 'We now welcome the head of the Bureau to speak.'

Not a single person clapped their hands. Eventually his 30 minute speech in which he instructed and reproved the prisoners ended, and the PSB chief climbed down from the platform.

'Bring forth Lin, so and so, so and so' (a total of 12 people).

Twelve believers were shoved by the prison guards and made to stand in front of these grim-faced interrogators. Sister Lin, whom they considered to be the leader of the believers, was the first to be questioned.

The head judge said to her slowly, 'Lin, will you honestly report to us how you preached Jesus in the prison? How many prisoners did you deceive? Who are your co-workers? You must be honest and thorough.'

'Please loosen my bonds so that I can read my confession.' After Sister Lin's ropes were untied, she held a stack of paper with both hands and, standing before the officials and all the prisoners, began to read her 'confession' in a loud voice. This was the content of her 'confession':

'On a certain date, I preached the Gospel to so and so and said, God created the heaven and earth and all things. God used the dust to create man, Man did not evolve from gorillas. The evolutionary theory of Darwin is totally bankrupt …. On another date, I told so and so, it is appointed unto man once to die and after death the judgment. On a certain date I also said to a certain person, Jesus is the Son of God and He came to the world to seek and save that which was lost, moreover He was nailed to death on the cross and rose from the dead. On another day, I prayed for so and so and said, Lord, I ask you to forgive this person's sins that she may be born again, and can enter the Kingdom of Heaven …. On a certain day I also taught so and so to sing this song, The Lord is coming, the Lord is coming, though we don't know when …'

She continued on and on for a long time.

Upon hearing this, the sisters were filled with joy and they all began to sing softly, 'Hallelujah!' The unsaved prisoners in their midst thought, 'What kind of a confession is this? She is simply preaching the Gospel to us!'

As for the officials they exploded with anger. 'Is not what she is saying also aimed at us? Is she trying to make us become Christians?' The officials were so angry that their necks turned red. 'You … you … you woman, we're going to lock you up until you die. Get out of here!'

Two other sisters were brought in and the content of their 'confession' was almost the same. The officials were all so exasperated that their faces changed colour. They did not know whether to weep or to laugh. They were confused and could not think straight. The chairman of the mass meeting stood up to lead the prisoners in shouting slogans.

With a booming voice he said, 'Down with those elements against reform!' Except for several officials on the platform and the prison guards, not one prisoner responded.

Angered, the guards lifted up their electric rods and threatened them. 'Why don't you shout the slogan? If you don't shout you will know what being electrocuted is like.'

'Down with the leaders of religious superstition!' he

attempted with a more forceful voice. There was total silence as all the prisoners kept quiet. Not one responded.

Of course the believers would not shout the slogan, but why was it that those who had not yet believed would not shout? The reason was they had already seen God at work and they were convinced at last that there was nothing wrong with those who believed in Jesus. Therefore they, too, did not open their mouths.

No one budged for several minutes and eventually the authorities were extremely embarrassed and realized they were in an awkward position. Their plan to increase the sentences of the sisters was therefore thwarted. They only recorded the names of nine sisters and the only action they took was to give a stern warning to six of them.

The meeting ended with just one threat. 'From now on you must keep your belief to yourselves and you are not allowed to preach to others, otherwise you will be severely punished.'

On returning to the cells all the believers knelt down and praised God. For in this large 'struggle session' meeting they had seen with their own eyes that He was in charge and once again Satan's scheme was foiled. After that, on several occasions when prisoners who were non-believers went to the administrative officers to accuse us, the warden would simply answer, 'Forget it. I see that those who believe in Jesus work harder than you do, moreover there is nothing else bad about them. To be honest there is nothing I can do about them.' Upon hearing this the prisoners who accused the Christians felt greatly ashamed.

Our God is truly omniscient. He knew my weaknesses and had mercy on me in my inabilities. In those depressing days when my faith was insufficient, I became discouraged and disappointed. Through His unlimited wisdom and power He gave me strength. My faith was greatly stirred up through the brothers and sisters visiting me in prison.

One day the prison guard notified me, 'Come out for a while for your family has come to visit you.'

I ran all the way to the meeting room, my heart was jumping inside me, for one brother and sister there were on the government's wanted list. Those who had come to see me were the key brothers and sisters responsible for the work in several counties. They had been faithful to the Lord's work and therefore were being sought by the government and had no fixed dwelling place. Due to the great concern they had for the work of the church they had not returned home to be with their families for several years. We knew that if any of these six people were arrested they would become martyrs for the Lord. Today two of those who came to visit me were among the six leaders. How could I not be deeply moved?

As we met together several guards were standing on the side watching, so we could not say very much. But their resolute and serene composure gave me great strength. They held my hand tightly and said, 'Sister, put your heart at ease and work hard in this place, make a contribution for the Superior and obtain merits. As to the children at home, the Father will take care of them.'

Chapter 5

Be Not Afraid, but Speak, For I am With You

(Acts 18:9–10)

The Lord lovingly watched over His children in prison. He knew that our spiritual lives were not that strong, and so He caused the situation in the prison to improve slowly. On Sundays, the authorities allowed us to take the day off. On this happy day we were so busy we had no time for the usual talk or eating. Many sisters who did not understand the Bible came to me with questions. Others who visited me either had problems or need prayer for healing or wanted to learn new songs. Though we were busy, our hearts were overwhelmed with joy.

One evening, the inmates went to watch a movie. I took several sisters who had not been baptized to the washing area where the water faucet was located. Some of the prisoners were washing there. As we washed our clothes we prayed that the Lord would cause those non-believers to leave and that every washbowl would be filled with water. Amazingly, water suddenly stopped coming out of the tap and they all left with their laundry undone. We began to dance and praise the Lord. We sent a sister to watch the door while we began our baptismal service. We took up a washbowl and poured the water on a sister and in the name of the Father, Son and Holy Spirit baptized her. We did the same with the second and third sister until all of them were baptized. The Lord protected us in a wonderful way. As soon as the last of the sisters had been baptized and they had all changed into dry clothes, water began to flow out of the faucet and the prisoners all returned to wash their clothes. This was how we baptized all the new converts.

After the great persecution, another affliction came upon me that I could hardly bear. One of the cell mates would humiliate me every day and I soon considered her my adversary. Because I loved the Lord, I showed love to her in every way. I served her, brought her tea, water and washed her clothes. I did not feel embarrassed at all to do these things, but she did her best to rouse my anger and continually cursed me. The most painful thing to me was that she would not allow me to pray, for every time I knelt down to pray she would stand at my side shouting and cursing me. Whenever I shared the Gospel with others, she would immediately interfere and create a disturbance. Then she would run to the administrative offices to report me.

One day, I was unable to bear it any longer. I fell on my bed and began to sob uncontrollably. I asked the Lord to take me home. 'Lord, why have you put me in this situation? I ask you to take my soul!' That evening, the Word of the Lord came to me: '*Verily, verily, I say unto you, Except a corn of wheat fall into the ground and die, it abides alone: but if it die, it brings forth much fruit.*' (John 12:24) Then I saw that I was weak and pitiful. I recalled all the work the Lord had done in the prison in the past.

I requested that the warden transfer me to another cell. The warden, aware of my situation, transferred me to cell number eight. When I arrived there I felt like I had 'crawled out of the pit to fall into the well.' For all the prisoners in this cell were extremely wicked and there was not one good person among them. I then realized that the persecution I received from my previous cellmate was of the Lord. The Lord had used her to force me to leave that cell and pioneer in this place. For in almost every part of the prison there were many believers, but this one cell was full of darkness. I earnestly interceded and fasted for the work in this new field.

The work was very difficult. Each time I began to witness to the inmates I met with opposition. I felt very discouraged and everything within me cried out to the Lord. One day, a young girl whose bed was next to mine fell sick. I was genuinely concerned, and took it upon myself to care for her. As a result she accepted Jesus. Then two more inmates believed. Soon, one of my cell mates reported my activities to the authorities.

'From the time Chan entered cell number eight, she has been preaching Jesus, praying and singing all night so that we are unable to sleep.'

The guards came to search my cell. In my hand was a copy of 'Streams in the Desert.' I quickly passed it to the sister two beds away and she hid it under her belt.

How I thank the Lord, for even with 20 pairs of eyes on me and under the hawkish glare of several guards none of them seemed to have seen me passing the book to the sister. Hallelujah! I immediately thought of the Scripture, '*If God be with us, who can be against us?*' (Romans 8:31) I was elated. The guards searched for a long time, but could not find anything. They led me to the offices where they reprimanded me. They then took me to the cell in the basement and prepared to lock me up there. But as the cell was flooded they took me to the observation room above where they keep criminals who have committed serious crimes. Prisoners who were especially stubborn or who had violated prison regulations were kept here as punishment.

The second day, four more people joined me in the cell. We were not allowed to speak to each other. The Lord especially watched over me. I took advantage of every opportunity to preach the Gospel and with great joy all four of them accepted the Lord. One night the Lord gave me a revelation in which I saw the prison warden wanting to speak to me and demanding that I confess all my activities in cell number eight.

The next morning I told the guard outside the cell, 'Today I will be brought out for interrogation.'

The guard asked, 'How do you know?'

'The Lord whom I serve told me so last night.'

At 8:00 a.m. I was summoned to the offices. Four cadres sat there waiting for me. I sat before them on a small stool.

'Chan, have you considered carefully?' they began.

'I have considered carefully,' I replied.

'You must honestly give an account!'

'What do you want me to give an account of?'

'You yourself know!' they retorted.

'I haven't done anything wrong or anything bad. What can I say?' I pleaded.

Suddenly, they all exploded and jabbing their fingers at me

one of them screeched, 'Chan, you are still so obstinate. You have an opportunity to speak, so why don't you speak? Since you have carefully considered, why don't you honestly give an account? Where did the book come from? Who gave it to you? Chan, if you refuse to speak you will get a thrashing.'

Then great joy filled my heart and I silently prayed, 'Lord, allow them to beat me and hit me! If they do this I will be greatly blessed to be considered worthy to suffer for your Name's sake.'

The cadres continued their verbal volley and after asking me several questions surprisingly said, 'You may return to your cell. Carefully reconsider and at a later date come back here to make your report.' That was how the interrogation ended.

Several days later, they called me in again in the evening and said, 'You should give an honest account! You have done nothing else, but just because you believe in the Lord you have caused us unnecessary work. Every day our time is taken up with dealing with this matter.'

I prayed, 'Lord, I obey You and I will do what You want me to do!' Then the Spirit of the Lord spoke to me, *'Be faithful unto death!'* (Rev. 2:10) Thus I was strengthened. Even though I had suffered much already the Lord especially protected me that day from further punishment. Many sisters had been praying for me.

On a third occasion I was asked about the book and my Bible. I did not give them any information. In the end they simply sent me back to the observation cell to 'reconsider.'

I thought of three things they could do to me: (1) I might be sent to the northwest. (2) They might increase my sentence. (3) Perhaps I would be given the death penalty. I prayed to the Lord and joyfully said, 'Lord, if they send me to the northwest, I can praise you aloud. If they increase my sentence, I can learn more lessons in prison. If they execute me, I will truly be grateful, for I can soon return to You and quickly end the pain of being separated from You.'

The fourth time the interrogating officials were demanding. 'You must give an account now. What book do you usually read?'

I remembered that when I first entered prison in 1982 I had

brought with me a certain novel. Then I did not know why I had brought it, but now I could answer, 'It is a certain novel. If you don't believe you can see for yourself. It is under the front of my bed.' They found the book and brought it to me.

I said, 'This is evidence that those who have accused me have fabricated false testimony to harm me.' There was nothing else they could say, so they allowed me to return to cell number eight. The Lord said, *'But when they deliver you up, take no thought how or what you shall speak ...'* Matthew 10:19–20. The Word of the Lord is so *real*!

I was in the observation cell for 50 days and in that period altogether five prisoners were brought in. I preached the Gospel and loved them and they all believed. One prisoner had been reported for stealing the clothes and food of other prisoners. She was brought here to consider her ways and had suffered much. I shared with her that 'all have sinned and come short of the glory of God .... If you don't believe in Jesus you will perish, so you should repent and accept Jesus ....' I also gave her the food which I had kept aside when I fasted and prayed for her.

With tears in her eyes she told me, 'In our family my mother believes in Jesus. She has urged me to believe and prays for me all the time. Yet I have had a hard heart and would not believe. Today in prison Jesus again is searching for me that I should know Him and turn to Him. In this hopeless prison, the only way out is through believing in Jesus.' Hallelujah, she received new life and to this day is one of the sisters in this prison who loves the Lord greatly and has led many to the Lord.

There was another prisoner who was very young, but was sentenced to four years for hooliganism. Because of all the scandal their daughter had brought to the family, her parents wrote a letter to her stating, 'You are no longer our daughter and after your release from prison do not return home.' In prison she had contracted meningitis, she felt that life was hopeless and that it would be better to die. So for several days she sat in my cell without any expression, contemplating suicide.

One morning, the love of the Lord overwhelmed me with compassion. I took her hand and gently said to her, 'Child, can you tell me your sorrows?' I gave her the food that my son had brought from home the day before. For the first time since she entered prison she sensed that in this world there is an unusual type of love. Greatly touched, she lay her head on my lap and poured out her heart.

'Child, though your parents do not love you, a loving Saviour has loved you for a long time. In order to seek and save you, He shed His blood and gave His life to bear your sins. If you only believe, He will accept you and take you in ....'

Her gentle weeping turned into loud sobs until she had completely repented. She wholeheartedly accepted the Lord, and was healed. Joy flooded her being. Later, I told her that she must fervently pray for her parents and to write them again, confessing her wrongs. Perhaps her parents might have a change of heart and love her again. She was very obedient and right away began to fast and pray for her parents. With tears in her eyes she wrote to them:

> Beloved Father and Mother, I have done you wrong. Due to the evil acts and scandals of this your dishonourable daughter, not only have I been sentenced, but I have brought disgrace to you. I have implicated the whole family and have brought reproach to the family. I don't blame you for hating me and I truly am not worthy to be called your daughter.
>
> But now I have met a great mother in prison who has helped me to obtain new life and understand the way to live and the significance of a person's responsibilities. Beloved Father and Mother, please come to visit me! You can beat me, scold me and release your anger toward me. I want to confess my wrongs to you and beg you to forgive me. I wish Father and Mother good health!
>
> Your dishonourable daughter (name and date)

After her parents received the tear-stained letter, they quickly came to prison to visit their daughter. The old parents and their young daughter embraced each other and wept. This moved many people to tears. Soon after, this sister met with persecution, but she remained steadfast. During interrogation she testified boldly, 'Nobody forced me to believe, rather it was because Jesus loved me first and, through the actions, moral standards and love of those who believed in the Lord, I was attracted to Him.'

The third prisoner, who was older, had been sentenced to life for murdering her husband. Not only had she done something that is not permitted under the laws of the nation, but murderers are despised and loathed by everyone. Not one relative or family member had ever visited her or sent her anything. Thus, she was poor and destitute and was unable even to purchase soap, hand towels, toothpaste and other basic items. To make matters worse, she became ill and her pain and loneliness was indescribable.

I gave her some things for her daily use and purchased other things for her. The Scripture tells us, '… *for in so doing you shall heap coals of fire on his head.*' (Romans 12:20) The love of the Lord melted this hard heart and caused her to turn to Him. She underwent a radical change.

The fourth inmate, a woman from a certain city several thousand kilometers away, had been sentenced for white slavery. She had an old mother in her 80s who did not know that she was in prison for crimes. The old lady thought she was doing business. This inmate wept constantly. I shared the Gospel with her and she received the Lord. Great rejoicing came to her and every day she would sing songs, pray, read the Bible and lead others to repentance.

The fifth and last prisoner sent to the observation cell was a kidnapper from a certain city in Henan Province. She was given a 15-year prison term and was extremely fierce and malicious. I prayed much for her and she eventually repented and turned to the Lord. After her release from prison she fervently loved the Lord and led her husband and family to repentance. She also led many others to believe in Jesus.

The 50 days I spent in the observation cell were not a punishment from the authorities, but rather it was the Lord who sent me there. In the end five prisoners who had committed severe crimes were saved. I thought of Acts 26:18, '… *I send you to open their eyes, and to turn them from darkness to light, and from the power of Satan unto God, that they may receive forgiveness of sins, and inheritance among them which are sanctified by faith that is in me.'* I sang hallelujah and gave the Lord the glory.

Our prison was one of the most famous in the whole nation with more than 4,000 women inmates. There were always new prisoners starting their terms and old prisoners who were being released. So there was no end to the work of the Gospel. During those days I witnessed at first hand, the filthy hearts and bodies of the prisoners, their fiendish natures and the most shocking of sins. I saw their future judgment and punishment in the eternal lake of fire and remembered the verse in Proverbs 24:11, *'If you forbear to deliver them that are drawn unto death, and those that are ready to be slain.'* I felt just like Jeremiah when he said, *'But His word was in mine heart as a burning fire shut up in my bones, and I was weary with forbearing, and I could not stay.'* (Jeremiah 20:9)

One night I woke up and went to the lavatory where I knelt before the Lord and with tears cried out, 'Lord, You came into the world to save sinners. I ask you to cause all the prisoners in this prison to experience your grace. Otherwise I am willing to perish in exchange for the salvation of these pitiful people!' Sister Sheng, Sister Lin and I were in constant communication so that all the sisters would pray for the Gospel to go forth in the prison. The Lord was faithful to bring in the harvest. Many were added to the family of God in that prison.

Chapter 6

As the Hart Pants After the Water Brooks, so Pants my Soul After You, O God

(Psalm 42:1)

As the number of believers rapidly increased, the scarcity of Bibles became our greatest problem. One day I noticed a sister crying as she was working. I gently asked her why she was unhappy. She said, 'Without a Bible how can I understand the Word of the Lord?' I felt a heavy burden in my heart and I could only call to the Lord. Other than copying the Bible by hand, we had one other method of getting His Word. Whenever my children came to visit me (they were allowed only one visit per month) they would first divide up the Bible and bring in the different portions each time.

After visiting for a while, they would say, 'Mother, I must go to the toilet.' The guard then permitted me to accompany them to the toilet. When the coast was clear they would quickly take out the portions of the Bible that were hidden in their underwear or strapped onto their legs. To hide the Bibles together with the food and clothing would be unwise as the guards normally checked these before they are allowed into the prison. Thus, we had been using the toilet method. When the sisters saw the Bible portions, they treated them as precious treasure, and would read them with tears.

Every morning at 5:30 before the morning call was sounded, the sisters would get dressed and be ready. As soon as the wake up call was given and the gate was opened, we all ran downstairs into the courtyard where we knelt in worship, praise and prayer. It was not time for the guards to come on duty (they start at 7:00 a.m.). They were still in their comfortable beds sound asleep. As for the non-believing prisoners they were usually physically exhausted and reluctant to rise so early. Hallelujah! This wonderful time was given to us through the Lord's grace. Each beautiful morning we had one precious hour with Jesus. We were tremendously blessed. During this time we enjoyed sweet fellowship with the Lord, prayed earnestly and praised freely. We received strength and light from the Lord. We had more freedom when the weather was very cold. When it snowed heavily it was a tremendous opportunity. We knelt down in the snow to praise God with a fire burning in our hearts. We did not feel the cold at all.

In 1983 God revealed to me that the prison was the third heaven, a paradise. It so happened to be that the place where I was locked up (including the large courtyard) was the location of the third sentry post and the Lord said this was the third heaven. Wearing the same prison uniforms we all knelt before the Lord and praised Him, 'Lord, we are all wearing the same "heavenly uniform" and in this "third heaven" worship you!' Hallelujah, this was truly inexpressible pleasure!

Besides doing manual labour during the day, we had to work until 10 o'clock every evening . More than ten hours of work every day led to extreme exhaustion. When we were dismissed from work, all the inmates would rush to bathe, wash clothes and eat their dinner. But the believers would go to their bunks and study the Bible or read other books. Only when our cell-mates returned would we go out to quickly wash ourselves and eat a little food before returning to sleep. These sisters with a burden would even study through the night to two or three in the morning.

Chapter 7

Be Strong and of a Good Courage ... For the Lord Your God is With You

(Joshua 1:9)

Do you think Satan would sit back and ignore the fact that this group of prisoners were freely worshiping God and preaching the Gospel? Of course not! As I said before, throughout this nation there is tremendous persecution towards Christians! Therefore, we believers expected persecution. Corporal punishment, raids, handcuffs, being locked in the basement cell and interrogation were 'normal' for us and did not surprise us at all.

In one particular brigade among 30 odd prisoners there were 17 believers. Even their monitor, who was a cadre, also believed. Their daily routine was the same as described above. Every day when they got off work at 10 p.m., they took the opportunity to diligently read the Bible. When the other prisoners finished their meal and returned to their cells the Christians would hide the Bibles in their sleeves. Now there was an evil prisoner who had been sentenced to a long prison term who reported them to the supervisor.

The supervisor said hesitantly, 'They do their work well, are polite and show love towards others. It is only that they persist in their faith. How can we deal with them?' Seeing that the brigade supervisor would not do anything, she went to the head of the prison.

As a result, the prison chief with a group of prison guards came to the believers' cells unannounced. They made a thorough search and found some Bibles. Two sisters were taken. One was locked up in the basement cell and the other in solitary

confinement on the fourth floor. The latter had just become a
believer a few days before. The rest of us sisters feared she
would be unable to stand steadfast so we prayed intensely for
her. Who would have thought that one morning, from the
small window on the fourth floor, she would wave her hands
and shout, 'You should remain strong!'

Hallelujah, praise the Lord. During several sessions of interrogation this sister did not say one word about how she
obtained the Bible. Though they beat her severely and handcuffed her, she would only say, 'I don't know.' After 20 or
more days she was freed and the head of the prison summoned
her.

He tried to dissuade her. 'You are very young. From now on
don't believe in this so called "Jesus".'

Standing tall, she said with fresh determination, 'Before I
was a secret disciple of Jesus, but after this time locked up in the
closed cell, everyone knows I am a Christian. Therefore from
now on I will openly believe and follow Jesus to the end!'

She not only declared this to the head of the prison, but she
was in fact making a declaration to all creation, the angels in
heaven and the forces of darkness. The prison chief simply
shook his head and sighed realizing there was nothing he could
to do to change her thinking.

The sister who was held in the basement cell was not released
until three days before Chinese New Year. She suffered much
during her time there and, before being released, the guards
said among themselves, 'Release her! Even if you keep these
believers in Jesus locked up until they die, or beat them to
death, it is impossible to force them to say "I don't believe".'

The day after her release she came out of the lavatory with
two other sisters, and stood there reading the Psalms. Someone
reported them to the guard. When the guards arrived the three
of them were so preoccupied reading a Psalm of David that
they did not realize what was happening until a guard sneaked
up from behind and grabbed their Bible. So she was hauled off
for interrogation. This time they imposed a fine on her. But
before very long she was again apprehended and taken in for
questioning for sharing Christ with an inmate. The Lord's
word came to her, *'For which cause we faint not; but though*

our outward man perish, yet the inward man is renewed day by day.' (2 Corinthians. 4:16–18)

When she arrived at the interrogation room, the guards stripped her bare and began beating her up. Her whole body was bruised purple. Then they tied her up and continued to assault her with leather whips and truncheons. She was beaten until there were open wounds all over her body and blood was streaming out of her nose and mouth. She was then taken to the observation cell where she was 'struggled against' with another sister. I fled to the lavatory and fervently prayed for her with tears asking the Lord to increase her strength and faith. She came out of this trial of her faith an overcomer, victorious in Jesus whom she had trusted.

Every day, the guards would deliver a newspaper to each cell for the prisoners to learn. We scoured the paper for news about the last days such as earthquakes, the AIDS disease, famines, wars, disasters, etc. We would show them to the other prisoners and used these events to preach the Gospel to them. In 1986 there was an article entitled *'The four great crises threatening human survival.'* I read it out loud and those listening were filled with fear. I then used the opportunity to tell them about the Lord's salvation.

Mark 16:15–18 tells us, *'Go ye into all the world, and preach the Gospel to every creature ... And these signs shall follow them that believe ... they shall lay hands on the sick, and they shall recover.'* It is a fact that the reason the Gospel caused such a revival in the prison was due to the power the Lord gave us to perform miracles and signs.

An elderly inmate, sentenced to more than ten years in jail, was seized by an evil spirit after starting her prison term. She was extremely violent. One day while at work she grabbed a sharp pair of scissors and threatened to kill everybody and destroy the machinery. The other prisoners were so gripped with terror that they all ran away. One of the sisters begged me to do something. I went to the factory immediately and in the Name of Jesus commanded her, 'Put down the scissors!' Very submissively she obeyed. Again in the Name of Jesus I commanded her to sit and she quietly sat. Then I prayed for her three times before the evil spirits left completely.

Miracles of deliverance and healing were a common occurrence in the prison. The Name of the Lord was thus glorified and many were added to His Kingdom. Another reason why the revival spread so fast was due to the light that shone forth from God's children. They glorified God in their testimony, on the job and in everything they did.

For example, there was a young sister who knew how to embroider, and she would embroider 20 pillowcases a day. The non-Christian prisoners were unable to complete that many in over ten hours. This sister sang as she worked and at times quietly quoted Bible verses. She not only fulfilled her daily quota, but exceeded it by seven or eight pieces more and the quality of the work was excellent. She was one of the three best workers in the factory, all of them being believers. Even the cadres could not help but admire her.

The brigade supervisor said to her, 'I see how you always sing as you work quietly. Your work is so outstanding. Probably the reason is your God helps you!' The sister smiled coyly and praised the Lord in her heart!

As for me, the Lord knew that I was always clumsy but He had mercy on me. He changed me so that I could do excellent work too, in fact it was superior to any other person in my group. My job was to sew hems on suit jackets. My quota was 30 jackets a day, and I far exceeded this quota, sowing the hems closely and evenly. This brought great satisfaction to the supervisor.

One time I was assigned to another job for several days and the hemming was done by a non-Christian prisoner. She completed only 29 jackets in three days, and her workmanship was rather shoddy. These were all returned for improvements, which made the supervisor furious. He then requested that I do the improvements. You can imagine the work of re-doing the hems was much more difficult than starting from scratch. They had to be unstitched, ironed, refolded and hemmed again. Though it was tedious work, I agreed to do it for the sake of the Lord's Name. That day I fasted, prayed and asked the Lord to help me. As a result, I was able to complete the work on those 29 jackets, as well as my own daily quota. This amazed the brigade supervisor who gave me the thumbs up and said, 'This

type of work can only be done by Chan who believes in Jesus!'
Hallelujah, glory to God.

Sister Lin had a very special testimony. They put her in
charge of the stock of cloth. She had to keep account of the
stock, and measure out the cloth. The non-believers usually sat
idly by. 'Lin is working so we can sit here and play while she
does the work!' they would say. Since she was not a calculating
person she was willing to put up with the hard work. Even
when she was totally exhausted and her thighs had become
swollen, she refused to stop and rest.

She would regularly lift bolts of cloth that were too heavy for
even two people to lift. Setting them on her shoulder she moved
them into the warehouse. Every morning she fasted and prayed
before starting work. The cloth that she measured out was
never short by so much as one inch. The authorities trusted her
completely and everyone admired her. The supervisors would
always say, 'Everything that Lin does is excellent and you
cannot find one fault in her, only that she believes in Jesus.'

Later they gave her another job to do and the authorities
transferred her out of the warehouse. Others took over her old
job. However they were very slow and they made many
mistakes. When the cloth was measured and cut they usually
came short by several dozen yards. This made the supervisor
furious and one of them exploded, 'What are you people doing
here? When Lin was here there wasn't a single problem, now
you people make mistakes daily and can't do anything right.'
So Sister Lin was transferred back to the warehouse where she
remained until the day she left prison.

Just as the revival was spreading like fire in the prison, the
devil did his best to destroy the work. The fiery arrow he shot
at the believers was formidable. One Saturday morning, the
department head transferred Sister Lin temporarily to another
place to take inventory for two days. The next day at noon, the
warehouse suddenly caught fire. Columns of dark smoke
billowed out of the windows and soon a black pall hung above
the warehouse.

The fire alarm was sounded and the cadres shouted a command to the prisoners: 'The cloth and finished items in the
warehouse are worth several hundred thousand dollars.

Whoever puts out the fire will obtain merit and not only will we reduce your sentence, but you will also be rewarded!' By that time the iron gate of the warehouse was red hot and the heat intense. Nobody could get near but everyone tried their best to pry open the door. Suddenly thick burning smoke and flames shot towards the door as more than ten prisoners rushed in. They had taken only a few steps when they suffocated and collapsed.

Soon several fire trucks arrived but by the time the fire was extinguished the warehouse was burnt to the ground. The ten prisoners were carried out unconscious and in a critical condition. They were rushed to hospital for emergency treatment in a fleet of ambulances.

A few days after the fire, a few prisoners who despised the Christians brought false accusations to the supervisors and the PSB. They blamed the fire on Sister Lin and several other Christians. The authorities immediately summoned Sister Lin and the other accused sisters for questioning. However they knew they were innocent and this was evident in their faces and composure. They relied on the power of the Holy Spirit and answered all the accusations and questions directed at them. Then the supervisor who had transferred Sister Lin testified on her behalf. 'At the time of the fire, Lin was at another place.'

As a result the PSB declared, 'This case has nothing to do with the Christians.' The accusers, who had evil intentions, were locked up for making false accusations. The news spread to every cell, which brought great joy to the sisters, and they gave thanks with tears in their eyes. The attacks of the devil served as fuel that caused the fires of the Gospel to burn even brighter. The revival in the prison flourished all the more.

The believers in each cell, whether in speech, behaviour, work or lifestyles, totally obeyed the prison regulations and lived for the Lord. The leaders clearly recognized this. As they compared the Christians to what they had been they could see the difference the Lord had made. When they compared them with the unbelievers, they could not help but admit that the believers were better.

Chapter 8

The Seed of the Righteous
Shall be Delivered

(Proverbs 11:21)

When I was arrested I had to leave my three children at home. The oldest was 14 and had frail health, and the youngest was only six. At such a tender age they had lost their father and now even their mother had to leave them. Then persecution swept through the church and many brothers and sisters were arrested and imprisoned. For a period of time there was no one to care for my children. They were all alone at home. They would go to the field to dig for wild cabbage to eat with mantou (steamed bread) made of flour prepared by grinding dried sweet potatoes.

Every day after school my children would take a hoe and dig for little potatoes about the size of a cocoon (they had been left behind by others). The oldest worked with the hoe while the youngest lifted up the loose dirt to search. They did this until they were exhausted, sweating and panting. When they had collected one basket it was as if they had found treasure and they brought it home for the evening meal.

When my daughter went to school her schoolmates would bully her. They would call her names like 'A wild girl without parents' or 'the daughter of a criminal.' Night after night my children cried themselves to sleep as they felt like orphans. They had frequent nightmares and the three of them would sleep huddled together.

But God did not forget my children, for He had promised, 'In the fear of the LORD is strong confidence: and his children shall have a place of refuge.' (Proverbs 14:26) Before long a sister took my children into her care. She was the wife of Brother Wu. The Lord had impressed on her to come to my house. Our homes were 1.5 kilometers apart. Brother Wu had been sentenced to seven years and the responsibility of caring for his aged parents and three young children (the oldest was eight and the twins were two) fell on his wife. Now she had the burden of looking after another family, which was truly too hard.

When my children returned from school they would go to the field to look for her and remain there until she finished her work. Then she would take them home with her. She taught them to do the house chores. Her daily heavy manual labour in the fields was exhausting enough. But now she had three more children to care for, meals to prepare, as well as the laundry, sewing and house cleaning. She loved to talk and her heart was full of goodness and sincerity.

Whenever my children faced difficulties or were ridiculed by other children they would cry, 'I think of Mother and I want Mother.' Sister Wu would cry along with them. She would hold my daughter in her arms and rock her to sleep. On Sundays or holidays when other children were taken out by their parents basking in family love, Sister Wu would leave her mother-in-law and children to take care of mine. In the eyes of my children Brother Wu's wife was like a second mother to them.

One bleak autumn evening, after she had finished a full day's work which left her exhausted, she came to visit my children. When they saw her approaching, my children refused to let her come in. They were about to eat their dinner but had hurriedly put away their food in the kitchen. Upon seeing these unusual actions she pushed the children aside, forced open the door, went to the stove, lifted the cover to the wok and looked inside. What she saw made her sad. My children, who were without parental care, would not let anyone know about their difficulties. That night they had tried to cook some wheat grain to satisfy their hunger. Raw wheat does not soften through cooking and it is nearly impossible to digest.

Eyes moist with tears, Sister Wu embraced them and soon tears turned into loud sobs. She prostrated herself on the floor before the Lord and asked Him to show mercy and to bless my three young ones. The next morning she brought a sack of flour and helped them to prepare a meal.

In this way, the Lord looked after me and specially had mercy on me so that I could devote all my time to the work of the Gospel in the prison. I did not have to worry about my children now that Sister Wu was caring for them. I am an emotional person. If I had to worry about my kids every day I could not have had the strength to continue. This was the wonderful protection and special grace bestowed by the Lord! I often wrote letters to my children. However, since it was forbidden to openly mention matters of religious faith in letters, I would use special phrases to communicate with them. For example, if I wanted them to bring a Bible I would write, 'Please bring Mother those several books that she likes to read.' When I wanted to remind my children to study the Bible and obey the Word of the Lord I would say, 'Read good books more and listen to what your father David tells you.' The Lord gave my children understanding and when they read the letter they knew what I meant.

They would often write me letters of comfort and exhortation. I could read between the lines what they were trying to say. Once, as I had mentioned before, a fellow inmate had humiliated and persecuted me, causing me such hardship. It was as Paul said, '... *we were pressed out of measure, above strength, insomuch that we despaired even of life*' (2 Corinthians 1:8). In my moment of weakness I had asked the Lord that I might die, but the Lord strengthened me instead through His Word. The letters written to me in prison helped me to endure this time of testing. I would like to share one such letter with you:

'Beloved Mother, How are you? We have received your letter and after reading it understand about your life in prison and know that you are doing well. Reading your letter is just like seeing you in person and the three of us have put our hearts at ease. Mother, we are doing fine and have done everything according to your instruction. We are of one heart and love one another. Uncle and auntie have come to help us and the "head of the factory" comes often to visit us.'

'Mother, **listen to the commands from above and obey them**. Work hard, **build yourself up and become a new person. Lastly love all those around you and strive for acceptance from above**. Please come home soon for a reunion. Mother, **be joyful and don't be sad** and don't worry about the affairs of the family.'

Your 15-year-old son

(Note the veiled meaning of the portions in bold.)

When I read this letter I dropped on my knees in gratitude and was unable to restrain myself as I praised the Lord. 'Lord, through the mouths of children you have established strength. Through children you have reproved, encouraged and comforted me and I have received new strength. You so greatly love my children and myself. Even if I were to have my body smashed to pieces for you, I would not ever be able to repay a small portion of your grace.'

The guards and cadres had also read this letter (note: the prison authorities always read all the mail first) and they had deemed this a good letter from the family of a criminal urging her to reform. So they copied the entire letter word for word on the blackboard including the underlined portion which they highlighted with red chalk. They then entitled it, **'Please read a letter by a 15-year-old boy to his mother.'** This showed the authorities thoroughly approved of it.

The letter caused a stir in the whole prison and all the inmates jostled among themselves to read it. The believers among them were touched as they read it and the characters that were underscored especially comforted and strengthened them. A few days later I was again locked in the basement cell and then they put me in the drain room. This letter was as someone delivering charcoal in the snow or as the dew in its season.

One afternoon the mild spring breeze blew upon several lovely little flowers and the beautiful pistils slightly bowed their heads as if to salute mankind. The golden sun shot forth gentle rays of light and the happy little birds began to sing on the branches. It was as if I were about to hear some good news.

Then a guard came to tell me, 'Your children have come to visit you.' I immediately stopped the work I was doing and sped towards the meeting room. My younger brother and my children were already waiting there. As soon as she saw me my youngest jumped into my arms and sobbed quietly. The two older children stood close to my side, looked up towards me and, biting their lips tightly, tried to hold back the tears as they carefully scrutinized my face. Had I lost weight? Was I in good health?

I tried to control myself from crying lest the children would feel sad and grieved. I prayed silently and asked the Lord to increase my strength and faith. I am not a person without emotion, on the contrary, I have abundant emotions and am full of a mother's love. How I longed to remain with my children, take care of them and raise them until they grew to adults. But how could I refuse the path that the Lord had set for me? The Lord said, *'He that loves son or daughter more than me is not worthy of me.'* (Matthew 10:37) How could I abandon this ministry of saving souls and only have concern for my children? Moreover, there were many more children who needed me in this place!

I held my young daughter tightly and pressed my forehead against her little cheeks that were wet with tears and said softly, 'Child, listen to Mother and don't cry. Do you obey your father David?'

She nodded her head obediently and said, 'Yes I do.'

'Do you pray daily?'

'I do pray.'

'Do you attend the worship meetings?'

'Yes I do.' With tears the child answered my questions.

The time passed all too quickly and in my heart there were thousands of things I wanted to say to my children, but I did not know where to begin. One hour soon passed and the guard indicated that the time had come. The youngest clung tightly to me fearful that she would lose Mother again. With great compassion the children looked at me and, as the guard once again called out, I held back the tears as I kissed the youngest. I said to them, 'Go home now! Beloved children, listen to uncle and auntie and I will see you the next time.'

My younger brother took the youngest from me and put her on his back. My children all bit their lips to keep from crying so that I might not feel bad. As they walked out they kept looking back as if it were very difficult to walk out of the prison gate. The group of more than 70 people outside who were watching felt very sad and wept silently. During my several years in prison, my children came to visit me often. Each time they brought a Bible that they cleverly sneaked in to give to me. Their physical stature and wisdom increased daily. I was full of joy and praised the Lord without ceasing.

Chapter 9

The Journey is Too Great For You
(1 Kings 19:7)

Six years of prison life passed quickly. March 19, 1987 was the day my sentence was up and I was to be released. For the past two months whenever the sisters saw me they would weep. During meal times they would put down their rice bowls and weep out loud. Many sisters held on to my hands and cried aloud saying, 'Mother, what will we do after you leave?' Some of them could not sleep at night. They would come to my bedside, gently pull away the bed cover, take one look at me and burst into fresh tears.

During that period my heart was torn and I cried every day not knowing what I could do. For the sake of the Gospel and the needs of the flock, I was willing to remain in prison. I remembered when I was arrested and left behind three small children, there were no sorrows nor tears. But now that I was to leave these spiritual children born in prison, it was as if a knife had pierced my heart.

For those two months I slept very little and all my time was spent wiping the tears on the faces of those sisters who came to weep. I comforted them with the Lord's Word, taught them and exhorted them. I commanded them to 'Live according to the call on your lives and for the sake of the whole prison be diligent in the work of the Gospel. Also pray much for our nation and our people ....' How I wished the sun would stop in the heavens and the day of separation would delay! Six years passed like a few days, and how much more quickly did two months pass by.

The day the sisters feared eventually came. The evening before I was to be released I was unable to close my eyes and at

142

daylight there was the sound of weeping everywhere. Many of the sisters did not eat breakfast.

At 9:30 a.m. the guard notified me, 'Those who have come to take you back have been waiting outside for a long time, so you must leave immediately.'

Some of the sisters embraced my head and others held on to my hands. Some of them grabbed hold of my clothes and began to wail. This was especially true of those sisters who had been sentenced to life in prison, for they felt the greatest pain as they would be spending their entire lives in this place.

With tears in my eyes I blessed them and prayed for them and committed them over to the grace of the Lord. At the constant urging of the guard, I could only pick up my belongings and walk towards the prison door slowly. The sisters I was leaving behind had cried until their swollen eyes were red like peaches. They paid no attention to the guard who was trying to obstruct them but insisted on seeing me off to the main gate.

The brothers and sisters who had come to receive me had been waiting since dawn and they first took my belongings. My feet felt as if they weighed a thousand pounds. As I was about to leave the main gate, an earthshaking wail rose up from behind me. The sisters imprisoned on the upper floors were unable to come down to see me off because the guards would not allow them to. They could only stretch their hands out of the windows and wave to me, sobbing out loud. The sound of wailing and the sight of many pairs of red swollen eyes and outstretched hands broke my heart.

So I ran back to the brigade head and said, 'I will not return home! I want to remain with my friends in adversity forever in prison!' But, without saying a word, the guard pushed me outside and closed the gate.

I did not have the strength to lift my legs and after a long time I found that I had taken only a few steps. I turned my head and saw the sisters on the upper floors still waving at me. I took a few more steps and I still could hear the sound of wailing, and I stopped again. Eventually, I walked quite a way and could not see them any more. Looking at the endless road before me, I could only pray, 'Lord, the road ahead is too great for me. I ask you to lead me step by step!'

PART FOUR

The Lily Among the Thorns

Chapter 1
Called as a Teenager

One day in June 1964, in a village commune near 'F' city, a baby girl was born. Her parents named her 'Sheng' (meaning holy). At the age of 11, she went with her mother to their grandparents' home to help them because her grandfather was old and physically weak. He was a very dedicated Christian and the brothers and sisters often met in his home for meetings. Therefore, as a young girl, Sheng had a good foundation in the faith. At 13, she regularly attended the meetings, but she still had not received the 'born again' experience.

When she was 15, she attended middle (high) school. She was mean, argued and fought a lot with other students and her teachers were always reprimanding her. One day, she knocked down a male student who was much larger than her, in a fight. She was filled with remorse and that evening she wept before the Lord in repentance and confession. Her heart was filled with a peace and joy that she had never known before.

From that day on, her life changed radically. She no longer argued or fought, and her schoolmates, even those students that she hated most before, felt she was loveable. She began to realize how precious their souls were and started to share the Gospel with them and taught them to sing choruses. As a result seven girl students accepted Jesus. Sheng saw how they hungered after the Lord's Word, so every Saturday afternoon she would take them to a meeting. They did not return to the school dormitory until Sunday evening. Several times there were special meetings that stretched past midnight on Sunday, and they did not return to school until Monday. And so the principal found out about their activities.

One morning, the principal assembled all the students and teachers on the field. He said, 'Our great country believes in Marxism and Chairman Mao's thoughts. We don't believe in God and there is no Saviour. However here in this school we have a student whose thoughts are backward. She not only believes in Jesus, but she has seriously deceived many students and caused them to believe. The school cannot allow this ....' After that he named 'Sheng' and gave her a stern warning.

Several hundred pairs of eyes fell on Sheng. Many students began to whisper about her, but she did not feel ashamed. She smiled, her eyes shining with love, challenging those who were staring at her disdainfully as if to say to them, 'Jesus is so loveable, come and believe!'

One day two old servants of God came to stay in Sheng's house. She was very excited and wrote out a request for absence from school to give to the teacher. As she entered the teacher's administrative office, she passed the note to the class monitor and said, 'Praise the Lord.' As soon as he heard it he said, 'What is this you are saying?' They all stared at her and all the teachers shook their heads saying, 'It is unbelievable how this student has changed.'

During the rest of the year, Sheng was constantly reprimanded for taking fellow students to Christian meetings. She was criticized and warned by the school. Eventually, Sheng was attending more meetings that studying. Finally, she left school and prepared to serve the Lord full time.

Most of the people at the meetings were old people. When the brothers and sisters saw how the Lord had called this young sister who fervently loved the Lord, they were extremely happy. They always took her with them to water baptisms, communion services and even asked her to teach them choruses.

In one meeting in the evening, more than 400 people gathered together. The brothers and sisters insisted that Sheng preach. So Sheng stood before them and preached with power under the anointing of the Holy Spirit. Many of the brothers and sisters were amazed and could hardly believe that such a young sister could stand before so many and preach so well. Before long their amazement gave way to tears of repentance.

Soon the whole meeting place shook with the sound of sobbing as the brothers and sisters unashamedly cried out loud before the Lord.

The situation at that time was very tense. Several of God's servants had to hide during the day and could only come out late in the night for meetings or to preach. The meeting places were usually packed. Regardless of how hot it was outside, they had to close the windows and doors tightly and cover them with black sheets so that no light or sound could get out. Outside there were sisters who were like 'Rhoda' in the Bible. Those attending the meetings had to wear slippers or walk bare-foot so that they would not be heard going to the meeting. For three years Sheng endured such circumstances.

When she was 17 she heard an old servant of God preach on Romans 12:1, *'Therefore, I urge you, brothers, in view of God's mercy, to offer your bodies as living sacrifices, holy and pleasing to God – this is your spiritual act of worship'*. As she listened to him preach there was a struggle in her heart and she felt great discomfort. After the meeting she knelt before the Lord, and prayed. 'Lord, my body has been purchased by the great price of your precious blood. From today I am willing to dedicate myself completely to you. Accept me as a living sacrifice!'

Sheng was inspired by several brethren who had just been released from prison, and a Sister Bai who was just a little over 20. Sister Bai had left her home to serve the Lord and her father had taken her picture to the Public Security Bureau (police) and requested that they arrest her. Even though she was in danger of being arrested at any time, Sister Bai and the brethren had no thought about their own safety and continued to gather together with the brothers and sisters. She encouraged them to be strong, bold and to love the Lord fervently. She said, 'If the PSB comes, they will not arrest you for they only want us.' Her words gave much strength and help to Sheng in her service for the Lord.

Chapter 2

Sent by the Lord

From the end of 1981 until the Spring of 1982, the church experienced a great revival. There was a continual increase of new believers. After the Spring holidays, the believers in a certain district came to Sheng's fellowship with an urgent appeal for workers to preach the Gospel in their areas. After much prayer, five brothers and eight sisters in 'F' city and 'G' county responded to the call. Sheng was one of them.

As they walked down the road they all sang Acts 20:22-24, *'And now, compelled by the Spirit, I am going to Jerusalem, not knowing what will happen to me there. I only know that in every city the Holy Spirit warns me that prison and hardships are facing me ....'* They sang and wept as they boarded the bus to go to that district. After two hours, they arrived at their destination. They split into five groups and went door to door preaching Jesus in all the villages.

It was amazing. On the second evening, without planning to do so, they all ended up in the same place after they had finished ministering in different areas. When they saw each other, the young sisters began to tell how the heathen turned to Jesus. Some of them were weeping as they shared about the difficulties they faced when preaching the Gospel. The oldest in the group was only a little over 20 years old and the youngest, 15 years old.

Sheng and the older co-workers reminded them what Jesus had to put up with. She said the birds of the air had nests, and the foxes had caves, but Jesus had no place to lay his head. He was constantly despised, and the people tried to stone Him and even spat at Him. She then related Paul's experience in preaching the Gospel as recorded in 2 Corinthians 11:23–29 to encourage them. This strengthened their faith and they once again boldly went into the villages to preach the Gospel.

They ministered for four days and the Spirit of the Lord moved mightily in every place. In one village there was a man who was possessed by evil spirits. He was so fierce that nobody was able to get near him. His family begged the brothers and sisters to pray for him. They first preached the Gospel to them and destroyed the idols in their house. In the name of Jesus they cast the demons out of the man and he was immediately set free. As a result the whole family believed in the Lord and were full of joy.

But an amazing thing happened. The demons left that man and entered another family and possessed them. The brothers and sisters went to that home to pray and they also believed in Jesus and the demons left them. They then had peace. The demons, however, plagued a third, fourth and fifth family. Ultimately, everyone in this village believed in Jesus and a meeting place was established. Every evening they would meet together, sing choruses, pray and worship God.

Brother Gui's group received a special anointing of the Holy Spirit. They had gone to a more distant village to preach and had begun by saying, 'The kingdom of heaven has come, you must repent and believe in Jesus ....' They had copied many Gospel tracts and gave them to whoever they met. They had also prepared many posters which they pasted on the walls along the roads. The posters declared, 'Believe in Jesus and you shall have eternal life,' 'Worship the true God,' 'Your soul is very precious,' John 3:16, Hebrews 9:27, etc. Therefore many believed.

In one village there was a boy a little over ten years old. He had contacted meningitis and would constantly make noises and cry all the time. Nobody could understand a single word he said. For the sake of their child this family believed in the Lord and asked the brethren to pray for him. Brother Gui laid hands on his head and prayed, 'In the name of Jesus of Nazareth we command you to speak.' The child ran around the courtyard once, came back to Brother Gui and said to him clearly, 'Uncle, how are you? Praise the Lord!'

When the young preachers first came to this place, nobody was willing to receive them including the older believers. But now things began to change. In every village they were warmly welcomed. The other believers invited them to come to their village to preach the Gospel. There were so many invitations that the brothers and sisters were unable to take them up.

On the fifth day, they left for a busy market in 'E' town. There were many people there, but their consciences were seared and there was great immorality. The people violently opposed the Lord and in the past those who came to preach the Gospel faced strong resistance. They would even beat the preachers.

A few years ago, a brother had passed through this town and had spoken a few words about the Lord to the people. As a result he was beaten so badly blood gushed from his head. Though there were a few believers in that town they were lukewarm and were Christians in name only. The young preachers felt their strength was inadequate and prepared to return home. After walking 2 li (Chinese mile: 1 li = 0.5 km.) they felt ashamed as if they were soldiers deserting a battle.

Brother Gui said loudly, 'Brothers and sisters, woe to us if we do not preach the Gospel. Why have we left 'E' town? There are many lost souls there and we must go and save them!'

Then the brothers and sisters knelt on the ground, cried and confessed their sin. They asked the Lord to give them faith and strength. They were immediately filled with joy and comfort, and as a result, they all returned to 'E' town.

Chapter 3

The Fire Burns in 'E' Town

At that time, Brother Atu from 'F' city came with seven brothers and sisters to join the original group of 13, a total of 20 people. They divided into five small groups and went into every street and alley preaching the Gospel. Sheng took one group and entered the restaurants, shops, workplaces and hawker markets. They preached to everyone they saw in every building they entered. The people who had gathered to listen to them were like 'boiling water in a wok'. The crowds were so large that hardly anyone could cut his way through. The many vehicles on the streets formed long lines as the drivers stopped with great curiosity and stuck their heads out to see what was happening.

So many people had gathered at the front of a food store selling 'mantou' (steamed bread) that they trampled the man-tou on the ground. Many stalls selling cigarettes and candy met with the same fate. It was amazing that the owners did not complain at all. In fact they closed their stores and stalls and went to hear the preachers. In one restaurant, someone had purchased a bowl of noodles and had eaten only some of it when the shop owner said, 'eat it quickly.' He then left half a bowl of noodles and ran out with the owner to the meeting.

What they saw was a 'little sister' of 16 years old, standing on a wooden bench preaching the way of salvation. Everyone was very quiet and listened attentively. After she finished speaking, a 15-year-old sister took a Bible and told the people about God's creation and so on. Then another sister stood up and sang:

> '*Life on earth is like grass and flowers,*
> *Why do people strive for reputation and riches,*
> *When the hands are folded and the eyes are closed,*
> *Nothing can be taken.*
> *The soul is very precious, very precious,*
> *The soul is very precious, very precious.*
> *Believe in Jesus and obtain eternal life,*
> *And avoid the sufferings of hell.*'

Many people looked at them with astonishment, for they had never heard the Good News before! As Gui surveyed the scene many questions ran through his mind: 'Is this the way to preach the Gospel? Is God in this? What will be the consequences?' Suddenly his stomach started to hurt so bad that he doubled up on the ground. He could not even move a foot.

Then Brother Lu came over and said to him, 'Look, so many are here to hear the preaching, and they are so hungry. These sisters have believed in the Lord for only a short time and they can only preach short messages. You must stand up and preach.'

Brother Gui said, 'My stomach is killing me. How can I preach?'

'Just look at the crowds. Stomach pains or not, you must preach. You can preach for only 15 minutes.'

Brother Gui stood up and said, 'I will obey the Lord, I will obey the request of the church.'

As soon as he stood up on the wooden bench, the pain completely left. The people were amazed as they watched him. He was about 30 years old, tall and skinny. He had a little bit of a hunchback, a plain face, high nose and thick eyelashes. From his bright piercing eyes glistened rays of love. The Lord gave him sufficient strength. As he spoke the words flowed from his mouth like the gushing rivers of living water. He spoke about man's fall, the salvation of the soul and the punishment of sin. He told how Jesus came for sinners and how He received stripes and punishment and was crucified cruelly for our sins. He told them how man should repent, leave darkness, enter the light and through faith be freely saved. As the people listened they began to weep.

Then they heard that one group of brothers and sisters had been arrested. Gui addressed the remaining evangelists, 'Brothers and sisters, we have heard that the first group that was with us has been arrested. We must preach openly outside all the more boldly with all our strength.' After the brothers and sisters heard this, they preached with all their might. The longer they spoke, the more power they had and the crowds swelled. The longer people listened, the more they were interested. As they listened they would bow their heads and that day many repented.

Sister Sheng also heard about the arrest. She and her group of brothers and sisters all ran towards the rural government offices. The courtyard of the rural government office was very large. The brothers and sisters who had been arrested were inside the PSB office. Those who had been listening to the preachers also gathered at the courtyard of the rural government to look.

The main gate was open so a crowd of 3,000 crammed inside the compound. The brothers and sisters cried out, 'Quickly believe in Jesus! The kingdom of heaven is near ...' The officer in charge of the PSB said to them sternly, 'You are not allowed to preach here. Who is your leader? Have him come forth and say a few things and I will release you.'

The Christians continued to preach and the number of onlookers swelled even more. This angered the PSB but they did not know what to do. Finally, they drove the people away and detained six brothers and sisters. But many who had accepted the Gospel refused to leave. With the six who were detained everyone knelt on the ground and took turns to pray. The person leading the prayer prayed one sentence, and they all shouted, 'amen.' It was amazing, for these people who had only just believed, all cried out 'amen' in perfect unison.

Sister Sheng prayed, 'Lord, I ask you to allow the seed of the Gospel to be planted in 'E' town that many will repent, believe and through grace be saved. We are more than willing to give our lives in this place ...' Another sister prayed: 'Lord, we ask you to cause the people here to accept the Gospel. We are willing to suffer for this and receive stripes ...'

The brothers and sisters with all the crowd responded,

'Amen! Amen!' This sound of 'amen' reverberated through the skies and shook the hearts of many people. The believers also prayed for the PSB men, 'Lord, forgive the sins of the PSB. Take hold of them today and don't let them go. Cause them to repent ...'

The PSB were interrogating the six detained brothers and sisters at that time.

'What have you come here for?'

'To preach the Gospel.'

'Who is your leader?'

'Jesus is the leader.'

'Where are you from?'

'We are heavenly people.'

Each of the believers gave the same response. When the PSB officials heard the Christians outside praying for them, asking God to illuminate and take hold of them, they were shocked and panic stricken. They dashed to the main gate and fled, together with the officials of the rural government.

Thus, the brothers and sisters escaped detention. It was already two o'clock in the afternoon when they left the rural government offices. As they walked out they saw a river embankment about ten feet high. Many people had gathered there. This meeting had begun at 10:00 a.m. and it was led by Brother Gui and his group.

There were young people, old people, women and teenagers. Those who were selling cloth and clothing had closed their stalls. Those who sold vegetables had piled the greens to one side and the restaurant workers had all stopped work. Merchants too, had quit trading and blacksmiths had deserted the foundries.

In 'E' town, the primary school students spilled out of their classrooms and headed towards the embankment. The teachers were left standing in the classrooms dumbfounded. Then they, too, followed their students. Even the workers with the rural government came.

A barber also came. In his wake was a customer who had half of his hair cut. He was wearing a short apron, with shaving cream still on his face and hair still wet. They all came to the river embankment. All you could see were masses of people.

There were already 7,000 to 8,000 people there. Yet, many others continued to come from all directions until there were more than 10,000.

On the eastern side of the embankment a salesman selling rat poison had attracted a large crowd. He used a monkey to make the people laugh and then sold his rat poison. When Brother Gui passed the people standing there he prayed for the man who was playing with the monkey, 'Lord, we ask you not to allow him to get away today.' After prayer that group of people also ran over to listen to the preachers.

Brother Gui stood on one side of the embankment and, holding a Bible in his hand, faced the crowd and read to them Deuteronomy 30:19: *'This day I call heaven and earth as witnesses against you that I have set before you life and death, blessings and curses. Now choose life, so that you and your children may live.'* The crowd became so silent you could have heard a pin drop. The people simply listened and soon the silence was broken by sobs as many began to weep softly.

All of a sudden, from out of the crowd, ran the man with the monkey. With one hand he held the monkey, with the other he was wiping away his tears. He cried, 'I am from a family of three generations of Christians. But I disobeyed God and I have become a tramp who doesn't believe in God. Please pray for me, that God would forgive me. From today on I will not frolic with the monkey. I will repent and return to the Lord.'

Then a butcher cried out, 'I didn't realize it was so wonderful to believe in the Lord. I, too, will repent and believe.'

Another person spoke up, 'I have never heard this before. Now I see it is so good to believe in Jesus. Today not only do I believe, but I will invite you to my village. I will gather my family and the whole village to believe in the Jesus you are preaching about.' There were also several people who were Christians in name only and they all repented with tears.

At 4:00 p.m. the believers prayed for the crowd and then closed the meeting with a blessing. The five original small groups prepared to return home separately. As they were leaving they were surrounded by many people who asked them, 'Where will you be preaching tonight? We will go and listen!'

Brother Gui replied, 'We have already been away several days and we must return home this evening. If we have a chance later we will return!'

Then they were approached by several more people who very earnestly begged them, 'Could you please come to our village this evening? We have many people who have not heard the Gospel. Whatever you do you must come at least once. We can rent a car to take you around.'

Brother Gui did not know what to do. The place was called 'M' village which was 22.5 kilometers from 'E' town and it was already late afternoon. However, they pressed Brother Gui to accept their invitation and he promised them.

Even as they prepared to leave, many people surrounded them and pleaded, 'Please tell us just a little more. We haven't heard enough!'

There was an old sister over 50 years old from 'F' city. She was one of the seven who was with Brother Atu. She was illiterate and had never preached before. But she came to pray for these young preachers. Then she was filled with the Holy Spirit and suddenly began to preach the Gospel to the crowd. Her voice penetrated the air and tears flowed.

Every word was full of power and pricked the hearts of the people. She preached about God's will, how to believe in Jesus, as well as the second coming of Christ. For the work of the Lord she had already prayed and fasted without food or liquids for the previous four days. Yet she preached for two hours and the power of the Lord was upon her. She was not the least bit tired and the longer she preached the more power she had.

As the sun was setting the people from 'M' village convinced her to stop so that the brothers and sisters could begin their journey to 'M' village by vehicle. The rest of the evangelistic team had gone no further than a few kilometers when the believers in all the villages persuaded them to stay. Some of these believers were revived that day, some had just repented. They were very hungry for the Word of the Lord. Therefore the five small groups ministered in different areas and preached the Gospel to the people.

Chapter 4
The Beginning of Persecution

Sister Sheng led the first group of co-workers and that evening they had a meeting in a village. Many came to listen. As Sister Sheng was speaking on how to obtain life, she suddenly received inspiration. The words gushed out of her mouth as she urged the crowd, 'You must be strong and courageous and don't fear any circumstance. He that endures to the end shall be saved.' Having said that, she handed her Bible to a local believer and led everyone in prayer in preparation to dismiss the meeting.

Just at that moment, a group of cadres from a brigade of the people's militia burst into the meeting place. In a very rude and unreasonable manner they commanded, 'All local people can return home, but outsiders must remain.' However the local brothers and sisters were not prepared to leave these young preachers from out of town. So even under pressure from the cadres not a single person was willing to leave.

The cadres then began to identify the individuals. Naturally they could single out the local villagers from the newcomers. They soon identified the young preachers.

With a stern voice they shouted, 'Where are you from?'

'We are heavenly people.'

'What have you come here for?'

'To preach the Gospel.'

'Ha, that's great. Move! Follow us to the police station!'

The four young believers (one was a brother) felt at peace and were not afraid at all. They said to the brigade cadre, 'We will go, but there is a condition. You must allow us to pray along the way.' Although the cadre did not agree, the four evangelists began to sing and pray after a few paces. And they continued till the cadre did not know what to do. Eventually they arrived at the offices of the brigade and the four knelt down to pray. They heard a brigade cadre on the phone say, 'Here we have also arrested four.' They then knew that members of the other evangelistic teams had also been picked up.

Late in the night, the cadres acting on instructions transferred the preachers to the rural police station. That evening there were no clouds in the sky and the stars twinkled brightly. The light of the full moon was almost like daylight. Along the road, the brothers and sisters sang out loud. Sheng had preached the most during the past few days and her voice was the most hoarse. However at this time her voice was especially resonant and full of power. She did not feel like she was in the police station at all, rather that she had gone to be with the Lord.

The cadre escorting them warned them again and again.

'It is already late and we have arrived at the police station. You are not permitted to sing any more.'

The brothers and sisters were strong and courageous and they sang all the louder,

> *'I have a glorious home over in heaven,* (2 times)
> *I have a glorious home over in heaven that I always*
>   *remember.*
> *Lord, Lord, do not reject me,* (2 times)
> *Lord, Lord, do not reject me. Always remember me.*
> *Jesus Christ has saved me and He also will save you, ...'*

As they sang they passed through the gates of the rural government. When they entered the courtyard they saw several PSB officers and several scores of the people's militia there. They were not afraid at all, moreover they sang very loudly Psalm 146, '... *Do not put your trust in princes, in mortal men, who cannot save ...*'

Then a man who was probably the chief of that police station emerged. He slammed the things in his hand on a desk in the room and glared at them ferociously.

'Do you know where you are? How dare you sing here!'

The PSB officials seemed to think they were facing a formidable enemy. They were fully armed and, working hand in hand with the officials and people's militia of each village, they had been riding around all night in PSB vehicles, on motorcycles and bicycles searching everywhere for the five groups of young Gospel preachers. They had not slept a wink all night.

Before the group with Sheng was arrested, several believers had already been taken in. One of them, a young sister, was singled out and put in a small room to write a 'confession.' The PSB officials used all types of threats and enticements. She was terrified and wrote down the details of the day's events, how many came, their names, addresses and the names of the leaders of the five groups.

Then she heard Sister Sheng sing Psalm 146 (*Do not put your trust in princes, in mortal men, who cannot save. When their spirit departs, they return to the ground; on that very day their plans come to nothing.*) This Scripture forcibly brought her to her senses and she ripped to small pieces the several pages of her 'confession.' She knelt, cried to the Lord with tears and confessed her sin. She asked the Lord to give her faith and strength to be victorious in this trial.

The PSB officials took Sheng to the second courtyard. The atmosphere was very tense and no believers were there. She was confronted by a group of fiendish looking PSB officials, with taut faces and glaring eyes. In the light of the moon she was able to see the whole courtyard and she was naturally very tense. Next to several large poplar trees were several wooden batons that were broken in half and several split leather belts lay on the ground. She realized that the brothers and sisters who had been brought here earlier had already suffered cruel beatings and punishment!

Sheng prayed earnestly that the Lord would give her sufficient strength and faith. Then a 16-year-old sister was brought in. She was short in stature and, as soon as she walked in, they beat up her face. They lifted her up as if she were a little bird and ruthlessly threw her down onto the ground until her clothes ripped apart. Then they crossed her hands and handcuffed her to a stone pillar. The metal handcuffs dug deeply into her wrists and cut into her tender skin until beads of cold perspiration broke out on her forehead.

Sister Sheng was cut to her heart, and ran towards the two men who were hitting her. 'Why do you bully this little sister? Come, put her handcuffs on my hands!'

So, four large men who were as ferocious as wolves and tigers, lifted Sheng up without a word as though she were a mere bird. They took her to a room and savagely kicked and beat her on her back. Sheng had not had much sleep during the past five days and so was on the verge of collapse. How could she endure the vicious beatings of these four trained fighters? She fell over on the floor unconscious. It was then about two o'clock in the morning.

It was early spring and a bitter cold north wind was blowing. The piercing cold revived Sheng. As she lay on the freezing wet floor, aching all over, she felt limp and very weak. She looked around at the small room and the events of the previous night flashed through her mind like a scene from a movie. She wondered about the other co-workers. How were they abused? She felt sad and lonely as she had lost all her strength and the road ahead seemed so uncertain. All of a sudden the Word of the Lord came to her: '*We are hard pressed on every side, but not crushed; perplexed, but not in despair; persecuted, but not abandoned; struck down, but not destroyed.*' (2 Corinthians. 4:8–9)

She could almost hear a graceful voice singing this scripture. She knelt before the Lord and cried out, 'Lord, I ask you to look on your child. Give me sufficient strength that I may overcome Satan's schemes and harm. Your Name to me is so important! Use me to glorify your name.' Then all weakness, regret, fear, and loneliness left completely. She felt that her whole body was renewed with the strength of the Lord. A little after four in the morning Sheng was taken into the courtyard. There she saw the third group of believers all tied up. She thought, 'Lord, how many of the brothers and sisters have already been arrested and brought here?'

Suddenly, there was a noise of something clashing against metal. It came from the main gate of the rural government. A 'lunatic woman' had a large stone in her hand and was smashing it against the large metal gate while shouting 'Those who came from "F" city are good people. They have come to preach the

Gospel to us. Why have you tied them up? You are evil men who should die. You and your children gamble, steal and commit all kinds of crime. Why don't you do anything about this ...?'

Sheng and the believers inside were dumbfounded. We were all detained in the wee small hours between two and three in the morning. How could this 'lunatic woman' hear about it so quickly? And who was this 'lunatic woman?' She continued to bash the gate and the clanging got louder and louder. She kept shouting, 'Open the door, open the door!'

This 'lunatic woman' was well-known by everyone near and far, and even the PSB knew her very well. Though they were heartless people, they did not dare to beat to death this person with 'mental illness.' She continued to shout loudly until they had no choice but to open the gate and let her in. Since they were afraid that this 'lunatic woman' would expose all their shortcomings, one by one they took off to hide in their own rooms.

The 'lunatic woman" found Sheng, sat down beside her and asked her gently, 'Child, where are you from and why have they arrested you?'

'I am from "F" city and have been arrested for preaching the Gospel.'

'Good! You are the servants sent by the Lord. Handmaiden, be strong and courageous. Don't be afraid and stand steadfast. Child, to be beaten with whips and rods doesn't matter at all, but never say you don't believe! I must go out to tell the brothers and sisters here to pray for you.'

These words of the 'lunatic woman' were like a powerful surge of current that flowed into the brothers and sisters. Her words were not at all like that of a 'lunatic.' What kind of a person was this 'lunatic woman?'

By then it was dawn. They brought in a fourth group of evangelists. The PSB official immediately asked one brother, 'What is your name?'

'My father is called Heavenly Father,' answered this young man of only 20 without hesitating.

The interrogator was enraged. Several men rushed over and started to hit and kick this brother in the back and abdomen.

He was kicked like a ball and hit the ground with great impact. After they viciously beat him they dragged him to the courtyard and forced him to kneel. After that they called an evil man to use his shoes to kick him violently until blood oozed from his mouth and nose. He could barely breathe. As a result he fell over on the ground.

These cruel, evil men would not let up and they dragged him and handcuffed his hands behind his back to a coarse concrete pillar from 5:00 a.m. to after 6:00 p.m. His face was drained of colour. He prayed, 'Lord, forgive the sins of these evil men. Protect every brother and sister who has been forced into this place that they may be strong and courageous.' This type of punishment is very painful. Eventually this brother passed out as he was praying.

Then Sister Li was brought in. The evil men used terrible, filthy language to curse and abuse her. She saw the brother tied to the pillar who had already passed out and she immediately knelt on the ground to pray. The evil men yanked her up sternly.

'What do you do?'

'Preach the Gospel and save souls.'

'Where are you from?'

'The kingdom of heaven!'

'In which district and village do you live?'

'I live in the elevated commune, the holy brigade, paradise village.'

The interrogators were so furious they kicked her over on the floor and made her kneel for two hours as punishment. However they did not realize that this punishment only gave her an opportunity to pray!

Then four sisters were brought in. Each one had been beaten until their faces were all swollen. Their clothes were ripped into shreds and their skin was cut open all over. Oh, when a Christian has come to this state, do they even consider him a human being? As it says in Romans 8:36, '... *we are considered as sheep to be slaughtered.*' This was especially true of the sisters, for if it were not for the protection of the Lord and their own boldness and courage, they would have been subject to greater indignities.

From that night until the next morning, nearly 20 brothers and sisters who had been arrested were held in different places. They would under no circumstance put two people in the same place. Not only were they afraid that the brothers and sisters would conspire together, but they were also fearful of the brothers and sisters looking at each other. They frankly admitted, 'Whenever these people look at each other they are able to strengthen each other.'

The PSB had planned at dawn to parade the believers publicly, so they brought out a large rope to tie up each one. Two strong robust soldiers bound up the first brother. With great force they twisted Brother Zhuzi's arms and tied them behind his back, pulling the rope so tightly that it cut into his flesh. From Zhuzi's throat came a gasping sound as he struggled for every breath of air. Just as he was on the verge of passing out, the rope suddenly severed in several areas leaving the soldiers dumbfounded. They produced more rope and tied up Zhuzi in the same manner as before, but it also broke into several sections. The same happened to the rest of the believers who were bound. Nearly all the ropes and cords mysteriously broke and the soldiers panicked. Doubt and fear filled their hearts. 'Is it true that these people have Jesus with them?'

They could only find some old ropes which they soaked in water for a time. This time, they did not dare to be as cruel as before because there was not enough rope so they tied up only the brothers and three sisters. When the Christians were brought out to the main gate of the rural government, everyone was full of joy and one with a moving voice led the group as they sang:

'When I meet testing and tragedy, and pass through the
   territory of thistles and wolves;
I have a sweet thought, that is the Lord remembers me.
Lord, you now remember me. (2 times)
What have I to fear, when you are near and remember
   me?'

Then the Spirit of the Lord fell on the brothers and sisters and they were filled with faith and strength. When the soldiers saw that threatening did no good, they changed their attitude.

They used very gentle words as if they were pleading with the brothers and sisters: 'Please, don't sing anymore. If you are asked the reason why we are parading you through the street, don't by any means say you were arrested and are being paraded for preaching the Gospel.' They said that because, just the day before, there had been great public indignation over the arrests.

The Christians stood up straight, smiling and nodding to all the people on both sides of the road. Sister Sheng began so sing,

> '*Take up the cross, preach the Gospel and you will be filled with peace.*
> *Jesus leads me down the heavenly road and it is joy without measure.*
> *Even though we have met with persecution and tribulation, the cross is my glory and crown.*'

They all sang together as they marched in step, their voices resounding. Was this a parade of criminals? It was literally as if they were participating in a wedding procession. The PSB officials and soldiers gazed at each other in speechless despair and dared not rebuke or stop them.

A huge crowd of people had gathered to watch this group of strong and courageous believers in Jesus who had been beaten, bound and 'struggled against' for preaching the Gospel. Compassion filled their hearts and their eyes filled with tears. This was especially true of the adults. Seeing how those young girls had been beaten until their noses and eyes were swollen and their clothes were ripped to shreds, they exclaimed angrily, 'These people must not have any mothers and sisters in their family! How dare they abuse these girls. This is despicable!'

The soldiers saw the outrage of the crowds and that the parade was proving counter-productive. So they quickly took the brothers and sisters back to the police station and locked them up in different rooms.

After several days of labour and the past day and night of affliction, everyone was physically so weak they could hardly stand on their feet. The brothers immediately lay on the concrete floor and fell fast asleep. Seven sisters were crammed into a single bed with no mat or blanket, but they slept as comfortably as if they were on a soft bed until the evening. The situation was somewhat like Peter in prison who was able to sleep sweetly between the soldiers!

As the sun was setting, the door to the room in which the sisters were locked flew open with a crash. Like lightning a rough voice roared, 'Who is Sheng? Come out!' The sisters awoke with fright and Sheng said, 'It is time for my interrogation. You must pray fervently for me and ask the Lord to give me strength and to know what I should say.'

Having said that, she stood up straight and with her head held high she confidently strode out of the door. She was taken into the third courtyard where she saw several dozen sedans parked which perplexed her. How would she have known that these few 'silly little girls' during the past few days of preaching the Gospel had shaken two districts and three counties? Due to the activities of this group of teenage preachers, PSB officials from these districts and counties had come together with many people from 'E' town.

Sheng was taken into the interrogation room. The room was full of imposing PSB officials. They directed Sheng to sit on a short bench across from a short fat man of over 50 years old. The interrogation began. This man had eyes that protruded like a frog and he had a vicious, hateful face. He was so amazed that a short, skinny, emaciated and unimposing girl of under 20 years old was responsible for 'turning the world upside down.' However, under her lashes flashed a pair of bright shining eyes that radiated resolution and steadfastness. She conveyed the sense that she was 'sacred and inviolable'.

In a very gentle voice he said to Sheng, 'Oh, I see that you are a good young person. Don't be afraid. Just tell me, what organization are you a part of? Who is the leader? How many members are there? What are their names? Where do they live? There will be no problem and you can be immediately released and return home.'

As soon as Sheng heard this she realized that this man was an insidious 'old devil'. He had a disgusting smile and was using sweet, enticing words to beguile her.

She stood up straight as a rod and without any hesitation

said, 'I don't have any organization and Jesus is our head. Jesus told us to come, for he said, *"Go into all the world and preach the Gospel to all people. He who believes and is baptized shall be saved and he who doesn't believe is already condemned."* (Mark 16:15–16) We have all been inspired, therefore we have come here.'

Her chubby interrogator saw that softness did not work. Immediately his face became taut, and hatred burned from his eyes. He belligerently pounded the table with his fist and roared, 'You are audacious in the extreme. How dare you use enticing words to try to fool me. I tell you, if you don't honestly tell me everything you are going to suffer greatly.'

Another younger official added, 'Our policy is to be lenient with those who tell us all and to punish those who resist. You can choose which road you want to take!'

Sheng answered firmly, 'It is appointed unto men once to die and after death comes the judgment. This is what we believe and preach.'

The face of that short fat man turned purple. He jumped up and pulled a pistol from his belt and struck Sheng's forehead with it. Gnashing his teeth, he threatened, 'I will execute you. Right now in this place we are implementing our birth control policy and you have a plan to sabotage it step by step.'

Unafraid, Sheng refuted his accusation, 'These past few days we have been teaching people according to the Bible. We have in no way violated any policy of the country nor broken any laws.'

The man exploded in anger and, using the barrel of his gun, struck Sheng's forehead with greater force. He used the most filthy curse words, 'You bunch of XXX (swearing), you have fouled the atmosphere and brought trouble to the people and government of these two districts and three counties. You have brought disorder to our work. Don't you realize how serious are the crimes you have committed?'

The interrogation went on for more than three hours, ending after 10:00 p.m. Sheng had answered every question according to what the Holy Spirit told her to say and they were unable to refute or argue with her. The interrogators were not able to obtain any of the information they wanted from Sheng.

After it was over, Sheng was taken to another room. As she entered she sensed that the atmosphere was much more tense. On the table were all types of items of punishment and torture: handcuffs, electric rods, whips with spikes embedded, etc. Beside the table stood two soldiers. They had rolled up their sleeves and glared at Sheng.

The man interrogating Sheng pretended to be very polite and asked her to sit down. Then he began, 'It is not true that God created the world, but the working class has created the world. Man was not made by God, rather he has evolved from the apes.'

Sheng contradicted him and began to debate. 'You say the world is not made by God, then what about the sun that is 1,350,000 times larger than the earth in which the surface temperature reaches over 6,000 degrees. Did man create this? If men have evolved from apes and monkeys, why is there no link in the chain of evolution to man? Why are there no monkeys turning into men today?'

Without ceasing Sheng explained to him how God created the heaven, the earth, mankind, and all things and how Jesus Christ came to save and so on. This went on till three in the morning and the interrogators were still not able to obtain any information. Very discouraged, they waved their hands in dismissal and allowed the soldiers to remove Sheng.

Sheng spent a total of eight hours in two interrogation rooms. Due to the stress and the fact she was so exhausted she did not want to move, and she could hardly keep her eyes open. She was put in a separate room and was all alone except for a male guard.

This man kept smiling and grimacing and softly spoke words that were absolutely disgusting. Although Sheng was exhausted, she realised immediately she could not sleep and became determined to remain alert. That guard was a devil with a man's face and an animal's heart and the words from his mouth were more to be feared than electric rods and leather whips. Sheng prayed earnestly to the Lord for protection.

The guard took out a notepad and pen and put it in front of Sheng. 'You are so young and beautiful and you shouldn't have to suffer here. Come, come, just simply write a few sentences, explain things and I will certainly speak to my superior on your behalf and you will soon be allowed to leave,' he smiled, leeringly.

Sheng took up the pad and pen and said formally , 'All right, I will write. Move away from me.' She began to write very quickly, 'God sent me here to save the souls of men, for all have sinned and need salvation ...' She also wrote John 3:16, Romans 3:23–24, Mark 1:15 and several other verses, filling several sheets of paper. After writing she felt extremely exhausted, but when she caught his lewd eyes staring at her, she remained wide awake, prayed and quoted scripture until daybreak. Thank the Lord, Sheng was able to pass victoriously this difficult and dangerous night.

The Chief of the PSB simply could not believe that nothing had come from a whole night of interrogating an 18-year-old. Was she some type of superwoman? He wanted to see person-ally how invincible this girl was so he had her brought into the interrogation room first thing in the morning. When she arrived Sheng saw people sitting there reading the 'self-criticism' that she had written the previous night.

As soon as the Chief saw Sheng, he raised his head and asked, 'Are you Sheng?'

'Yes!'

The Chief jumped up. He was tall and large and he had an ugly and fearsome face. He reminded Sheng of Goliath, the Philistine. His hairy arm shot out towards her collar and she was seized by him, lifted up and thrown onto the ground. As he kicked Sheng he cursed, 'You so and so, you were told to write a confession. How dare you preach Jesus to me. You have a lot of nerve that you would dare to pull hairs off the tiger's face.' (to do something extremely foolish and dangerous).

Sheng remained silent and allowed him to hit her. He did this over and over again to no avail. The Chief ran out of methods of attack and could only allow the soldiers to take her out. In that room Sheng had to endure another two nights without any sleep. Her suffering during these two nights was indescribable. In order to avoid being 'devoured by wild beasts', she dared not lie down to sleep. To prevent herself from getting sleepy she bit her tongue and lips until the skin was broken. But thank the Lord, He give her sufficient strength and faith and she was able to completely overcome the snare and temptation from the Devil. Later, she began to keep her thoughts on the brothers and sisters who had been arrested. She felt discouraged and overwhelmed with loneliness.

All of a sudden, a very loving voice from outside the room called out, 'Daughter, daughter, where are you?' When Sheng heard it she knew it was the old mother whom they called the 'lunatic woman'. That evening, this 'lunatic woman' brought her seven-year-old daughter and a bucket of rice to the rural government to give to the brothers and sisters who had been detained. As she had done before, she took a large stone and began to beat on the gate of the rural government shouting, 'Open the door, open the door! I am bringing food for the children who believe in Jesus.' When the soldiers heard it they retorted, 'They have already eaten their evening meal. Go home!'

But the 'lunatic woman' persevered. 'I don't believe you. Your words cannot be believed. The children are starving for sure. Open the door! Open the door!' She then pounded against the door with great force. These PSB officials and cadres who were armed and feared by all because they acted like tyrants, amazingly had no way of dealing with this 'lunatic woman' so they obediently opened the door for her. She set the rice before the believers and tenderly entreated, 'Children, quickly eat! You have been starved for the past few days.'

Turning to the soldiers, in anger, she asked, 'Hey, something is not right. Why are there only seven children? Where is the other one? Where is that girl? Quickly give her back to me!' At first the soldiers paid no attention, but she continued to cry and shout and they did not know what to do, so they told her where Sheng was detained. She ran straight to Sheng's room and frantically called, 'Child, child, where are you?'

Sheng quickly responded. She demanded that the soldiers open the door immediately, but the soldiers lied to her saying, 'We don't have the key to this door for it was taken away by the guard.' The 'lunatic woman' climbed up to the window and said to Sheng, 'Child, be strong and don't be afraid. The people here are very wicked but outside many brothers and sisters are praying for you.' Sheng listened intently to every word and was once again strengthened.

Chapter 5

Cruel Persecution

That night in order to prevent the sudden attack of those 'wolves', Sheng sat there and prayed the whole night. When dawn came she sang Psalm 150, *'Praise ye the Lord.'* As soon as she had sung one sentence, she suddenly heard the sound of people singing *'Praise ye the Lord'* from all directions. She was amazed. With her hands she pushed open a window that was a little larger than a fist and saw several hundred brothers and sisters swarming like a flock toward the rural government. They walked and sang and the sound of singing shook the earth.

These were the brothers and sisters from 'G' and 'F' counties. They had heard that these young people were arrested by the PSB from 'E' town and they hurried all night from a district more than 50 kilometers away. Then all the people from 'E' town came as well and they gathered from the gates of the rural government all the way to the embankment of the river. The people were solidly packed there. It was as the Chinese saying, 'The wind sweeping through the tower heralds a rising storm in the mountains (a storm was coming).'

The Christians who had been detained heard the majestic sound outside of singing and began to sing along with the crowd. The sounds blended into an earth-shaking musical composition that could be heard far off. A directive came from the county PSB over the telephone to the 'E' town local police station that they were to organize the militia. They were directed to beat the Christians savagely, and if anyone was beaten to death the county would bear the responsibility.

Soon several hundred core members of the militia, well-trained in martial arts, had been organized and with their full armour fell into companies. A loudspeaker from the rural government called on those who did not believe in Jesus to leave. Many onlookers, smelling trouble, quickly left the grounds. Still, many people stayed and the majority of them were local people. They were the ones who had believed after hearing the Gospel for the first time or older believers who had been revived. Part of the crowd were believers from 'F' and 'G' cities.

As soon as the order was issued, the soldiers began to move towards the group of innocent brothers and sisters and beat them. First they drove the believers to the river bank. Two large, strong men then twisted Brother Gui's arms and began to beat and kick him viciously. One lifted his foot and kicked him down an embankment that was more than ten feet high. Gui landed on sand and gravel on the edge of the river. Then the two men jumped down and continued to kick him with all their might. Although Brother Gui could hear them beating him, he felt no pain whatsoever. He was prostrated on the ground and he cried out, 'Lord, their feet have trodden on your head and their fists have beaten your body for you have used your hands to protect me.' Without a doubt, if it was not for the Lord's protection, even if he had a body of steel and bones of iron, he would have been beaten to a pulp.

The monsters were sure they had beaten him to death, so they left Brother Gui and looked for other victims. Brother Gui pulled himself up and looked up. How terrible! Everywhere he saw soldiers savagely using their fists to attack the believers. Then they kicked them over the embankment. The soldiers below the embankment would continue beating and kicking them. They aimed at their heads, backs, chests, and abdomens without any mercy, beating them so viciously that one by one the brothers and sisters fell unconscious.

The soldiers kept throwing people down the river bank. Brother Gui wept as he counted. At least 70 people had been beaten until they fell over. The older aunties and ten-year-old little sisters received the worst beatings. It was too cruel to behold. If it were not for the protection of the Lord, several dozen people would have been beaten to death that day.

The beatings continued unabated. Old Auntie Fang was beaten until she fell. They yanked out much of her hair, leaving her head a greenish colour and her eyes swollen. Blood was coming out of her nose and mouth. She called out to the Lord, 'Lord, I ask you to protect this group of brothers and sisters and forgive the sins of these evil men.'

Children of God, think of it. In this 20th century in a nation where the government advocates 'Five ways to speak politely and four superior ways of living' (a courtesy campaign) and 'spiritual civilized behaviour', this type of extreme cruelty still exists. And this is only one small example of millions of cases of persecution of the Christians in this nation.

As the many new believers in 'E' town witnessed this savage attack, there was not one who did not cry. Many angrily said, 'These are all good people and they have been beaten without cause. God will certainly punish the people in this place!' Hearing this, many who had not yet believed ran over to help those who were injured.

Brother Gui saw the injuries inflicted on the believers and he began to beat his chest, weeping and wailing. He rushed to the brothers and sisters who had been beaten unconscious and touched their swollen faces and hands tenderly. He cried over them, his tears splashing onto their foreheads and faces. They lay very still.

Then a young sister from 'E' town who had just believed came running over and grabbed Brother Gui's hand urgently, 'Run quickly! The PSB men are looking for you everywhere, for you were the one who was seen and preached the most at the river bank.'

With tears in his eyes Brother Gui said, 'I cannot leave. How can I bear to leave these beloved brothers and sisters and my unconscious "flesh and blood" here?'

The sister spoke firmly, 'You shouldn't speak this way. If you are arrested, a lot of unforeseen things may happen. The brothers and sisters in 'F' city are unable to take over from you. Consider the overall situation and leave here immediately. Come with me.'

As Brother Gui agonised over what to do, he prayed and the Holy Spirit prompted him to leave immediately. So he followed the sister and sought refuge with a family nearby. Several brothers and sisters came and Gui spoke to them with tears in his eyes saying, 'You brothers and sisters here are so lukewarm. You don't consider smoking or drinking as something wrong and have committed many sins. That is why the Gospel is not spreading here. This time the brothers and sisters from "F" city and "G" county have suffered for you.' Hearing this they, too, began to weep, and they knelt down and confessed their sins.

Suddenly a brother ran over to them and said, 'Quickly leave, quickly leave. The men from the PSB are leading the militia and are going door to door searching for you.' The believers immediately whisked Gui to another family located some distance away. Soon another brother brought a report that those who were beaten unconscious had almost all revived. However, three of them were seriously injured and are still unconscious. Among them was a young brother who was near death.

'What shall we do?' he asked.

The brothers and sisters who were with Gui all began to cry out loud. Then another brother came and told Gui, 'Two of the brothers after prayer have already awakened, but we are afraid there is no hope for the young brother.' Gui immediately called them to prepare a hand cart to bring that brother to him.

Sobbing, they pulled that brother home. Gui immediately came out, lifted the blanket and looked at him. His face was beyond recognition. His head had swollen like a gourd and he had already stopped breathing. With the others Gui knelt down in the presence of the Lord and wept, 'Lord, how can we bear this heavy burden? Have mercy on us and cause this brother to rise from the dead.'

After prayer that brother suddenly took a gasp of air. Gui immediately gave thanks to the Lord. The brother began to open his eyes and slowly sat up. Everyone wept as they praised the Lord with a loud voice.

The brother opened his mouth to speak, 'When I was by the riverside and was beaten, I saw a man whose beard and hair was white and who was clothed in white raiment right down to his feet. His face was like that of the sun and light shone from His whole body. He held in His hand a book and with a pen quickly recorded what was happening. Then He said, "Young son, today I have recorded all that you have suffered".' Upon hearing that all the people sang, danced and praised the Lord.

Gui left that family and met Brother Ming, God's servant from 'F' city. Gui was like a child meeting his mother after being bullied. He wept as he told Brother Ming everything that had happened. Then he said, 'I have seen you today and commit everything to you. Now I must go to the police station and suffer with the other members of the body. I just cannot forsake them!'

Upon hearing this, Brother Ming wept and said grimly, 'There are already more than 70 brothers and sisters who have been arrested. Now there is much work waiting for us to do. To go to prison is for the Lord and work outside is also for the Lord. Now we have to leave this place immediately.' Amid the sound of the local brethren weeping, the two mounted their bicycles and returned to 'F' city.

They had not gone very far when the PSB vehicle from 'E' village caught up with them. The two brothers prayed as they pedalled their bicycles with all their strength. They thought, how can a bicycle compete with a PSB police jeep? In the natural, there was no way these two brothers could escape. Then an amazing thing happened. The PSB jeep could not catch up with the brothers on their bicycles! After chasing them for many miles they got farther and farther away from them and the PSB jeep had no recourse but to return. With tears the two brothers praised the Lord and rode their bicycles back to 'F' city.

As they pedalled their hearts were very heavy. Their greatest concern was they did not know the present situation of those 70 brothers and sisters. They had been in the police station in 'E' town for six days now. The policemen had used every scheme possible, employed many personnel, threatened and tempted them. Yet they were not able to move the faith of these 70 people in the slightest. Who knows how many batons had been broken in half and how many leather belts they had worn out? They even used guns, electric rods and other instruments of torture. The only result was to bring bodily injury to the believers, but they were unable to shake their faith in Jesus. In the end it was the police officers who were absolutely exhausted. They had a discussion and decided to send the believers back to their original counties thus ridding themselves of this responsibility.

That day the weather changed. A freezing cold wind was blowing. Sheng and the 70 believers gathered in the large courtyard. Each one was bound with ropes and those on Sheng were particularly tight. Upon seeing this a brother said to the PSB officials, 'She is only a 17-year-old girl. Why have you tied her up so tight? Come, loosen her ropes and bind me tighter.' Several soldiers immediately slapped him on both cheeks. They kicked him to the ground and tied him up very tightly. After that they took pictures of the 70 believers and pushed them onto a large truck. With several armed soldiers guarding them they were sent back to 'F' city and 'G' county.

The truck drove slowly out of the gates of the rural government and a large crowd immediately swarmed it. They were all brothers and sisters from 'E' village and the neighbouring areas. The majority of them were those who had heard the Gospel and believed in the Lord. A small number of them were older believers who were lukewarm and backslidden. Due to the preaching and testimonies of the brothers and sisters, and especially due to their suffering, God moved these who had been sleeping for many years.

The Christians did not know what was going to happen today, so they had been waiting at the gate from early morning. Upon seeing the brothers and sisters all tied up standing in the truck, they surrounded the vehicle so that it could go no further. They all stretched out their hands and grabbed their clothes and began to wail very loudly. Even those passing by on the road were moved and wept along with them.

The 'lunatic woman' held onto the side of the truck and stuffed ¥60 RMB into Sheng's pocket and put into the truck a large packet of cakes. Weeping, she said, 'Children, this is a little token of appreciation from the brothers and sisters in "E" village. May the Lord give you peace on your way!' Sheng and the brothers and sisters wept, but they were greatly comforted. Even though they had to put up with physical sufferings during the past few days, the fires of revival had already begun to burn in 'E' county and the neighbouring areas. They had already seen the fruit of their labours and had with their own eyes seen the mighty works of God. Hallelujah, glory to the Name of the Lord!

Because the truck was unable to move, many cadres and soldiers came running out from the rural government building. They used their guns to force back the crowd that came to send off the brothers and sisters so that the truck could leave. The brothers and sisters from 'E' town, seeing the vehicle leave, wept and chased after it. How could man's legs race a vehicle? However they continued running after the truck till it disappeared around a mountain bend. Only then did they stop and, beating their chests, wailed loudly. Some of them knelt on the road and prayed for these young people.

The believers in the truck all looked back at 'E' village, memories crowding their minds. Suddenly, Sheng led them in singing Hebrews 10:32–39:

> 'Remember those earlier days after you had received the light, when you stood your ground in a great contest in the face of suffering. Sometimes you were publicly exposed to insult and persecution; at other times you stood side by side with those who were so treated. You sympathized with those in prison and joyfully accepted the confiscation of your property, because you knew that you yourselves had better and lasting possessions. So do not throw away your confidence; it will be richly rewarded. You need to persevere so that when you have done the will of God, you will receive what he has promised. For in just a very little while, "He who is coming will come and will not delay. But my righteous one will live by faith. And if he shrinks back, I will not be pleased with him." But we are not of those who shrink back and are destroyed, but of those who believe and are saved.'

With weeping the brothers and sisters sang this Scripture. The longer they sang the more strength they had. The sound of singing resounded from the sides of the road through to the mountains and up to the clouds. The soldiers took the brothers and sisters who had been bound to the PSB offices of 'G' county and 'F' city. The reason is that this Gospel team was organized by brothers and sisters from these two counties.

Chapter 6

Imprisoned in 'F' City

It was already six in the evening when they finally arrived at 'F'
city. It was amazing to see so many brethren turn out to meet
them. All were weeping. As soon as the evangelists alighted
from the PSB truck they were immediately whisked to the
courtyard of the PSB offices.

As news of their arrest spread, the believers in other counties
went into prayer and fasting together with the Christians in 'F'
city. Oh, the depth of the riches of the wisdom and knowledge
of God! How unsearchable are His judgments and His ways!
Who knows His thoughts and who has ever been His coun-
sellor! Who would have thought that God would use the
tribulations of His children to bring revival to the churches in
town 'E', county 'G' and city 'F'? Hallelujah! Praise Him for
His might works!

The authorities, however, were furious with the young
evangelists because what they did in the other counties had
caused the authorities to 'lose face'.

Their trial began that very night. First to be called to the
stand was Sister Sheng. Her interrogator employed different
tactics in questioning her. He was at times gentle and coaxing,
at times harsh. Then he would scold her and beat her into
telling him who her 'leader' was. But the Lord gave her strength
to overcome it all.

Next to be tried was Brother Atu. He was very calm and did
not say a word. This made his interrogator very angry so that
he banged his pistol hard on the table, sending a teacup flying
and landing with a crash, splashing tea everywhere and especially on the prosecutor's face!

Purple with rage by now, he lashed at Atu's legs and chest with an iron rod. He summoned two other agents who used a piece of wood to thrash Atu at his ankles. As a result, Brother Atu suffered serious injury. Even years later, his health was to be affected by frequent chest pains because of this one incident.

The other 12 brothers and sisters, meanwhile, were thrown into a small room with a large iron gate. Their bonds had been tightened even more, turning their hands black and draining their faces of colour. The pain was unbearable. They had barely recovered from being bound up like this in town 'E' when they found themselves in bonds again, this time even tighter.

As the gate clanged and locked them in the darkness, they began to understand how Jesus must have felt when He was whipped and crucified on the cross. Weeping, they mustered whatever strength they had left to sing:

> *'Saviour Jesus wore a crown of thorns, bearing the cross to Calvary.*
> *Roman soldiers whipped His body, Precious blood was shed on Calvary.*
> *Saviour Jesus, Saviour Jesus, How can I ever forget Calvary?*
> *There you were crucified on the cross, Your precious blood was shed for my redemption ...'*

As they continued to sing, the pain left. They wept. Then they could sing no more. The torture and abuse of the past few days had left them totally exhausted. Although it was freezing, they all slept on the cold, stone floor. Their rest was short lived, however. They were awakened by the chilling cold in the middle of the night. Suddenly, they realised were not bound! Their bonds had fallen off beside them! They remembered how Peter's chains fell off while he was in prison. Their joy was unspeakable! Abandoning all caution they danced and praised the Lord.

The next day, they were brought out to be tried but the authorities could not squeeze anything out of them. Instead, the PSB ordered the families of the evangelists to bear the cost of feeding them in prison. The believers collected an offering for them. The amount should have been more than sufficient to buy the best meals, but what they were given was worse than pig food! One night, before they went to bed, Sister Sheng took out a pocket-sized New Testament which she had taken from the prosecution room in town 'E' when nobody was watching. She opened it to Revelation 2:10–11 and read out loud:

> '*Do not be afraid of what you are about to suffer. I tell you, the devil will put some of you in prison to test you, and you will suffer persecution for ten days. Be faithful, even to the point of death, and I will give you the crown of life. He who has an ear, let him hear what the Spirit says to the churches. He who overcomes will not be hurt at all by the second death.*'

This word from the Lord was so precious, it was like morning dew to all of them.

Three of the sisters stood to their feet and began dancing and singing loudly, 'Hallelujah, praise the Lord!'

They then began to sing a song they had never sung before:

> '*The way of the cross is the way of sacrifice,*
> *Everything must be offered to God,*
> *All must be laid on the altar of death,*
> *Before fire can come down.*
> *This is the way of the cross, Are you willing to tread this way?*
> *Have you ever carried the cross for your Lord?*
> *You who have given everything to God, Will you be faithful to Him?*'

When the guards outside heard it, they were shocked and rushed into the room immediately. But all they saw was just several women singing and dancing. They simply could not understand how they could be so joyous in such circumstances.

> '*All things work together for good for those who love God and for those who are called according to His purposes.*'
> Romans 8:28

How true this scripture is! Before this group of evangelists went to town 'E', there were divisions among the believers in county 'G' and city 'F'. But now that the co-workers had been arrested, there was unity among the churches again. They all fasted and prayed in one accord for those in prison. As a result, there was great revival in the home churches and many new believers were added to their number.

While in detention, the evangelists received many visitors daily. Some days nearly a hundred believers would come to visit them! They all stood outside the PSB office, and when asked who they wanted to see most of them said they came to visit Sister Sheng. The PSB men were surprised. 'Why, this girl is only 18,' they said. 'She must be a leader of these Christians or there wouldn't be so many people wanting to see her.'

Soon, no visitors were allowed at all, especially for Sheng. The authorities believed that 'even if you don't allow Christians to speak to one another, they can still gather strength just by looking at one another.'

But God is a wonderful God! There was a small hole in the wall at the back of the room where Sheng was held. Brother Ming and the other sisters would talk to her through this hole, comforting and encouraging her.

The 12 evangelists were held for 19 days altogether. Although they were interrogated over and over during that period, the PSB could not get anything out of them. So they had to release them for a while.

On the day they were to be released, the PSB chief called them in and said, 'What you did in town "E" has upset our work in many places. The case is not yet closed. For now, we'll let you go home but we'll call you in future. You have to come as soon as you are called. Go home and be good citizens, obey the rules! Do not speak to anyone along the way!'

As soon as they walked past the PSB gate Sister Sheng broke into song,

> 'The Spirit of the Lord is on me, because He has anointed me to preach the good news to the poor. He has sent me to proclaim freedom for the prisoners and recovery of sight for the blind, to release the oppressed, to proclaim the year of the Lord's favour.' Luke 4:18–19

Chapter 7
More Persecution

Not long after her release, Sheng was again picked up by PSB officials from 'F' city. They took her to the local government office and locked her up in a dirty store room. At first, she felt all alone. Then she knelt down to pray, asking the Lord to strengthen her. Suddenly, she heard a familiar voice calling her gently, 'Sister, Sister, where are you?' Sheng listened carefully at first before responding. She recognized Xiaohong's voice. 'I'm here,' she quickly replied.

Xiaohong was only 16 then. But she was very mature for her age and loved the Lord dearly. Sheng treated her like her own younger sister and regarded her as a noteworthy co-worker as well. Despite her youth Xiaohong was always faithful to complete whatever task the church gave her to do. And she always did a good job too.

Today, Xiaohong brought Sister Wei with her to see Sheng. They had looked all over the place for Sheng and finally tracked her down in this store room.

Sheng jumped up with joy and praised the Lord! She knew it was the Lord who sent Xiaohong to strengthen her. Her fears dissipated and she was greatly encouraged.

The next day, Sheng was taken out for interrogation. She recognized the official at once. He had interrogated her before. He was nicknamed 'Ku Da Tou', and was a mean character with a violent temper. The average criminal was terrified of him. During the past decade how many believers had suffered torture at his hands? How many more Christians have been given harsh prison terms and languished in jail because of this one man?

Now Sheng found herself in his grip again. She was well aware that 'Ku Da Tou' was full of the devil and hated Christians intensely. Sheng could only pray earnestly.

Ku reached for a document case and took from within a stack of photographs. They were shots of Sheng and 17 other people in town 'E'.

'Do you recognize the people in these photos?' he growled. 'What you did in town "E" was counter-revolutionary. It was a very serious thing you did in that it shook the whole country. We understand that you are all very young and have been used by other people and there's an organization behind you. We have decided to give you a chance if you will only be honest with us.'

Then he went on, 'What kind of an organization is this? Who is behind all this? Who was the leader of the five groups that went to town "E?"'

Sheng was frantically praying all this time. She did not feel led to say anything so she maintained silence. The Holy Spirit reminded her of Jesus before Pilate.

Her silence, however, aroused Ku's anger. Enraged, he shouted, 'You said so much in the streets of town "E"; why don't you speak today? Many people have already confessed to me that you are the leader. Are you still denying this?'

Sister Sheng refused to speak. Ku Da Tou stood up and slapped her hard across her face. He insulted her, using foul and abusive language.

Then, at the prompting of the Holy Spirit, Sheng spoke. The words came tumbling out of her mouth like rushing water. She began by telling how God had sent them to town 'E', how sin came into the world and the result of sin, and how man could flee from judgment, etc. Sheng spoke for more than two hours under the anointing of the Holy Spirit. It seemed as if it was someone else saying all those things and not her. Ku had tried to stop her several times but she would not let him until she had well and truly finished.

By which time Ku shot up from his chair and screeched, 'Take this girl away! Let her have a taste of what she deserves!'

Two men sprang forth and dragged Sheng to the courtyard, where they whipped her viciously with a leather belt. She was forced to lift her hands while they whipped her. And if she were to drop her arms ever so slightly, they would hit her with a staff. This went on for two hours until Sheng could no longer lift even a finger.

She simply sat down, and did not care a jot about the two men. Seeing her exhausted, they then tied her to a tree.

They only untied her at midnight and then locked her up in the store room again. The guard assigned to watch over her looked very much like the wicked man who had guarded her cell several months ago in town 'E'.

Sheng prayed as she looked him in the eye with authority and quoted Bible verses to him. The guard found her rather extraordinary and, seeing her purity, left in shame as he could not possibly violate her. So Sister Sheng sang, '*You have prepared a table for me in the presence of my enemies.*'

Four days later, Sheng was released.

Chapter 8
Arrested and Put in Prison

The authorities in the various counties and districts considered the young Christian preachers' activities in town 'E' as 'counter-revolutionary'. So they brought the case to the attention of the provincial and central government. Two months after Sheng was released (in late October, 1982) the provincial government issued a warrant of arrest for the evangelists who went to town 'E' charging them with belonging to the 'counter-revolutionary' group, the 'Yellers Sect'. Sheng and the other co-workers were back on the wanted list.

As a result of the beatings she received in prison in town 'E' her health deteriorated. After the warrant was issued for her arrest, Sheng left home to avoid capture. She worked with Sister Bai and the churches in 'F' city and she would preach at the meetings in the nearby counties.

Once, she was leaving a village after preaching there when the PSB sent its men on motorcycles to catch her. Naturally, she made good her escape. She was to evade arrest several times in a few months.

One miraculous escape occurred when she was cycling on a highway and turned a corner into an approaching PSB car with two armed police officers inside. Sheng thought, 'If I turn my bicycle around they will surely recognise me.' So she pedalled faster *towards* them. Sheng was only a few meters from the car, all they had to do was compare her photograph with the rider and Sheng would have been done for. Just at that crucial moment, there was a loud bang! The police car had a flat tyre and the PSB men got out of the car to inspect the damage! Sheng simply cycled past, relieved for the narrow escape.

Another time, the police jumped into their car as soon as

they received a tip-off about Sheng's whereabouts. They were so eager to arrest Sheng that somehow they careered off the road and into a ditch. Several of the PSB were injured, one of them suffered a broken leg. This put Sheng high on the hate list of the police!

As it was, they would search her house every night. By then, several believers had already been picked up.

Nine months passed. Then God revealed to Sheng that it was time for her to suffer for the Lord again. She was at peace about it and tried to use her time wisely, helping the churches with the work.

On the evening of June 30, 1983, Sheng was arrested after a village meeting. When the armed PSB officers snapped the handcuffs on her, the brothers and sisters felt heavy in their hearts. But Sheng remained calm. She simply said 'goodbye' to them.

On the way to prison Sheng looked up into the heavens and found stars shining brightly. Her eyes brimmed with tears as she said a prayer, 'Lord, this world is really in darkness. Try me and purify me that I may become a star in your right hand that shines forth in this crooked and perverse generation. Also, raise up more brothers and sisters to shine for you.'

Sheng and her captors walked for about two kilometers before they reached the main road where a PSB car was parked. She was shoved into the vehicle. Sheng closed her eyes and began to pray. The heroes of the faith flashed through her mind … Joseph in prison … the three men in the fiery furnace … Daniel in the lion's den etc. She then began to sing with excitement.

> 'Of old there were three men of faith, they were thrown into the fire but were not hurt.
> Where are they now? In the Promised Land!'

Sheng continued singing despite her captors' efforts to stop her, including beatings and curses. Her heart was just filled with the Lord's love!

They arrived at 'F' city at 3:40 in the morning. The courtyard was floodlit, despite the hour, and a group of PSB men were waiting as if for a VIP.

Sheng was perplexed. 'It's so early in the morning, what are these people standing here for?' Little did she know that they were brought here to see her, since they had gone to great lengths to arrest her. Why, she had become quite a famous criminal!

When Sheng emerged from the car, the PSB officers gasped and said, 'Is this the one who made us suffer for nine months? We had thought she was a great heroine, but she's only a girl!'

Sheng was thrown into the women's prison. At daybreak, many PSB men came to see Sheng, among them an officer on crutches.

Sheng was singing, 'I am a little bird in a cage' just as he arrived. With great fury he dragged Sheng out of the cell and forced her to kneel. Then he whipped her with a leather belt and yelled at her, 'You XXX, you have caused me much misery. In our efforts to catch you several of our motorcycles have been damaged, one PSB jeep was overturned, and I broke my leg in the process. Now I'm going to break your leg!'

He thrashed Sheng until he was exhausted. Her clothes were torn into shreds and she was a bloody sight. He pushed her back into her cell.

In July of that year, the number of prisoners suddenly increased. Every cell was packed with inmates. Crammed into Sheng's cell were more than 20 women prisoners.

The food given to prisoners was worse than pigs' feed. All they had was a small bowl of noodles or simply soup for their meals. The inmates who had hearty appetites were always starving, so they cursed and cussed and, as a result, they were often punished and beaten.

Sheng felt sorry for them. She often prayed for them and for their souls. So she decided to eat only one meal a day and share the rest of her food with the other prisoners. Although this did not amount to much per person still they felt blessed to have the extra portion. They could see that Sheng was no ordinary person and they gave her the utmost respect. Before long, the majority of them accepted Christ. Sheng would then lead them to pray and sing hymns. In that short time, their lives were changed.

Chapter 9

The Trial and Sentence

Fifty days after she was arrested, Sheng was sentenced. During that time, she had been interrogated numerous times but the authorities never got anything out of her. This made her interrogators very mad. Many teacups were smashed, and all kinds of ways were employed to coerce Sheng to talk, including torture, threats, and bribery. But she would not yield.

The government had wanted this case to close soon. Therefore, the People's Court in 'F' city decided to pronounce a verdict in an open court on August 20.

The day dawned bright and promising, with clear skies and brilliant sunshine. Sheng was brought out of her cell handcuffed.

It was a 50 kilometer walk from the prison to the courtroom. Sheng had not seen the sun for many days, so now it made her feel dizzy to be walking in the dazzling sunshine. She prayed, asking the Lord to be with her. Suddenly, she heard a very gentle, small voice saying, 'My child, do not be afraid. I will be with you today. It's time for you to glorify My Name. Be bold and courageous and a good example.'

Bubbling with joy, she strode into the courtroom with her head lifted high. She looked around and saw many familiar faces of the servants of God. They looked at her with encouragement and hope in their eyes. Her parents and younger sister, Xiaohong, were also there. There were altogether ten court officials present.

Sheng took her place behind the defendant's bench. The judge gave her a quick glance and then proceeded to ask her routine questions about herself, her age, address, background, work unit, and so on.

Then he asked her contemptuously, 'Are you the master-mind behind the counter-revolutionary riot in town "E" which shook the entire province?'

'No'

'Your fellow worker has accused you of being the leader.'

'Show me the written accusation,' Sheng responded without fear. The judge did so. She took the paper and saw a very familiar signature and a red finger print. She was taken aback. But she regained her composure and said, 'I demand that my accuser be brought forth to testify. And even if he does, the testimony of only one witness is not valid and cannot be the basis for a verdict.'

'Then who is behind the incident in town "E"? Who is the leader of each group?' the judge asked, perplexed.

'I don't know.'

The trial went on for more than an hour. In the end, there was no hard evidence with which to convict her. The authorities had no legal case but because of pressure from the government they had to have a verdict. So they sentenced Sheng to two years' imprisonment for disturbing peace and disrupting the traffic.

Then the judge asked Sheng, 'Do you need a lawyer?'

'No.'

'Do you want to appeal?'

'No,' Sheng said with a smile.

On the way back to the prison, Sheng saw many, many believers in tears waving at her. The two armed guards escorting her seemed to be very nervous. They were sweating profusely as they used their guns to keep the mob away from Sheng.

Her little sister, Xiaohong, rushed to her side. And it made Sheng think of the church as scattered sheep without a shepherd. Her heart was heavy. Tears began to well up, and she said to Xiaohong, 'Though you are young, look after the family and take care of the sheep.'

Weeping, Xiaohong nodded, 'Don't worry, I'll certainly do as you say.'

Just before Sheng disappeared behind the prison gates a cry went up from the brothers and sisters accompanying her. Sheng turned and shouted, 'Do not worry about me, just pray for me.' The iron gate clanged shut.

Ten days after she was sentenced, Sheng was removed to a women's prison to be reformed through hard labour. Her family was not notified about it. As she was being taken to the bus station by two armed guards her heart felt like stone. She begged the Lord to let her family know. He is wonderful!

While Sheng was boarding the bus, Xiaohong had come to visit her with another sister in the Lord. They had gone to the prison and hence had found out that she had been taken to the bus station, so they rushed there. Xiaohong and Sheng embraced each other and wept aloud. Sheng was about to tell Xiaohong about the church when the guard shoved her sister to one side and bundled her into the bus.

The bus lurched forward and Xiaohong ran after it, weeping and shouting, 'Sister, serve the Lord and serve Him well'.

Xiaohong was out of sight but Sheng could still hear her last words – 'serve the Lord, and serve Him well.' She thought of her little sister who now had to care for the church at such a tender age, and the condition of her sheep. She began to cry.

Apart from Sheng, Brother Gui and four other brothers were also given prison terms of three and four years. Another three brothers who were caught in town 'E' preaching the Gospel were sentenced to five, four and three years respectively.

Not long after, a severe drought hit town 'E'. For three consecutive seasons there were no harvests. Many of the farmers in town 'E' complained to the government, 'It's because you have persecuted the Christians that this disaster has befallen us. You are responsible for this.'

The cadres retorted by saying, 'The past is past, there is nothing we can do about it. In future we won't bother the Christians anymore.'

Interestingly, the official chiefly responsible for beating the Christians involved in the town 'E' incident fell off his bicycle and broke three ribs right at the spot where he had beaten the believers mercilessly.

Chapter 10

Hell on Earth

At the women's prison Sheng could feel the oppressive darkness. It was like hell on earth. The air was so dank Sheng could hardly breathe.

There were 20 inmates in Sheng's cell, 12 of them had been convicted of murder. Most of the prisoners were immoral, cheats, robbers and prostitutes. Cursing and filthy language was the order of the day in those cells.

Many inmates sent there were never reformed but became worse instead. Surrounded by every imaginable wickedness their hearts and minds just grew more and more depraved.

A young thief of only 18 learned in prison to become a bigger thief. She would steal from anyone, both guards and fellow inmates. She would be beaten and punished but still she would not change her ways. A few days later, she would be doing it again. But praise the Lord, Sheng eventually led her to the Lord, and she was delivered of this sin. She became a very good Christian helper in the prison work.

Then there was a village woman who was sentenced to one year in jail for fighting with her neighbour. At first, she was very quiet and would blush whenever she heard all the cursing and swearing. But within a month she had become like all the rest of the inmates.

One day, one of the young prisoners in her twenties attacked another middle-aged inmate with a beer bottle, hitting her on the neck and gashing her throat. The older woman almost died. For this, her young attacker had her prison term increased by five years.

Some very strange things happened in this 'hell on earth'. As this was a women's prison, there was not a single man. Many of the inmates were lesbians and their scandals should not even be mentioned. During one of the 'struggle sessions', the prison head, who was a heartless woman, read out their 'love letters'. She blushed a deep red even before she could finish reading half of them. She was so angry she reprimanded and cursed them.

There was always the sound of beatings, cursing, wailing, shouting and fighting within those walls. The inmates would destroy public property, trample on the food, and commit all kinds of vandalism. There was no evil under the sun that they would not do. At times, the prison guards were quite helpless. Oh, how tragic, that God's creation should fall into such a state!

Now Sheng had grown up in a Christian environment all her life and she was used to life in the Spirit. Imagine how she must have felt in such a horrible place. She was lonely, sad, shocked and fearful.

Her sorrow was great. She always prayed that the Lord would keep her and use her. She asked Jesus to change the entire prison and pour out a spirit of repentance so that they might know Him.

Chapter 11

Three Visions and the First Persecution

When Sheng first arrived in this prison, she had no idea if she would find other believers. Two months later, a brother in Christ came to visit her and told her about 'Auntie Dong', who was also in that prison. Sheng was excited. She wanted to meet her as soon as possible so that they could begin the prison work together.

However, there were thousands of inmates and security was tight.

Looking for someone you had never seen before is like looking for a needle in a haystack. Sheng prayed, therefore, that the Lord would bring them together.

One beautiful morning in March, when warm sunshine replaced the chilly air and spring blossoms were everywhere, their fragrance carried by the gentle breeze, Sheng was on her way to the canteen to get her quota of rice. She passed a woman of about 40, with big eyes and a smiling face. She looked like a warm and kind-hearted person. When Sheng glanced at her name tag and saw 'Dong XX', her heart leapt with joy! 'Auntie Dong' also looked at Sheng's name tag and they both simultaneously asked each other,

'Are you Auntie Dong?'

'Are you Sheng?'

Both women burst into tears. They had been wanting to meet each other for four months and now the Lord had arranged for them to meet on this beautiful day! Hallelujah!

Sheng was thrilled beyond words. They quickly got down to business and began to share about their respective Gospel work

194

in the prison. Sheng could not stop praising the Lord for the sheer blessing of meeting a 'mother' in the Lord and co-worker in His vineyard.

Two days after their meeting, Auntie Dong gave Sheng a little notebook full of scripture verses and scripture songs. Sheng knew instantly what she had to do – make as many copies by hand as possible.

The work of the Gospel began to develop in that labour reform prison. The number of converts in both sisters' cells grew steadily. Sheng prayed earnestly for a Bible. Auntie Dong soon gave her one.

In spite of the risk of being found out, Sheng would diligently copy scriptures under her quilt every night. Then, when she was done she would pass the copies to Auntie Dong while everyone was watching a movie. Auntie Dong would, in turn, distribute them to the other new Christians.

One evening at about seven, Sheng looked out of a third-floor window and saw a whole crowd of inmates milling around in the courtyard. They were using abusive language. Sheng felt a rush of compassion for their souls and asked the Lord to save them.

At that moment, she saw a vision: all those prisoners standing in the courtyard became Christians!

Then she saw another vision. Many of the prison cells were golden lamp stands and all the people in them were believers.

In yet another vision, Sheng saw the entire prison reverberating with praises to the Lord. Sheng became so excited she began to dance and praise the Lord!

The inmates were given jobs to do during the day. They were all employed in the different stages of garment-making – designing, cutting, sewing, ironing, buttonholing, etc. The prisoners were divided into groups and each group had a quota.

In her sewing group, Sheng led many to the Lord. An inmate who wanted to be on the good side of the authorities told on her. The response was quick: Instant interrogation.

Sheng was punished and duly transferred to another work group. But she continued sowing seed, and was again transferred for the same reason. Finally, she was transferred to six groups altogether in a few months and the seed of the Gospel went forth.

Each work group was given a heavy quota, working 14 hours a day. The highlight of the day for Sheng was to copy the Bible at night when everyone was asleep. She hardly slept. As a result, her health suffered and she came down with hepatitis.

One day, on the way back to her cell after getting her meal Sheng fainted on the stairs. The other sisters had to carry her to the clinic.

The doctor at the clinic, Dr Lan, had been sentenced to life imprisonment for killing a cadre who attempted to rape her. While in prison in County 'X', she was in despair and tried many times to commit suicide. But the Lord saved her from the brink of death. An old sister who was imprisoned for the Lord's sake shared the Gospel with Lan and she accepted Christ. The Grace of God changed her life.

When Lan was transferred to this labour reform prison for women her life glorified the Lord and edified the believers. She was so grateful to the Lord for her new life.

So when Sheng was brought in Dr Lan prayed over her and gave her first-aid. She had heard of Sheng for a long time but this was the first time they had met. Oh, how she wished they had met sooner! They just loved each other!

The prison chief had sent a 17-year-old girl named Xiu to look after Sheng. She was also a believer and had suffered greatly for the Lord.

The clinic provided the opportunity for all three of them to meet and pray together. They pressed in on three prayer goals: that the Lord would pour out His mercy on this prison, that He would turn it 'upside-down', and that all the prison officials, too, would repent and believe in Jesus.

The prayer assaults launched from the clinic were instrumental in bringing revival to the prison.

Since Sheng was laid up in hospital it fell on Xiu to seek out the Christians imprisoned for the Lord's sake. She came up with a list of 21 sisters' names, their ages and cell numbers. Sheng would pray for each one by name, asking the Lord to keep them and revive them, and that the Gospel would be preached in every cell.

Thus the fire of revival was kindled, and the Spirit of the Lord worked mightily in the lives of many prisoners. One day, a 23-year-old inmate came to see Sheng. She was in despair and poured out her predicament.

'I have been sentenced to 20 years in jail. My life is finished! I might as well die than suffer in this prison.'

Sheng said to her firmly, 'You mustn't die. Believe in the Lord Jesus. He will save you. He will comfort you and give you joy. Tonight, you can kneel and ask Jesus to save you.'

She left and returned the next morning, full of joy. 'I have found Jesus and my heart is full of joy now. I want to introduce Jesus to my friends. Please pray for me.'

Sheng was ecstatic. She prayed for her and blessed her. This new baby Christian came back the same night with eight other prisoners who were her close friends. They had committed terrible crimes but when their friend shared with them about Jesus they wanted to accept Him too!

Sheng explained the plan of salvation and prayed with them. Later, Sheng said to them seriously, 'You all have a job to do. You must pray for all the prisoners and the prison guards to repent and turn to Him.'

They received her words gladly. 'Jesus is really wonderful, He loves even people like us! We can also pray for others.'

Hence, the Gospel was preached behind prison bars and daily the Christian population grew.

When these desperate, hopeless inmates heard about Jesus they gladly received Him and were filled with joy. The incredible thing was that, as soon as they were saved they would share the good news with others immediately, with exceptionally clear understanding of salvation in Christ.

Good news kept filtering back to Sheng as she recuperated in the clinic: Five people came to the Lord in cell number X today; three more accepted Christ in group Y today ... it was entirely the work of the Holy Spirit for He had prepared the hearts of the people.

There was a 17-year-old girl, Li, who was jailed for ten years. She was a nuisance, always quarrelling with everybody and screaming her head off. Quiet she was not. Neither did she fear punishment.

Whenever she was hauled into the prison office to be reprimanded or disciplined she would bother the officials so much that they would be at a loss as to what to do with her.

But the Lord even had mercy on such a one, and Li eventually accepted Christ. And the whole prison knew about her decision!

One day, she went to the offices to preach to the cadres there. Curious, the cadres asked her, 'We have heard that you now believe in Jesus. Is it true?'

'Yes, otherwise things wouldn't be so quiet around here,' she replied with a twinkle in her eye. 'I was so bad before that neither electric rods nor punishment could change me. Only Jesus could save me and change me. If all the prisoners believed in Jesus, you would have less trouble from us. So, repent, and believe in the Lord Jesus and you will be saved.'

Many others were as bold as Li in their witness. The new believers would diligently hand copy scripture portions on pieces of cloth or paper to share with the lost. They would even scribble them on their arms and legs or on their trousers! This way they could easily read and memorize the verses during their break or after work. It also came in handy when evangelising in the prison.

The most popular Bible verses were John 3:16, Romans 3:23–24. Praise songs were copied on pieces of paper then wrapped around stones to be thrown out of the windows on the upper floors to the inmates below. The Christians used all kinds of ways to spread the Gospel, and the Holy Spirit was with them.

If the guards came to search their cells, the believers would swallow all these incriminating notes. Sheng had to do this many times before she was admitted to the sick bay.

According to the doctor, Sheng was supposed to be seriously ill. But as soon as she began to 'work', she seemed quite well! This was because the prison was experiencing a revival which left Sheng excited and rejoicing. God's ways are marvellous! Here she was, recuperating in a ward, and openly receiving many visitors who could come and fellowship, pray and be taught the Word of God by her. And they came from different cells, too! The ward provided a wonderful meeting place for the new Christians.

Sheng would often teach them songs such as these: 'The way of the cross is the road of sacrifice,' 'Forward, follow the Lord and go forward,' 'Be Bold and Courageous,' 'Psalm 146 and 84,' and so on.

One spiritual song that they liked to sing goes like this:

> *'To pray is to breathe, everyone agrees*
> *If you want more grace, more often you should pray,*
> *Your spiritual life is like a lamp,*
> *If you don't pray it will soon end!'*

Most of the believers came to see Sheng after work hours. They could only stay till 10 p.m. as the iron gates on each prison floor would be locked at that hour, and anyone not in their cells by then would be punished. These baby Christians, however, were not afraid of anything. They were so hungry for the Word and had regretted not knowing about Jesus sooner. Now they wanted to learn as much as they could about the Lord.

One night, 16 sisters from the third floor prison ward asked Sheng to teach them the Word. So Sheng found a quiet spot in the courtyard and began preaching the Truth. Suddenly, three guards armed with electric batons walked towards them, having just left the isolation room. It was too late to disperse and they were coming nearer and nearer. Sheng asked the Lord for help. She abruptly changed the subject and began to talk loudly to the girls about increasing their efficiency and improving the quality of the products and meeting the quota. When the guards heard this, they were very pleased, and they walked on.

The sisters still would not leave. They urged Sheng to come and teach them in their cells and preach to the girls there. Thirty-one of the 32 inmates had accepted the Lord, and some of them were graduates or had worked in the PSB before. But Sheng cautioned them to be wise as serpents and harmless as doves. After much persuasion from Sheng the sisters reluctantly returned to their cells to rest.

Two days later, more than ten other sisters from the fourth floor prison ward were on their way to visit Sheng in the evening when they were stopped by guards. It was already past nine but they really wanted to see her. One of the sisters, Li, had a brainwave. She feigned a tummy ache and the other girls had to carry her to the clinic.

When the guards shouted, 'What are you all doing?' the girls simply chorused, 'She's sick, we are carrying her to the clinic.'

At the sick bay, they woke Sheng. There was an empty room adjacent to the clinic but the door was locked. However, as it was an old house, there were three small holes in the wall below, each large enough for a person to crawl through. So Sheng, Dr Lan, Xiu and the 14 sisters crawled into the room. Later, another three sisters from the kitchen joined them. All 20 of them had a wonderful time of fellowship, singing and praying. They could hardly contain their joy!

But somebody else heard their singing. An unsaved inmate had popped into the clinic and saw what was going on. 'The Christians are having a meeting here,' she said to herself. 'I'll report this to the warden!'

Sheng saw her pop her head round the door, and immediately ended the meeting. She told the sisters to return to their cells quickly.

Now, when leaving the room, they should have headed west but, prompted by the Holy Spirit, they turned east instead and walked back to their cells.

No sooner had they left than the tell-tale inmate returned with several guards to catch the believers in the room. The guards shone their torches into the room and found it empty. Furious, they turned to the woman prisoner and scolded her, 'You wicked woman, why do you always accuse the Christians and make a fool of us?' One of them smacked her across her face.

'We will never believe you again.' They stormed off. The 13 sisters had to carry Li back to their cell, to make it look like their original ploy of feigning sickness. When the guard spotted them, she yelled out, 'How is she now? Is she any better?'

'She is much better now. She has taken some medicine and was given an injection,' they all chorused.

Revival was spreading like wildfire in the prison. For two months, innumerable prisoners were being born-again every day. In some cells, all had become Christians; in others most of the inmates were believers.

A Catholic nun was astounded at what she saw happening. She knew it was the work of the Holy Spirit. She even talked with Sheng a couple of times about it. She emerged from those discussions a changed person! She began to encourage the other Catholics to join the Christians and attend the meetings led by Sheng. She herself became Sheng's valuable co-worker.

The entire prison had been transformed. In place of cursing and obscene songs and language, songs of praise to the Lord could now be heard. Wailing and screaming gave way to joy and peace. And instead of beatings or fighting one another the prisoners would now be encouraging, comforting, edifying and praying one with another.

In the canteen, workrooms, cells, washrooms or laundry room, all they talked about was the Lord Jesus! The sound of praying, singing and praising God could be heard throughout the prison.

The power of darkness had been broken. The first two visions had come to pass, glory to God!

Chapter 12

Visiting the Prison and Delivering Bibles

One reason why revival broke out in the prison was because the Christians were willing to suffer and lay down their lives for the Lord. The prayers of the saints also played a big part. They would frequently visit the believers in prison and bring Bibles to them despite the risk of being discovered.

One day, Sheng's sister, Xiaohong, came to visit her with three other believers. They were ushered into the reception room under the ever watchful eye of the guards, then body searched. Even the gifts of food they brought for Sheng were scrutinised carefully. Even though their conversation with Sheng was limited in the presence of the guards, Sheng was nonetheless greatly encouraged to see them. When it came time for them to leave, they sang loudly outside the prison gates.

Sheng rushed upstairs to the balcony to enjoy every note as they sang:

> 'I'm a little bird in a cage, away from the trees, flowers and
> fields.
> To be in bonds for you, Lord, how glad I am to sing and
> pour out my heart to you all day.
> You like to hold my wings that like to fly.
> Listen to the songs that I have to sing;
> Your great love constrains me, I'll be your love slave who
> will never run away.
> Who will understand the bitterness of prison life?
> But the love of the Lord can make it sweet;
> Oh, Lord, I love the road You have prepared for me.
> May the whole creation praise Your wonderful deeds.

They sang beautifully, Xiaohong's melodic voice leading. Though they could not say much to Sheng during their visit, they 'spoke' their love and concern for her through their song and tears.

Oh, saints who are in chains for the Lord, have you ever experienced such blessing and grace from our God?

Sheng stood on the balcony and wept, touched beyond measure. One of the brothers who had accompanied Xiaohong was also crying. He cried because he could not sing the songs. Later, he wrote to Sheng in prison and shared with her his concern for the brethren in the prison. He encouraged her to be strong and courageous in the Lord and bear much fruit for Him.

Months later, the words of the song and the melody were still etched in her heart, and she would sing it over and over again, and was greatly strengthened.

Visits from the Christians outside prison were very precious to Sheng. This was because the revival in the prison had spread in such proportions that it had created a desperate need for Bibles. But the Lord knew about their need for His Word, so He sent brothers and sisters to bring them copies of 'manna'.

Many were being copied by hand by the new believers, but with many new babes in Christ being born daily, it was impossible to keep up with the great demand for God's Word.

One sultry afternoon at the end of summer, the sun was blazing hot and everyone was feeling the heat. The oppressive air was still and no man nor beast stirred, except the prisoners who had to carry on working in the factory to meet the daily quotas. Some were drenched in sweat, and some were feeling dizzy because of the heat.

A guard came into the workroom and called out to Sheng, 'You have visitors.'

Sheng immediately dropped whatever she was doing, and ran excitedly to the reception room. Inside were three people fanning themselves vigorously with their straw hats.

When Sheng saw who they were, she was stunned. Brother Ming and Sister Bai were still on the PSB's wanted list, and Brother Bing was one of the main co-workers from 'F' city! She was greatly encouraged that they had taken the risk of visiting her.

Upon seeing Sheng, the three of them quickly stood up and shook her hands. Touched, and with tears already brimming in her eyes, Sheng said, 'Brothers and sister, thank you for coming to me in such hot weather!'

Brother Ming and Sister Bai both said, 'We miss you! We have always wanted to come and see you but we didn't have the time until today. Listen to the "leader" and do your "work" here well.'

Brother Bing then handed a tin of biscuits and a coat to her. Sheng took the tin and was surprised that it was so heavy! Usually, the guards would check every item being brought into the prison but this time they did not seem to bother at all. They just sat there, chatting away.

Soon it was time for them to go. Ming grasped Sheng's hands and said, 'Don't worry about us at home. Everything is well. The "flock" which you looked after before is doing well, and we're having many "baby lambs" this year.'

After they had left, Sheng ran as fast as she could back to her cell. Trembling with excitement, she opened the tin of 'biscuits' and found three Bibles tucked inside. A fourth copy was hidden in a pocket of the coat! Sheng jumped with joy and kissed the Bibles. Then she quickly hid them, knelt down and praised the Lord, singing:

> *'No man could stop me.*
> *No hand could prevent me;*
> *The thorns on the way would only be a help,*
> *I'll press on and gain my crown;*
> *My spirit, my soul revived.*
> *Let this world pass away,*
> *Lord of my life,*
> *Come back soon and take me home!'*

By His mighty hand, the Lord used the brothers and sisters to bring Bibles into the prison, despite the tight security. Oh, how great and wonderful our God is!

Chapter 13

The Second Persecution and Great Revival

It says in Revelation 1:15, *'The voice of the Lord was like that of many waters.'* The power of the Gospel was like that of many waters in the prison, and it could not be stopped. The more the authorities persecuted the Christians in jail, the more the Gospel prospered and more people accepted Christ.

The prison authorities were greatly concerned but did not know what to do. So they reported the situation to the PSB.

One day, several PSB vehicles drew up at the prison gates. The police and prison guards then surrounded the entire prison and made a thorough search of every prisoner and every cell.

It was simply miraculous that they did not find a single Bible, only a few song booklets. Those on whom they were found were punished.

One of them, 33-year-old sister Xia, had been given a life term. She had not been a believer for long but there was a radical change in her heart. She was always bubbling with joy and would witness to the other inmates everyday.

Now, they handcuffed her and put her in solitary confinement in a fourth-floor cell for a fortnight. Whenever the other prisoners were allowed into the courtyard each day, she would linger at the balcony, hoping to see a familiar face. Sheng would use sign language to encourage her.

Another sister found with song books was Chen. She, too, was handcuffed and locked up in the basement cell. Although a new believer, this was already the second time she had been punished because of the Gospel.

Chen had two other companions in the cell. One was a

205

woman of 22 who had been sentenced to 17 years. She was an exponent of kung-fu and could jump over very high walls. Once, she climbed over the prison wall and escaped. The prison authorities informed the PSB, which sent a posse after her.

She was eventually caught and taken back to prison, where she was beaten mercilessly until she was almost dead. Then she was chained hand and foot in the basement cell.

But two weeks later, she somehow managed to break free from her fetters and escape again, breaking the lock on the prison gate and leaping over the seven-meter-high wall.

During her brief spell of freedom, she robbed, cheated and became a prostitute. Her run from the law ended 11 months later when she was apprehended in 'H' city. Back in prison she was again beaten to a pulp and this time heavier handcuffs were used, while a guard watched her day and night.

The other prisoner, a teenage girl of 19 called Bai, was serving a 15-year prison term. She had run away from home at 11 and mixed with bad company. Her new companions had committed many crimes. Seven years later she returned home one day with her clique of 'friends'. When her father heard she was in town he came to her and persuaded her to return home. But the young rebel hissed at him, 'Who is your daughter? You are not blind, are you?' And with that she hopped on her bicycle and took off. Her poor old father fainted in distress.

Not long after, she was arrested and imprisoned. She seemed to be incorrigible. Swearing, cursing and scolding people had become second nature to her.

One day, she took it out on a fellow prisoner and almost beat her to death. The guards marched her to the prison office. They were about to punish her with the electric rod when she snatched it and screamed, 'I've had enough! If I kill one of you we'd be even. If I kill two of you, I win!' And she began attacking the guards with the electric baton. The guards were shocked beyond words. But they finally tackled her, got her down to the floor, bound her with a big heavy chain, and locked her up in the basement cell.

Now Sister Chen was thrown into the same cell as these two ruthless women. Sheng was extremely worried but all she could do was pray earnestly for her.

These two hardened women appeared heartless but they were both afraid of death. All day, they would wail and cry making a frightful sound in the cell.

Sister Chen was broken with compassion for them, and poured out love and concern towards them. Sometimes, she would fast and share her food with them. How true is the saying, 'Love and sincerity can melt stones and gold.' Not having known kindness in their lives, the two wicked women were touched deeply and before long they, too, accepted Jesus as their Lord and Saviour!

Whenever dangerous prisoners like them were confined to a cell it would usually be for more than a year. But after their conversion, they were so radically changed that they were released from confinement a month later!

Bai met Sheng soon after coming out of confinement. Excited beyond words, Bai hugged her and said warmly, 'Praise the Lord, Sister Sheng, I have become a Christian!' Sheng was taken aback, and thought to herself, 'Could such a person actually become a Christian?'

Seeing the incredulous expression on Sheng's face, Bai said, 'You don't believe me? Let me sing you a hymn!' And she began to sing:

'To be born again is to repent, Repentance without fruit is
   dead;
'The Lord wants us to be born again, Brothers and sisters,
   let's listen to what He says.'

She continued the conversation. 'Please pray for me,' she asked of Sheng. 'I'm going to the office to witness to them about what Jesus has done in my life!' Then she ran off.

A few days later, Sister Chen was also released from confinement. She went directly to see Sheng and they both praised and worshipped the Lord together for His goodness.

Behind bars the Gospel prospered beyond expectations. The prison authorities were very concerned about the mass conversions. When they saw that persecution did not work they tried another way to thwart the Christians' efforts. They separated the believers, scattering them in cells where there were few or no Christians. They had thought this would curb the work of the ministry.

But it worked to the contrary because the believers zealously preached to the unsaved inmates and gained more converts! As a result, prisoners on the entire fourth floor and almost all the inmates on the second and third floor cells received the Lord!

Chapter 14
The Third Persecution and the Fourth Vision

Sheng had been in the sick bay for two months when things began to get rather tense. Sister Xiu was summoned for interrogation, during which she was questioned closely on Sheng's activities in the clinic. 'Who did she see in the two months? How many meetings did she conduct? What else did she do?' All to which Xiu simply said, 'I don't know.'

That was her stock reply to every question they threw at her. Finally, unable to coax any evidence out of her, they had to let her go. But on one condition: she was not allowed to see Sheng.

Next, the authorities conducted a massive search of the entire prison for Bibles and Christian literature. By then, many of the sisters had transferred the Bibles to Sheng for safekeeping in the clinic.

However, several guards demanded of Sheng, 'Where are the Bibles?'

She had hidden them in a card-board box and put canned food and cutlery on top. Now she proceeded to pull out the box from under her bed, but the guards did not seem interested in it at all. Instead, they searched through her clothing and bedding and other boxes of belongings but found no Bibles.

Clearly dissatisfied, they said to her, 'We don't believe you do not have a single Bible!' Then they turned on their heels and left the clinic.

Sheng, however, knew they would be back. She did not know just how soon. Quick as lightning she hid the Bibles somewhere else and was about to shred to pieces the song sheets and dispose of them when the guards returned!

It was too late. Sheng was caught in the act.

'What are you doing?' they shouted at her. They snatched the song sheets from her hands.

Triumphantly the guards marched her to the offices. The prison chief exclaimed in disbelief, 'I can't believe you are the leader of the Christians! Because you are sick we put you in the clinic on humanitarian grounds. But now the sick bay has become your "command centre".'

'You must be honest with us today. How many Bibles do you have, and where are they?'

'Who do you work with?'

'How many people have you converted?'

Sheng's answers were simply 'No' or 'I don't know.' She was duly handcuffed and locked up in solitary confinement in a cell on the fourth floor. No one was allowed to visit her, except for the prisoner who would bring her her meals. To crown it all, Sheng had to write a letter 'confessing' her 'crimes'.

The authorities tried various methods of reforming Sheng, to no avail. How could they understand that nothing could separate her from the love of God?

One night, at about nine o'clock, when all the prisoners were in their respective cells, the whole place shook with the praises of God as the inmates just praised the Lord from their hearts.

Stunned, the guards were livid but did not dare do anything. Sheng ran to the window of her cell and listened intently. She was beside herself with joy and lifted up her hands in praise even though they were still bound. This was what happened in her third vision! Now it has come to pass!

Right there, she had another vision. She saw the words 'Jesus' appearing on a prison notice board.

Sheng befriended the woman who brought food to her every day. And because of her love and witness, this inmate became a believer. Soon she proved to be a valuable co-worker like Xiu, and helped to deliver notes of encouragement to the other believers from Sheng.

It was not easy for Sheng to write as she still had handcuffs on. But she had only to think of Jesus and His crown of thorns, His scars and wounds, and she would be renewed in her strength.

Thus, she picked up a pen and wrote seven pages of 'confession' – basically, when she became a Christian, why she believed in Jesus, and the ultimate purpose of believing in Him. She even exhorted the prison Chief and the cadres to believe in Jesus!

Winter soon came. It snowed hard one day but despite the blizzard a fleet of provincial PSB vehicles made their way to the prison.

A bench and table was set up on the north side of the courtyard under a banner which read, 'Down with the destructive elements!' 'Down with the Christians!' It looked like the prisoners were in for another of those 'criticism meetings' again.

All the inmates trooped out into the courtyard and sat on the floor, surrounded by armed soldiers and prison guards. Taking up the seats on the judges' bench were cadres from the PSB, the prosecution and legal offices, the courts and the prison.

Then the names of 12 prisoners – all Christians – were read out. Sheng was among the 12, and they had to stand facing the bench. To set the tone for the meeting, and to show who had authority, a PSB officer struck one of the sisters with his baton. She fell to the floor, knocked out by the hard blow. All the believers prayed for the 12.

Then the prison Chief stood up. She read Sheng's 'confession' out loud but halfway through, she banged her fist on the table and screeched, 'How dare you! You even want to convert us!'

Eyes flashing, she was not to be outdone.

'I have been in the prison business for more than 30 years. I have never seen anyone the likes of you!

'You Christians have turned this prison upside-down. You are not afraid of beatings or confinement. Nor are you afraid of being "struggled against".'

'You have a nerve! I am going to write down what you have done and have it printed and circulated in the other prisons. They will put it up on their notice-boards and serve as a warning to other prisoners.'

'Shame on you!' she almost spat out the words.

When the believers heard this they were thrilled to bits!

Why, the prison Chief was not 'struggling against' them at all, but she was actually helping them to spread the Gospel!

Praise God, the revival fire could not be quenched. Two thousand years of Church history taught us one thing: that wherever there is persecution, there is revival. The greater the persecution the greater the revival. Like a ball. The harder you hit it, the higher it will bounce. If you do not hit it, it will not bounce.

From that day onwards, the activities of the Christians were posted on the bulletin boards everyday. Just as in Sheng's fourth vision!

Sheng, now identified as the ring-leader, was kept in solitary confinement for another six months. She was handcuffed all this time, until just a few days before her release from prison.

Chapter 15

Leaving Prison

The Lord's mercy and protection enabled Sheng to complete the task He asked of her in prison.

August 22, 1985, was a landmark day for Sheng. At last, she was allowed to go home. Her last few days in prison was spent comforting the 'flock' she would be leaving behind. Even the unsaved inmates bade her a sad farewell. 'You're so nice to us,' they told her. 'We really don't want to see you go. We hope you'll come back.'

The night before her release from prison, many sisters swarmed around her, crying unashamedly. They had no words they could speak.

Finally, a sister said, 'Sister Sheng, do not forget us. Please ask the brothers and sisters outside to pray for us ...' Her voice broke into heart-rending sobs.

It was quite late before they dispersed and returned to their cells for the night.

Before dawn broke the next day, all the 32 inmates who shared Sheng's cell were already up. They crowded round Sheng and wept. Sheng could barely hold back her own tears as she exhorted them to love the Lord with a fervent heart, and to pray diligently, and to work hard in prison, and to ask the Lord for their prison terms to be reduced so that they might live for Him the rest of their lives.

At daybreak, they carried Sheng's belongings and accompanied her downstairs. All the other believers on the same floor – there were a few hundred of them – came to say goodbye. There was not a dry eye in the place.

The guards would not allow all of them to see Sheng to the

gate but Sheng kept turning round to look at them. When she saw all their tears, she did not want to leave.

She had reached the courtyard but her steps were heavy. There were more believers there, all of them crying.

'Lord, how can I leave these beloved sisters here? I wish I could stay!'

She walked past the first gate and, before she went through the second gate, several sisters could not resist rushing out to hug her one more time. 'Sister, don't just pray for us. Work hard for the Lord and do that which we cannot do.'

Sheng could not linger any longer. She walked out through the iron gates and they shut behind her. The sound of weeping could be heard throughout the prison.

She walked on, but turned to look up at those waving at her from the balcony and shouting, 'Sister, do not forget us!'

She remembered the day she had arrived at this prison. How strange and full of darkness and filth it was to her then! And now, she was loath to leave.

So Sheng sat down, facing the prison, praying for and blessing those still inside. It was quite a while before she left for home.

PART FIVE

The Execution

Preface

A rough dirt road runs to the east of Shanzui town in southern Henan province, passing under a rail track to continue northwards by a disused factory and then winding on to the hills.

A small, barren hill stands about half a kilometer from the south side of the abandoned factory. It is desolate with no man in sight and only the rare vehicle or two passing through. Walking past one feels a sense of overwhelming loneliness. Only the croaking of frogs from the ponds on both sides of the road punctuate the dead silence, moanful gusts of wind make an eerie cry as they sweep across the valley, making ripples on the pond's surface.

East of the road is a depression covered with scattered vegetation. A few wild gourd plants have sprouted there but their leaves have long since dried up. On top of a foot-high stalk, 18 little white flowers with octagonal petals stand mournfully, as the breeze gently caresses them.

Behind the depression to the north is a small dirt hill. It has lain barren for years. This desolate hill stands as a silent testimony to the tragedy that took place on its soil.

Several years ago, two people met their death – an outstanding mother and her son – right where the white blossoms are now flourishing. They were cruelly executed for the sake of God's Word and their blood was shed on this desolate piece of ground. Their blood dyed the earth red in this depression. They used their blood and tears to write a chapter in the history of the Chinese Church.

Chapter 1

A Family Who Loves the Lord

The following events took place in September of 1983. There was a family of 11 by the surname of Shi who lived in Zunzhuang village in the rural district of the same name. The father was Shi Gushen, his wife Lishi, and their three sons were Wuting, Wuming and Wuhao. Their oldest daughter, Xiaoxiu, youngest daughter, Xiaoqiu and daughter-in-law, Meiying, also lived with them, along with a grandson and a granddaughter. The last member of the family was Mr Shi's brother, Guzhen, who was still unmarried and so he lived with the rest of the family.

The Shis lived in several dilapidated huts in the village. But though they were poor and life was bitter, the entire family feared God. Therefore, they loved one another and lived in harmony. Even in bitterness, they experienced a sweetness that brought them much joy.

Mrs Shi was 58 years old that year. Of medium build, her compassionate face was tinged with a smile all day long. There was such love and compassion in her eyes!

In 1976, Mrs Shi became seriously ill. And though several doctors attended to her, her condition deteriorated until there seemed to be no hope of recovery at all. Then, at the urging of an old grandmother who was a Christian, the Shi family believed in the Lord. Mrs Shi was soon healed of her sickness and recovered totally.

She became very fervent for the Lord and would bring her family to meetings to worship the Lord. Sadly, the believers in the church went the way of the world and established an official

'Three-Self Patriotic Church'. Although it had formal Sunday worship, it had no life whatsoever.

After attending these meetings several times, Mrs Shi and her family felt very troubled. Her oldest son, Wuting, began to study the Bible and discovered that the Three-Self Church was not a true church. From then on, the Shis stopped going to the official church. Instead, they invited the brothers and sisters to meet at their home and so they began a house church.

Naturally, this was opposed by the so-called Christians from the official church, who regularly reported the Shis to the Public Security Bureau. They accused the family of opposing the leadership of the Communist Party and of organising illegal 'underground' meetings. For this, the Shis suffered unending persecution.

In the summer of 1983, the older sister of Meiying fell very ill. Doctors treating Meichun diagnosed a terminal disease and gave up on her. Her only hope was to go to Meiying's house where the believers could come and pray for her.

Several days went by, and Meichun's condition fluctuated between satisfactory and poor. Her mother prepared to find a vehicle to take her home but Meichun suddenly stopped breathing and died.

The family, realising the sober consequences and the gravity of the situation, determined to remain strong and not be afraid. The whole family prayed and committed it to the Lord. Whatever happened next, they would still follow Jesus to the very end, even if it meant spilling their blood and giving their lives for the Lord.

The family appointed second son, Wuming, to go to the brigade to report the death. The rest of the family remained at home and packed up their clothes in preparation for imprisonment or death.

Village folk soon got wind of what had happened and came crowding into the house, eager for some excitement. They were making all sorts of accusations against the Shis. One would shake his head and sigh, while another commented, 'They have packed up their clothes in order to escape!'

Chapter 2

One Family in the Court

By four in the afternoon the brigade cadres had arrived in the Shi home, along with several PSB officials. After searching the house, they brought out ropes to tie up Mrs Shi. But Wuting jumped up and declared loudly, 'I am the head of this family. I am responsible for this incident. This has nothing to do with my mother!'

His wife, Meiying, interjected, 'The deceased is my sister and it was I who brought her here. I should be the only one responsible for this. It has nothing to do with the others.'

Her younger sister, Meizhen, immediately piped up, 'The deceased is my older sister. I brought her here to second sister's home. I am wholly responsible.'

The PSB officials' response to all that was icy indifference. 'Stop pretending. We will show you a thing or two!' They then proceeded to tie up the four of them. But the rest of the family, led by Mr Shi Gushen, stepped forward and said, 'We are all instigators. If you must take anyone away, take us also!'

As the PSB men led away Mrs Shi, Wuting, Meiying and Meizhen, the two grandchildren tried to follow after them. Aged four and one-and-a-half years old, the toddlers were pushed to the ground by the heartless official. The rest of the Shi family followed behind the four to the police station.

There eight members of this one family were locked up in one room and forced to kneel all night long. Mrs Shi, Meiying and Meizhen were tied up. Meizhen's bonds were specially tight and she eventually fell unconscious for a long time.

That night, in the large household of 11 people, the only ones left were 12-year-old Xiaoqiu and the two toddlers. Xiaoqiu was unable to comfort the babes as they cried all night for their mother. All three of them eventually fell sleep, exhausted from crying. But at midnight the two little ones awoke with fright as they recounted the nightmare of the day seeing their mother being taken away. They began to cry right through until the morning.

The next day, all three of them were taken to other relatives where they stayed until Mr Shi and his brother were released two months later.

The next day, the husband of the dead girl and both their families lodged a formal charge in the court. Mrs Shi was accused of collaborating with her son, Wuting, and the entire Shi family in preventing Meichun from going to the hospital. They were also charged with using force on Meichun and murdering her with intent. The deceased's family demanded that the legal authorities conduct a thorough investigation of the case and bring the accused to justice by executing Mrs Shi and Wuting. This would subdue the anger of the people, they said.

Several days later, the authorities cleared the Shi home of household items, food, and even the two oxen which they used for ploughing, and sold them for a princely sum of ¥2,000 RMB. This was used to pay for Meichun's burial expenses.

Their trial soon began. The courtroom was a fearsome sight. The judge sat high up on a bench with the 'jury' behind him. The court secretary and other officials sat on the either side of him. Several armed policemen stood on guard at the sides and behind them, on the walls, hung leather whips, electric rods and other torture instruments. It was truly a fearful scene.

First to be questioned was Wuting's mother. She was just a simple village woman and had never dealt with officials before. But she stood calmly before all the court officials without any fear at all.

Opening the case, the judge asked her routine questions like her name, age, address etc. Then he asked her directly, 'Did Meichun die in your home?'

'Yes,' Mrs Shi replied. 'It happened yesterday at noon.'

'Who is the main offender? What method did you use to cause her death?'

'I was the one who prayed for her,' said Mrs Shi. 'However, we who believe in Jesus have no other method other than singing songs and praying for her.'

'According to the coroner's report, the victim was beaten to death by you. Do you still insist on denying this?' the judge's voice rose in anger.

Mrs Shi calmly answered, 'The deceased was diagnosed by the doctors as having a terminal illness, and so she was sent home from the hospital. She died because her years were up and nobody could do a thing about it. Besides, everyone will have to die one day, which is why we believe in Jesus. As for accusing me of beating her to death, that is utterly impossible!'

The judge struck the table and, jumping to his feet, pointed his finger at Mrs Shi. 'I see if one doesn't pull the muzzle of a cow it will not voluntarily go into the water. Come, teach this treacherous old woman a thing or two.'

They kicked Wuting's mother to the ground. Then they whipped her and beat her with the batons until she fell unconscious. One of them brought a basin of cold water and splashed it over her. She came round, and the judge cackled, 'Ha ha, what did you think of that? Are you going to deny to the end, or are you going to confess your crime?'

He pursued, 'The policy of the Party is one of leniency to those who confess and to deal severely with those who resist.

'Confess! How did you murder Meichun?'

Mrs Shi said, 'We only prayed for her, we have no motive for killing her nor is there any evidence that we harmed her.' The interrogation continued well into the day to no avail.

Eventually, Mrs Shi was sent back to the prison. Her children ran up to her when she entered the cell, pained to see her bloody face. Weeping, they took her hands and held her up, asking her what had happened. Meiying, especially, held her mother-in-law close and, using her handkerchief, tenderly wiped away the blood oozing from Mrs Shi's lips and nose. Meiyings' tears streamed down her face as she did so, splashing onto her mother-in-law's forehead.

The older woman whispered, 'Children, remain strong. We are considered worthy to suffer reproach for the Lord ...'

Suddenly, the prison door flew wide open with a loud bang.

It was Wuting's turn to be interrogated. After him, they came for Wuming. When the two brothers returned to the cell they were an unrecognizable mass of purple bruises and bloody wounds.

The youngest son, Wuhao, was treated a little mildly by the judge. He said to him, 'Shi Wuhao, you had previously received long-term government education (Wuhao had graduated from a certain teacher's college) and are a teacher of the people. Of course you will not follow superstition like your mother and older brothers.

'You have never been against the leadership of the Party, nor have you been against the government-established Three-Self Church.

'Concerning your family establishing and illegally organizing underground meetings, and concerning this crime in which Meichun has been murdered, I am sure you know about all that has occurred.

'All you have to do is to deny belief in Jesus and honestly tell us how your family killed Meichun. If you do this you will be absolved of this case and you can continue teaching. We hope that you will cooperate with us in this matter.'

Wuhao lifted his head and said, 'Jesus is not only the Lord of my family, but he is also my personal Saviour. There is no way that for the sake of my position as a teacher I will go against my conscience and deny my faith.

'As for Meichun, because she had a terminal disease she would have died anyway, whether she remained in hospital or stayed at home. It is only by coincidence that she died in my home. You have blamed this on my mother, but I am equally responsible as I did not send her back to her house sooner.'

His little speech left the judge in a royal rage! Eyes bulging out of their sockets, the judge exploded, 'The Party has trained you for so many years. It appears to be all in vain. You are hopeless! Come! Get rid of his haughty attitude!'

What a pity that such a learned and refined young man should be beaten until his flesh ripped open and his wounds covered with blood.

Meiying's turn came next. She, too, was not exempt from punishment. During interrogation each member of the Shi family claimed responsibility for Meichun's death, which left their interrogators quite amazed. Then Meizhen was brought into the room.

Fearlessly she reiterated her position. 'The deceased is my elder sister. I alone was responsible and it was I who brought her to my house to be prayed for. I was closest to her. If someone must be responsible, it should be me. It has nothing to do with anyone else.'

Lastly, 16-year-old Shi Xiaoxiu was brought in. The judge, thinking he could take advantage of this small and skinny teenager, said confidently, 'Your whole family has confessed. Now what do you say? Who really caused the death of Meichun?'

Xiaoxiu said calmly, 'Meichun died of a terminal disease. What do you mean, who caused her death? If you want to find out who was responsible for praying for her then it was my little sister and I. We were closest to the patient and we prayed the most.'

Infuriated, the judge again struck the table and cursed, 'You have the nerve! You are so young and yet you dare to deceive the People's government. How could two mere children cause someone to die?'

'Little child, I promise you there is no heaven for you here. If you continue to be stubborn and resist I will sentence you to eight or ten years in prison. Your future will be finished! Don't think this is some game.'

Still maintaining her composure, Xiaoxiu replied, 'My future is not determined by this world but by heaven.'

Jabbing his finger at her the judge cried out, 'Do not think that because you are young you can resist to the end. I tell you that you are not going to leave. This time I am also going to sentence you.'

Xiaoxiu answered lightly, 'Since I have fallen into your hands I have no plans to return home. My family is prepared to finish the course our Lord Jesus has determined for us.'

That afternoon, all nine members of the Shi family were paraded in the streets, tightly bound and with placards hanging from their necks on which was written, 'Intentional murderers'.

The social climate in that year, 1983, was chaotic. Crimes shot up like never before and murder, rape, armed robbery, theft, drug trafficking, hooliganism, prostitution and kidnapping, were the order of the day. In many areas women dared not walk the streets at night and the wealthy would not even venture outside their homes.

To restore order the government launched a campaign against crime. As a result, mass executions of criminals took place in most cities. Thousands of people were executed throughout the country.

In an ancient capital city, it was reported that in one day alone 700 executions were carried out. The central authorities issued a 'quota' of criminals to be executed in each area and district. When the wrongdoers were children and relatives of cadres, their parents would frantically search for substitutes to fulfill the quotas. Tragically, many innocent people were killed along with the wicked during this anti-crime drive. Miscarriages of justice were all too prevalent in those days. As a Chinese saying goes, 'A conflagration at the city gate will burn to the fish pond'

Over the past 90 years it has been proven that the Church has always been the target of any political movement. This anti-crime campaign was no different. The government singled out a certain Christian group, accusing it of being 'counter-revolutionary'. It also accused many of the faithful servants of God with being 'counter-revolutionary elements' of this sect and proceeded to arrest and persecute them.

And so it was that the Shi family's 'murder' trial took place during these turbulent times. In the world's eyes, Christians were often considered weak and easily taken advantage of. Thus the authorities found in the Shi case an unexpected opportunity to make them the scapegoats!

The Shi family were forced to go through four or five interrogations. The one who suffered most next to Mrs Shi was Meizhen, who was only 24 years old then. Blessed with a pair of charming eyes, her ruddy face was always wreathed in smiles. When she spoke, even her eyes seemed to smile! She conveyed affection and a genuine personal interest in people.

Her fiancé was a primary school teacher and they had

planned to marry in the autumn of that year. Now, for the sake of the Lord she was sacrificing her youth, her love, and her position. After she received her sentence, her fiancé broke off their relationship. During each interrogation she had tried to take the blame upon herself in order to lessen the charges and punishment on her older sister, Meiying. Therefore, after several such forced confession sessions and severe physical punishment, Meizhen was so badly beaten that there was not a square inch of her body where her skin had not been broken or scarred.

225

Chapter 3
Love Knows No Bounds

On the morning of August 30, 1983, officials from the legal
department used a theatre in Shanzui village as the setting for
sentencing the Shi family. There was not an empty seat in sight.
Everyone had turned up for the event.

The bigwigs in the legal branch, justice branch, Public
Security, investigative branch, jurors, secretaries and other
court officials took their seats behind the judge's bench with all
pomposity. Outside the court door, several scores of PSB men
patrolled the compound with submachine guns.

The temperature outside was sweltering. Inside the courtroom the atmosphere was tense and intimidating, so much so
that the crowd of several thousand sat hushed with apprehension. The silence was unnerving to anyone entering the room.

First the PSB chief stood up and gave a report. He spoke
glowingly of the significance of the anti-crime campaign and
about a certain 'anti-revolutionary' sect of Christianity which
the government was determined to suppress. Then the nine
members of the Shi family were brought out bound.

The chief judge, a balding man of 45, stood up and pronounced judgment on the Shis. He spoke forcefully, shaking
his head with great emphasis and showering spit all around.

'The criminals Shi Lishi, Shi Wuting, Shi Wuhao, Mu Meiying, Mu Meizhen ... the nine of them are leaders of such and
such Christian sect. They have always been opposed to the
Party leadership and the People's government as well as the
Three-Self Patriotic Church that is under the Party.

'On July 30, 1983, Shi Lishi and the other eight accused,

using the excuse of "casting out demons and healing the sick", prevented Mu Meichun from going to hospital for treatment.

'Moreover, they used an atrocious method to beat Meichun to death. After investigation, we have found stark evidence. According to the criminal code of the Republic Number ... this constitutes murder with intent. With the approval of the legal courts of the Central People's Government, the sentences are as follows:

'The chief criminal, Shi Lishi, 58 years before arrest, lived at Zunzhuang village located in Zunzhuang rural district belonging to "P" city and is the leader of "such and such" counter-revolutionary organisation. Lishi has always opposed the Party leadership and the Three-Self Patriotic Church. In the case of Mu Meichun's death, Lishi with her son and daughter-in-law beat Meichun to death. This is a very serious crime. In order to pacify the outrage of the people against this criminal act, I now sentence Shi Lishi to death and strip her of all her political rights for life, according to article ... of the People's Republic.

'The criminal Shi Wuting, oldest son of Shi Lishi, aged 35, is also a leader of "such and such" counter-revolutionary organisation. He was a chief conspirator in the murder of Mu Meichun. He has committed a very serious crime and unless we execute him we cannot justify the anger of the people. Therefore, I sentence Shi Wuting to death by execution and I order that he be stripped of all political rights for life.

'As for the criminal Mu Meiying, now 31 years old, who is the wife of Shi Wuting and the third sister of the deceased Mu Meichun, I sentence her to life imprisonment. She will also be stripped of her political rights for life.

'The criminal Mu Meizhen, 24 years old, is also a sister of the deceased and is a chief conspirator in her murder. I sentence Mu Meizhen to 15 years imprisonment with no political rights for the same number of years.

'The accomplice to the crime, Shi Wuhao, 24, was a teacher at (village name) People's Middle School before his arrest. The criminal was one of the people's teachers and should not have had such backward thinking and belief in superstition. He actively participated in the murder of Mu Meichun. Therefore, he is sentenced to ten years in prison during which time he will lose all political rights.

'The accomplice Shi Wuming, Shi Lishi's third son, is 28 years old. I sentence him to four years in jail with no political rights during that time. The accomplice Shi Xiaoxiu is now 16 years old and is criminal Lishi's daughter. She is a student at (village name) Middle School. I sentence her to two years in prison with no political rights.

'The accomplice Shi Gushen, 58, is the husband of criminal Lishi. According to the law, he will be detained for two months. His brother, Shi Guzhen, 55, will also be detained two months.'

As the lengthy sentencing was being read out in court, cries of 'aiya!' and 'O God', came from the gallery when the fate of Meiying and Meizhen was made known. Then there was the sound like a thud, and someone fell on the floor, followed by cries like that of a pig being slaughtered.

'Daughters, Mother has done you harm!' wailed Meiying's own mother. 'Judges, I ask you to deal leniently with my two daughters!'

During the past month, she had daily visited the PSB offices and courthouse with other members of her family, demanding justice be done over the death of Meichun. They did their level best to bring accusations against Shi Lishi and Shi Wuting. They were bent on seeing them executed. But she never imagined the high price she would have to pay. Her oldest daughter was to die, and her second daughter would soon be 'dead' (being sentenced to life), and her youngest girl might as well be 'dead', since she was given 15 years. As Mrs Mu was getting along in years herself she may probably not live to see Meizhen released from prison.

Ignoring her pleas, the PSB guards took away the 'criminals'. Mrs Mu was filled with shame but there was no turning the clock back. She could only give vent to her grief by pounding her chest and wailing loudly.

As the court spectators left the auditorium they were buzzing with comments. In their eyes, the mother and son who were to be executed had lost all their dignity. Those who did not understand the facts agreed scornfully that they deserved to die. Others with a little bit more brain, and those who knew the truth, could only look on and sigh helplessly.

Two of the spectators were caught in this conversation: 'Hey, what do think of the sentences? Can you believe it? Where under heaven has there been an entire family – not for money nor immoral reasons – intentionally murdering a family member who was about to die anyway? I don't understand why the authorities used the term "intentional murder"?'

His companion continued, 'Even if it were "intentional murder", what law is there that states two people must die for the death of one? Moreover, why should a whole family of nine, including a mere 16-year-old, be sentenced?'

'This incident is as minor as "a lice on the head of a monk". As though we don't have enough murderers, thieves and rapists who kill their victims as it is! They go free while this pitiful Shi family have become scapegoats. How pathetic! How dreadful!'

'Say no more,' his friend said fearfully. 'This incident has nothing to do with us. As the saying goes, "sweep the snow away from your front door and don't be concerned with the frost on the roof of others".'

'That's right. Let's not say any more about this, lest disaster falls on our own heads. Come! Let's go to my house and have a drink!'

The Shi family were locked up in separate cells after the sentencing. Handcuffs and feet stocks were put on Wuting, who shared cell number two with another death-row prisoner. His wife Meiying and his mother shared cell number one across from him.

When her mother-in-law, also with handcuffs and feet stocks, passed out from the weight and tightness of her bonds, Meiying had a moment's reflection on how such a warm, blessed family could now be facing such tragedy?

She thought of how a loving, old couple were soon to be separated forever, and how her beloved mother-in-law and husband were soon to become martyrs for the Lord. She realized she would be spending her entire life in prison and that her two lovely children would lose their parents. Only two old folk and three children would be all that was left of the Shi clan. Just to think about it caused her heart to break, and her sobs broke out uncontrollably giving way to mournful wails.

Suddenly, she heard coughing from across the hallway.

Wiping her eyes, she looked out of the prison bars and saw her husband, his body covered with wounds. He was lifting up his handcuffed hands trying to beckon to her.

Now Meiying had been a very simple, serious and diligent farm girl. Previously she seldom paid any attention to her husband's looks or build. But now that she was soon to lose him, she lifted up her face and scrutinised him carefully.

He stood 1.72 meters tall, of lean build, his large fiery eyes conveying strength and intensity. She considered his kindness, affection and devotedness. She cried out in her heart, 'Oh, such an esteemed husband. Why do we have to be separated by death?' The tears flowed without ceasing.

Wuting comforted her in a gentle voice, 'Meiying, my beloved wife, why are you crying? How can I not drink the cup that the Lord has given me? Don't you realise that we live for the Lord, and if we die, we die for the Lord? Therefore, whether we live or die we are the Lord's? Beloved Meiying, it is only that I will be one step ahead of you. Before too long, we will be together again, never to be apart. Don't be sad. Be strong and courageous. Whatever happens, you must live fully for the Lord. Don't waste any time.'

Though they were simple and plain words, his exhortation was powerful. Meiying felt as if an intense fire burned in her heart, flames of love, hope and revival. She was greatly encouraged and sustained by his words all through the long years in prison.

She spent as much time as possible looking out through the bars at Wuting. He was so great, loving and affectionate. She would have given anything to run through the prison door and into his arms and kiss him passionately!

For two weeks, Wuting and Meiying, faithful children of God, continually beheld each other through the bars. This was how they comforted, encouraged and strengthened each other.

During the night, Mrs Shi regained consciousness. Meiying cradled her mother-in-law's head in her bosom and gently treated her injuries, even though she herself suffered many wounds. Their relationship was already one of mother and daughter. But now in this 'hell on earth' their hearts were knit even closer.

During the precious time they shared before the execution how many final wishes, how many words from the heart were spoken!

From the time of sentencing, they had two precious weeks together before death separated them. It was very difficult for Mrs Shi to move, with handcuffs and chains and severe injuries. At meal times Meiying would kneel before her and feed her each mouthful with a spoon. Then, using a comb, Meiying would gently comb the older woman's hair. When she had to go to toilet, Meiying carried her on her back and helped her.

Sleep did not come easy either. Because of her extensive injuries, Meiying had to help her lie down slowly and carefully. In the silence of the night the two women would draw near to God in prayer. They prayed for the country, the people, the authorities, their persecutors, the church and their family. Mother also used God's Word to continually encourage, exhort and comfort Meiying.

Her daughter-in-law would listen respectfully and weep, while holding on tightly to her. Then both of them would fall asleep.

One night, they both dreamed that they saw themselves dressed in white robes with beautiful wings flying through the dark clouds above the atmosphere to heaven! They flew higher and higher! Then they saw 'The Beloved'.

His hands were stretched out to receive them. With great emotion they went towards Him, and He stretched out scarred hands to wipe the tears from their eyes. Then He lightly touched their heads. Fearful that He would leave them, they held on to Him tightly.

Chapter 4
Mother and Son Enter the Execution Ground

On September 14, 1983, the PSB's legal department in 'P' city arranged a propaganda stunt to boast of its great achievements during this political movement. It held a huge public trial in the People's Hall of the city. More than 30 truckloads of criminals from different districts were paraded through the streets. In each vehicle were ten criminals guarded by two triumphant guards wearing steel helmets and holding guns with live ammunition.

After the public display the criminals were all taken to the People's Hall. More than 40 prisoners had been sentenced to death and were to be executed immediately. Several prison trucks sped to the execution ground with these on board, their placards hanging from their necks signifying they were death-row prisoners. Wuting and his mother were among them.

When they reached their destination, most of the prisoners were so gripped with fear their faces turned an ashen gray and they fell on the ground as if paralysed. Only Wuting and his mother remained calm, kneeling and waiting. More than 40 soldiers lifted up their pistols, each one aiming at his target.

At the command, all the pistols fired with one loud sound and the criminals all fell over dead. How strange! Why was it Wuting and his mother did not fall over? The two were still kneeling on the ground. They looked at the execution squad, but they had already laid down their pistols.

These rulers were not going to let them die so easily. They still had to be publicly paraded and 'struggled against' in another place. Wuting and his mother were put through a 'mock execution' that day. The weak-hearted, when put through this, often pass out from fear at the crack of the gun and die with those who have been shot. How many rulers in the world today still use such inhumane torture?

That evening, seven members of the Shi family (Father and Uncle were exempted) were heavily guarded by armed guards. The next day, all seven of them were separated and put into different trucks to be taken to Shanzui town. Mother and Wuting, still wearing their placards which condemned them to die by execution, were bundled into a truck with another two death row prisoners. Meiying, Meizhen and Xiaoxiu went together and the two younger boys were put in another vehicle.

All the way on the road, Meiying kept her eyes fastened on her husband and mother-in-law following in the truck behind hers. When the public display ended, the prison trucks drove towards the place where the 'open trial' was to be held.

In a joyful spirit, Wuting smiled at his wife and said, 'Meiying, I will go first. I will wait for you in Father's house. Goodbye!' With a smile, her mother-in-law nodded her agreement.

It was not at all like they were going to the execution grounds. It was more like they were going to a large wedding banquet! Meiying and Meizhen also nodded their heads and smiled. Meichun, especially, wished she was privileged enough to stand with the condemned pair to meet the Lord together!

The 'open trial' was held at a crossroad in Shanzui town, where four major highways came together. Each highway was about 30 feet wide, and in the middle of the intersection was a public square. Tens of thousands of spectators crowded the place to watch the proceedings. The judgement bench was set at the southwestern edge in front of the courthouse gates, elevated on the steps above the people.

Ninety criminals were brought out. The head of the department made a report, then the head judge read out the crimes of each criminal and their sentences. Finally, the 'murder case' of the Shi family was read out. In a loud, authoritative voice, the chief judge said, 'Take Shi Lishi, Shi Wuting and the other two criminals to the execution ground for immediate execution!'

Two guards grabbed Mother and Wuting by their collars and

arms and pushed them off the 'stage' and into a truck with the other two condemned men. Meiying went up to a soldier and begged him. 'My mother-in-law has been better to me than my own mother. Before she dies, please allow me to say a few words to her!' The soldier glared at her without so much as a blink, and shouted, 'Shut up. Don't speak again!'

Meiying then watched her husband and his mother being pushed into a truck. It was to be her last glimpse of her beloved. The truck started up and the crowd moved back. As it sped off towards the execution ground, scores of people ran after it.

The truck went through the underpass beneath the rail tracks and up the uneven dirt road. Eventually, it stopped at a place called 'Frog Mountain'. The other two prisoners were so consumed with fear they passed out. The soldiers carried them to a small, red, dirt hill and dumped them there.

But Wuting and his mother were smiling and walked calmly without assistance to the plot. As far as they were concerned, they were going to meet their heavenly Father, the Beloved, and all the saints who were waiting to receive them. The believers have a saying, 'The ancients say life is but a dream, but to the saints death is only returning home.'

It was noon. The sky was clear and there was not a cloud to be seen. Then suddenly, dark clouds gathered and a strong wind began to blow.

Mrs Shi turned towards the soldier at her side and smilingly asked him, 'Can I be allowed to pray?' The soldier nodded his silent approval.

Mother and son knelt down, lifted up their heads heaven-wards and prayed to the Saviour who created heaven and earth: 'We ask you to forgive our country and our people for the sin of persecuting us. Save our country and the people. Forgive the sins of those who harmed us. Lord, we ask you to receive our spirits.

Bang! Bang!

Blood spurted out of Mother's head and her soul entered Paradise. Wuting, however, was not yet dead. He turned to look at the soldiers behind him and saw they were so frozen with fear they could not fire a second time. But two other soldiers, after they were done executing the other two criminals, raised their pistols and fired at Wuting. He slumped over, his brains and blood splattered all over the ground.

Suddenly, there was a heavy downpour, with thunder and lightning flashing. But all the rain could not wash away the blood of the innocent that was spilled there on the execution ground.

Just then, a train passed by. The train whistle mingled with the sound of the rain and rolling thunder, making a somewhat sorrowful cry. The locomotive slowly disappeared into the horizon.

The Execution

Conclusion

After the public trial, Meiying, Meizhen and Xiaoxiu were taken to a women's prison. Before their transfer, however, Meiying's mother and older brother came to see them. They embraced the two sisters and wailed loudly. But they looked toward heaven as if they didn't hear a thing. Mrs Mu and her son refused to leave, and the PSB guards kicked them to the ground. There they sat and sobbed hopelessly. When they next looked up, the two girls were already on their way to the women's prison.

Meiying and her sister obeyed the last words of Mother and Wuting. They remained strong and lived for the Lord. Together with several other believers, they became messengers of the Gospel to the thousands who were in that prison. When several key workers completed their prison term and left, Meiying and Meizhen took over as leaders of the church in prison.

Six days after the execution it was the mid-autumn festival. Mr Shi and his brother were released and allowed to so home. It was to be a time of family reunion and laughter and happiness. But these two brothers sat under a tree in the courtyard, pondering the events silently.

This once warm and happy family was now reduced to only two adults and three children. They could not stop from crying. But as they thought of the Lord's imminent return, their hearts were comforted.

Relatives of the Shi family retrieved the bodies of Mother and Wuting for burial. In Wuting's coat pocket they found a letter written to the family: 'It is now finished. Do not be sorrowful for me. I am only going to that place before you. Love the Lord fervently and hold steadfast to His Word. Later, you will also go to the Heavenly Father and meet me. He that endures to the end shall be saved. For my funeral, make it very simple. Take care of the two children and let them know that I died for the Lord ...'

PART SIX

The Soldier of Jesus Christ

Chapter 1

The Soldier of Jesus Christ

In a certain village people heard the explosive news: Qinlu (Chin-lu) has believed in Jesus. But many people did not believe it, for Qinlu was a morally corrupt person who could inflict terrible hurt and damage on others.

However he truly repented. It was Christmas of 1971 when, with joy, Qinlu was baptized in water and took identification with Christ. He received water baptism in an icy river, and the brethren had to break open seven inches of ice before he could be baptized. When Qinlu came out of the water, every hair on his head became an icicle. His clothes froze as if they were armour and it took much effort to remove them. After that, he immediately took part in a communion service. After he had received communion, the Holy Spirit came on Qinlu and several brethren like fire falling. They were anointed with the oil of gladness and began dancing and praising the Lord. Then they began speaking in tongues.

Three months later, the Lord clearly called Qinlu to preach the Gospel. One day, he was in a meeting when the commune authorities organized a group of soldiers and surrounded the meeting place. Angrily, the cadres came into the meeting and commanded that the people report their names one by one. Qinlu immediately stood up and said very loudly, 'I am Qinlu, from Dalian Shan (Dalian mountain).'

The rest of the brothers and sisters were afraid of the consequences, and dared not give their names. As a result the soldiers bound them and took all who attended this meeting to the re-education classes of the commune. But they did not tie up Qinlu as he had reported his name. For ten days they laboured during the day and read newspapers and documents about Party policy in the evening.

Though Qinlu was oppressed physically, his heart was not oppressed. He constantly led everyone in prayer and through the Word of the Lord encouraged the believers to be strong and love the Lord. As a result many became fervent believers. Qinlu took advantage of lax supervision at the commune to send the brothers and sisters out to preach the Gospel. He himself did this often and, as such, was an example to others.

Late at night Qinlu returned from re-education classes to his home to see the many preachers from other districts who came to his house to avoid arrest. During the night he fellowshipped with them and learned from them. Every day in the early morning hours he had to climb over the wall to return to the re-education school, but the authorities never discovered him.

After ten days, the cadres asked everyone in the re-education classes to discuss the benefits of their learning. They said, 'Those who have learned well can return, but those who have not yet learned must remain here to learn more.' Qinlu was the first to rise and say, 'I have learned well.' They said, 'If this is the case you can discuss what you have learned.'

Qinlu continued to say without hesitation, 'During the past ten days of learning, I have come to understand more clearly what kind of a person I was before, but now I'm saved by Jesus. The people in the world love good people, their friends, those who are handsome. Only Jesus came to the world and loved sinners. He loved enemies, in fact He loved to the extent that He shed his blood. Due to this wonderful love He is willing that everyone should repent, for those who love the Lord shall obtain eternal life, but those who do not believe shall be condemned ...' The cadre interrupted Qinlu, 'Enough, enough, don't say any more. Take your bedding and return home.'

After one year, the commune and brigade realized that Qinlu had changed greatly. Not only was he straightforward and impartial, but his ability to handle affairs was excellent and he had many talents. Therefore they appointed him to be the leader of the production brigade. Qinlu refused to do so three times. After that he realised that being the leader of the brigade had many benefits, therefore he agreed to be the brigade leader.

After he became the leader, due to the presence of the Lord, he was selfless, put sacrifice before pleasure and had great concern about the members. As everyone respected him, his words had authority. During the rest time he continually preached the Gospel to the members of the commune and encouraged them to believe in Jesus. Due to his love and inspiration, many believed in Jesus. Before very long his neighbours and the vast majority of the commune members believed in the Lord. He constantly organized the people to come to meetings to worship the Lord.

The production output of this brigade was fantastic, and brigade members helped others and taught three other brigades. Originally, these three brigades were not of one heart. They always fought and had differing opinions. But when Qinlu became the leader of the second brigade, they all came together and increased their production, submitting to the leadership of Qinlu.

The Lord chose Qinlu's family and they willingly received others into their home. During that time there were few preachers of the Gospel. In an area of 19 districts in this province, there were only about ten workers to feed the flock and preach the Gospel to people. These workers stayed in Qinlu's house where they had their devotions.

During one tense period, the house churches were continually under persecution. Many workers from that district and several outer provinces went to Qinlu's house to hide. Thank the Lord for his protection, for these people in Qinlu's house hid for one month and then returned home safely. Therefore it was the Lord's will that Qinlu had become the leader of the brigade.

At that time, food supplies were very short. Qinlu's family had only one meal everyday so that they could share their rations with the workers. The God of Elijah is also our God, and was the God of Qinlu. Because of the kindness of his family in receiving others, God remembered him and many wonderful things took place.

One day, Qinlu came upon two brothers from outside the area. He thought of every method possible to serve them. His family had only a little flour, but he used it to make one small bowl of jiaozi (dumplings), and prepared to receive these two brethren. Who would believe that after these jiaozi's were put in the wok to cook, he would take out enough to feed these two brethren until they were full, with still two large bowls left?

Once, Qinlu's sister took one basket of wheat to make flour, who would think that, when this one basket of wheat was milled it would become two full baskets of flour? There were more amazing things. Qinlu's house had only one small wok, and usually when they made porridge, at the very most, it could only provide food for six people. With ten or more preachers, there were always twenty people who ate, and they always had leftovers. For many years there were meetings in Qinlu's home. Sometimes there were 40 or 50 people, sometimes over 100. Qinlu used his wok each time to make food and everyone ate until they were full. Hallelujah!

In August of 1973, a Judas reported to the PSB in the city that preachers were staying with him every day. They then sent seven PSB officials who came to his house on motorcycles to make a search. Thank the Lord, when the PSB men came Qinlu had already moved the preachers elsewhere, so they did not find anything.

They then took Qinlu to the brigade headquarters for questioning. 'Do you have people living in your house?'

'Yes, people who pass by on the road stay there, how can I refuse them?' he replied.

'Then who are those people, and what are their names?'

Qinlu laughed loudly and said, 'Over such a long period so many people have come, how can I know where they are from and their names?'

The PSB officials continued to question him, 'You mean to tell us, you don't know the name of a single person? How can that be?'

Qinlu again laughed saying, 'I don't know. You yourselves go and investigate.'

The PSB questioned him for a long time, but got no results. They were so angry they hit the table and reprimanded him.

After that, the PSB sent people to watch him continually for 74 days. During this time, Qinlu was called in daily 'to consider his ways and tell the truth'. But they obtained nothing from him. They were unable to find anything against him. They went back to the PSB office and said to Qinlu, 'We have investigated you for a long time, and you are not corrupt. You have done nothing bad, and you do well the work of the brigade. But it is too bad that you stubbornly hold on to this religious superstition.' Qinlu laughed and said, 'If I didn't believe in the Lord, I would be a stubborn man, and how would I do the work of the brigade well?'

In April of 1974, Qinlu was arrested because of his involvement with a certain preacher in another city. The day before he was arrested, Qinlu was working when he heard a small voice say to him, 'Son, your heaven is in the cross, and without the cross there is no heaven.' Qinlu immediately knelt down and with tears he said, 'Lord, it is true, I am willing to follow you down the road of the cross.'

Qinlu was the first brother to be arrested from the church in 'F' city. Before very long, Brother Ming was also arrested. They were together in detention for seven months. In the detention centre, Qinlu had a dream: A man with white hair and a long beard came to him with an open book and asked, 'Are you Qinlu?' Qinlu said, 'Yes I am.' That old man then opened an ink box and had Qinlu put his hand in the ink box and said, '21 months.'

After he woke up, Qinlu immediately told this dream to Brother Ming. But he said, 'I don't believe that we must be here 21 months. I see it as three or four months, the most five months and then we will be set free.'

After that, Qinlu counted the time – one day, two days, five days, one month, two months, five months. After one year he stopped counting. In the end, Qinlu's time in detention was lengthened to two years, and the day that he left the detention centre it was exactly 21 months.

The detention centre where they were kept was truly hell on earth. The way they treated the prisoners is frightening to anyone who hears it. They not only received much punishment, but they were only given a little to eat each day. The prisoners were always starving, so much so that when they could leave their cells they rushed outside to eat grass. The most terrifying thing was that some people ate their own excrement and as a result went insane. There was one prisoner who ripped up his shirt to eat it. Before very long he had eaten half his clothes. As a result every day he excreted blood and it was so painful that he fainted. Due to starvation every evening more than ten prisoners would faint.

During this period of 21 months, they questioned Qinlu daily, sometimes twice a day. He was not only questioned by the PSB officials of that province, those from other provinces also came to question him. Everyday Qinlu had to kneel in the PSB office. You can imagine the physical punishment and pain that he experienced.

In January of 1976, they formally sentenced Qinlu to two years in prison. The PSB bound him up tightly on the day of his sentencing. After that they took him as a common criminal to a public 'struggle session.' Many people gathered there. The people's militia had guns to keep order. Many armed PSB men had weapons pointed at the prisoners and there were many with machine guns.

Many students threw stones at Qinlu and spat on him. At this time Qinlu saw his parents, brother and sister. But he was not sorrowful or in any way ashamed, rather he smiled broadly at them, for he considered it a glory to suffer for the Lord. Thus, their hearts were put at ease.

During these 'struggle sessions', the other prisoners were ashamed to let people see them. Therefore they lowered their heads as the PSB forced them onto the platform with their pistols. Only Qinlu acted like he was going to receive a prize. With confidence he walked up the platform. When he got there, his two hands held up a placard that said, 'Qinlu, the counter-revolutionary who has put on the garments of religion.' He looked at everyone with a smiling face.

After they sentenced him they sent him to a labour camp. After a short time, Brother Ming was also sent there. The two met each other, were encouraged and prayed together. Qinlu had to fire bricks in a kiln. But he had a heart of love for the Lord and for others, even as Jeremiah said, 'there was a fire in his bones.'

In spite of the hard labour, in the evening when he went back to the camp, he took off his prisoner's clothes, put on the clothes he brought from home and sneaked out to the neighbouring villages to preach the Gospel. He returned the next morning before the cadres found out. If he had been discovered he would have had his sentence increased by one to two years and would be put in an isolation ward for two to three months. Eventually Brother Ming also went with him to places up to 15 kilometers away to preach the Gospel. Many came to hear the preaching.

After Qinlu was arrested, in order to find out about the preachers from the other provinces who had lived in Qinlu's house, the PSB sent several men to live there for two years. The whole family of six were often questioned and the PSB men were very vicious toward them. They frequently took his parents, brothers and sisters to the brigade headquarters and severely beat them up. But the family was protected by the Lord and each time they were questioned they were bold and did not divulge any information.

Once Qinlu's sister was taken to the brigade, and she did not answer a single word. The interrogator took a pistol and beat her around the mouth until her teeth were shattered and dropped out, leaving open bleeding wounds. When Qinlu's sister was taken to the brigade headquarters, her mother opened the door of her house and knelt there and prayed, asking the Lord to protect and give strength to her daughter. She continued until early morning when her daughter returned.

In 1978 Qinlu eventually returned home. At that time in the southern part of Henan, the churches were in a pitiful state. Several old servants of God were arrested and put in prison. The remainder became fearful and unwilling to minister. Many believers stopped their meetings. They could not live normal lives, were fearful and there was no one to shepherd and comfort them. They were as sheep without a shepherd. Qinlu could not believe that the church had come to such a condition and it was very painful for him.

Every day he took his bicycle and went to many places to exhort the brothers and sisters not to stop meeting. He encouraged them to love the Lord fervently and to remain alert and pray. He travelled in the middle of the night, facing all kinds of dangers and freezing cold winds, as he went from family to family and from village to village. As he rode his bicycle, he thought about the sorrowful state of the Church and began weeping. He finally stopped cycling, knelt down on the ground and wept before the Lord.

> 'How often has his shadow shown under the light of the stars and the moon.
>
> How often has his voice of wailing been heard deep into the night and in the early hours of the morning.
>
> How many times has he been under the winds and in the rains.
>
> How many times have his footprints been left in the icy snowy ground.'

After this time of difficult work, the churches began to experience revival. Every time Qinlu held a meeting, many people came together. God gave him great strength and every time he preached many people were moved and repented with tears. Once, he went to Wanhe to preach on a mountain slope, and about 2,000 came to hear the preaching. The Holy Spirit moved mightily in the meeting and many were enlightened. They repented before the Lord with weeping and untold numbers were greatly revived.

Qinlu began to preach at 6 p.m. and went on until 11 p.m., but the people were not willing to leave. He continued to preach through midnight until 1 a.m. Several thousand people in this large meeting place were so quiet it was unbelievable. You could even hear a pin drop. The brothers and sisters were so hungry for the Word they sat there without moving. The longer Qinlu preached the louder his voice became. He had much to share. He preached until the morning of the second day.

Before long, all the churches in each district experienced revival. Qinlu went to the churches in each area and through the leading of the Holy Spirit appointed workers in each area. In the spring of 1983, due to the moving of the Holy Spirit, Brother Qinlu brought a group of young brothers and sisters to a certain district and began a work that had an impact that was beyond description.

Then he was persecuted with the brothers and sisters and they were severely beaten. Because of this incident that took place in 'E' district, they were arrested and forced to take part in learning classes. More than 200 brothers and sisters were arrested and a total of eight were sentenced.

As Qinlu was held responsible, he began to live as a fugitive, avoiding arrest and preaching on the run for two years.

In order to arrest Qinlu, the PSB sent several special men to live in Dalian Shan village. During those two years, Qinlu and several others who were wanted by the PSB, slept in ditches, in the forest or in the fields. Only when it was raining did they return home to sleep.

Once, the PSB suspected that Qinlu was sleeping in his home and sent several cadres and people's militia army with several dozen rifles, pistols and electric cattle prods, to arrest him. They came in several vehicles but were afraid the noise would waken Qinlu, so they parked two kilometers away from his house.

Like a tiger stalking its prey they moved toward the house. Each person had three hand-carried lights like spotlights. They divided into three groups. The first group watched the roads leading from the house; the second group watched the wall surrounding the house. The third group rushed through the main door leading to the house to arrest him. Who would believe that it was all in vain?

Qinlu was on the small hill behind his house and saw and heard all that they said. He heard their curses and the questions they asked his family. He watched them most of the night until they finally cursed and left.

Qinlu's wife not only responsible for taking care of the whole family. Her house was regularly searched by the PSB. They beat her and she had to face much punishment and suffering. But the Lord was with her and gave her sufficient strength to overcome all. Whenever she was with the brothers and sisters, she was never seen looking sorrowful. In fact she was full of joy and encouraged them to be strong, not to fall back and to watch and pray.

In 1983, the government came against the 'Yellers Sect' and the whole church went through a time of severe persecution.

The PSB of 'F' city declared that Qinlu, Brother Ming, Brother Bai and the others were the leaders of the 'Yellers Sect' and cruel persecution came to the Church. They declared that the leaders were to be arrested. The local authorities felt that the numbers to be arrested were too small and that it should be at least doubled. They then said, 'In "F" city we need to execute 14 Christians.'

At that time the situation was unbelievably adverse and the heavens were full of dark clouds. The PSB made up their minds that they would use every way possible to arrest and execute Qinlu and the group of believers. Qinlu and the 14 brothers and sisters daily played hide and seek with the PSB. God miraculously protected them and they were always able to escape even when they were surrounded.

Daily they were on the run, but this did not hinder them from the ministry in each district. They went from this district to that district and this commune to that commune. At that time their lives were very difficult because they had no money for transportation and often had to walk 200–300 kilometers.

When they were thirsty they had to drink from the streams, and when they were hungry they could only tighten their belts. Some were so weakened from the lack of food they could hardly move. They would sleep under vehicles beside the roads or under tractors in the fields. Then one evening, it began to snow heavily and they were so cold they shook. Several sisters took a canvas bag and wrapped themselves in it. Only in that way could they survive through the freezing night.

During those days, one worker had no trousers to wear for five months. Several brothers had no money for a haircut and did not cut their hair for over five years so it grew very long. They were like a show to the people of the world to look upon.

Everywhere they were sought after; everywhere they were despised. But the world was not worthy of these people. They did not consider gain or loss. Every day they risked death that they might save lost souls. Though they risked death, had no certain dwelling place, were poor and had no livelihood, they were full of joy. Peace is something that no amount of money can purchase, but it is something that the fearful and those who covet pleasure cannot understand.

In this way Qinlu wandered for a full two years. To edify Qinlu and for the sake of many souls in prison, the Lord allowed him to be given over to evil hands. One day, Qinlu went with a brother in 'F' city to the bus station to catch a bus to another place. He then saw a 'Judas' looking at him. He told the brother who was with him to take the first bus, and he would wait for the second bus and leave quickly.

After the bus was a little over ten kilometers from the station, several PSB vehicles came up with their sirens on and forced the bus to stop. Several PSB men then entered the bus and began to check the identification of the passengers. When they saw Qinlu they asked, 'Where are you from and what is your name?'

Qinlu said very calmly and deliberately, 'I am Qinlu, from Dalian Shan.'

They immediately pulled him off the bus and cursed him saying, 'Qinlu, these several years you have been running very fast. But it doesn't matter what tricks you try, you cannot get away from us now. This time we have come to ask you to eat some 'red soup pills' ('Red soup pills' is the local slang for 'bullets').

Qinlu laughed and said, 'Don't be so uptight. If I wanted to take off and run I would have done so.' After they heard him, they were astonished. They thought this man they had been seeking for years would resist them. They politely said to Qinlu, 'All right. Do you want to be bound today?'

Qinlu said, 'Go ahead.' Then they bound Qinlu to a motorcycle and took him away. Along the way Qinlu happened to see a sister and loudly told her, 'Go home and tell the brothers and sisters that I have been arrested.'

When they arrived at the main PSB station, many PSB officials turned out to see him. These included the Chief of Police and the Department Head. One cadre said to him, 'You are truly a VIP. Even the Chief and Department head have come to welcome you!' A policeman asked a cadre: 'Where should I take Qinlu?' That cadre said very calmly while pointing at him saying, 'Please take him to Nanlao!'

Qinlu was shocked. He knew that the prison in 'F' City was known to be the worst in the whole province for its torture of the prisoners; the conditions in Nanlao were inhuman beyond any description. In that place a minor slip by the prisoners would result in them being stripped naked, their arms pulled apart, and they would be bound to a wooden cabinet. The police would use a bamboo rod to viciously beat the prisoner's head, hands, feet and body until there was no unbroken skin and they were covered with fresh blood. Then they used a hard piece of wood to beat the prisoner's palms, knees and ankles. Cruelty like this is seldom seen in the world today.

Qinlu was immediately taken for judgment. The courtroom was full of instruments of torture. The judge was the same man who judged him in 1974. He said, 'Qinlu, you have come again.'

Qinlu very calmly said, 'Yes, I have come again.'

'Do you still believe in Jesus?'

'I can lose my head and my blood can flow, but I can never lose my faith in Jesus.'

'OK, we'll not talk about believing or not. You are a labour reform prisoner who has been released. After your return home in 1978, you not only did not change your philosophy, but you recklessly carried on counter-revolutionary activities. You are the main organizer behind the incident in 'E' village. We have investigated thoroughly and already have a large amount of evidence. Now your only way out is to confess to the government and ask us treat you with leniency. Otherwise you will learn something today.'

Several policemen, hearing this, stood up and with eyes full of murder started staring at Qinlu. Qinlu coldly laughed saying, 'Don't try this one again! I have already been in prison once. I understand the policy of the Party and country towards one who has been arrested. You say your policy is fair and based on evidence and that you are opposed to torture. However, here before me what are these instruments we see? I want to say to you gentlemen standing here, it is clear that it is not me who is a criminal, but you. You just said I was the main person responsible for the incident in "E" village. Bring forth the evidence!'

The power of the Lord was mighty on Qinlu. He spoke with authority and his words burned the ears of the judge so that there was nothing he could say. The judge was silent for a long time and finally said, 'The trial is temporarily suspended for today. After you have gone back, carefully consider this and we will resume your trial in seven days.'

Qinlu was taken to the second ward of the prison. It was a very small room crammed with 14 prisoners. When the door was opened a nauseating smell came out. The prisoners inside had been beaten nearly to the point of death. Some were famished to the point of fainting. Some were struggling just to stay alive while others wanted to die. All the prisoners hung their heads with sorrow written on their faces. Several had pounded their heads against the walls in an effort to kill themselves, but without success.

When Qinlu saw the condition of these prisoners, the Lord immediately gave him the burden for these souls. He fervently prayed and asked the Lord to show his grace and send help. As Qinlu began to preach the Gospel to these pitiful people, their hearts were drawn by the love the Lord. As a result this group of over 40 prisoners, with the exception of two or three, all believed. Some of the prisoners came to visit Qinlu immediately upon their release from prison. Needless to say, in order to save these souls, Qinlu paid a great price in his body and suffered much.

After three months, God's work for Qinlu in the prison was completed. The plan of the authorities to have Qinlu executed was thwarted by the Lord. To everyone's surprise, Qinlu was not executed, moreover he wasn't even sentenced. After three months he was released!

On the day of his release from prison, the two highest authorities of the detention centre brought Qinlu forth. Mustering all their authority, they shouted, 'Who is Qinlu?'

Without hesitating he answered, 'I am.'

'Why are you in prison?'

'For believing in Jesus.'

The Assistant Supervisor, hearing this, gnashed his teeth, cursed him with a curse phrase that translated means: 'I hate you so much! To execute you with a gun cannot satisfy my anger. I want to have you shot with artillery!'

Qinlu lifted up his voice and said, 'Don't be so frenzied, for if

I hadn't come to your prison, you wouldn't even have anything to eat.' Hearing this the Assistant Supervisor was so enraged that he ran towards Qinlu but he was stopped by the Supervisor. He said, 'Enough, enough! The thinking of this Qinlu is already like a rock. You can't do anything with him.'

He then said to Qinlu, 'Your case is finished. Today you can return home!' When Qinlu returned home, he was amazed as he found many brothers and sisters there waiting for him. When they saw Qinlu had returned peacefully, their hearts rejoiced and they all praised the Lord very loudly. They asked Qinlu to preach to them and tell them about his experiences in prison. In that way they happily conducted a meeting in Qinlu's home that lasted for three days.

PART SEVEN

Of Whom the World
Was Not Worthy

Preface

For nine days, in the northern part of China on the plains of Fanda every drop of water had turned into ice. The temperature had fallen to −19°C. There was a very strong Northwest wind that blew the snow around like cotton balls. After several hours, snow of several feet covered the whole area like a thick white blanket. It was as if it covered all the sin and filth of mankind.

At 2 o'clock in the morning in a certain district in 'Love' Village, a middle aged man, over 40, knelt down in the snow in the courtyard to pray. He prayed for over two hours. He prayed earnestly to the Lord for the sake of his country, his people, the souls of thousands and the work of the Church. As he was praying his ankles fell deeper and deeper into the snow. He began to weep and his tears started falling into the snow.

He continued to pray and all of a sudden, in his heart, he heard a still, small voice; *'Within three days you will be arrested for the sake of the Lord.'* He thanked the Lord from the depth of his heart and rose up to his feet. By that time his trousers had already become like ice. Who was he? Where was he from? Why did he come to that place to pray?

Chapter 1

To Them Which Sat in the Shadow of Death Light is Sprung Up

(Matthew 4:16)

The beautiful, clear water from the river was shining like flames under the morning sun. You could almost see light coming forth from the river as it flowed slowly from north to south. The little fish were jumping under the light of the morning sun and, when some shepherd boys came by, they jumped into the river to play.

To the east of the river there was a small mountain. Even though it was not very high, it was part of a mountain range that seemed to extend a thousand miles. The mountain had thick shrubbery that gave it a very special appearance. There were four thatched houses by the river in the village at the foot of the mountain. There lived a couple and their five children.

The head of that family was Cheng Jian. He was medium-built but very strong, with thick eyebrows, sparkling eyes, a round face, a big nose and a wide mouth. He was full of energy. Even though he was over 30 years old and he had had a hard life, he was just as open, cheerful and optimistic as he had been when he was young. He was a delightful person, even in the midst of great difficulties, you could still hear his laughter.

Because of the tragic state the nation was in, life was very hard for everybody. Jian's wife was very weak and was always ill. They were so poor that often they had to go without food. That lasted for six to seven years. A couple of times, when Jian walked past his relatives' house he wanted to go in just to say 'hello'. His relatives were afraid that he would borrow money from them. They would relate how hard up they were before Jian even said anything. That made Jian very embarrassed and he did not know what to do.

During the Cultural Revolution, it was very common for Christians to be taken to the street to be 'paraded.' It was the spring of 1974. One afternoon, Jian was walking past a village. He saw an old woman being taken to the street to be 'paraded.' She was about 60 years old. Jian heard her say; 'My family was very poor and we were always ill. Even I had seven different kinds of sickness. I spent a lot of money on medicine and I have suffered a lot. But since I came to the Lord, we have had peace in my family.'

After Jian heard that, he thought to himself; 'Well, believing in Jesus can make you well.' So he ran home and went to find the people from the Church. He said he wanted to believe in Jesus and he asked the Church to pray for his wife. But the brethren did not believe him. Yet he was persistent. He went to the brethren's house three to four times a day to ask for prayer.

Finally, the brethren were moved. They went to his house to pray for his wife. They did that for three successive days. Praise the Lord! Jian's wife was completely healed. She did not look as if she had been ill for a long time at all. She went to the fields to work on the fourth day and the people from the production team were very surprised. She used to complain a lot and she was difficult to deal with. But now she had changed completely. People asked her, 'Have you believed in Jesus?' Jian's wife just smiled; she did not say a word.

But Jian himself had not come to the Lord yet. His heart was still quite hard. He thought because his wife had been healed, she should be the one to believe in Jesus, but not him. One night, Jian's wife came home from a meeting. She knelt down in her room and prayed earnestly for Jian while he slept in another room. It was then that Jian began to feel very uneasy. He knelt down and started to cry. He cried for a few hours before he had peace in his heart, and accepted the Lord that night. Jian used to be a 'big-kid' and was well-loved by people. But after he was saved, people began to despise him.

Chapter 2

When Thou Art Converted, Strengthen Thy Brethren
(Luke 22:32)

One day, while Jian and his wife were working in the fields, two men started to make fun of them and said mean things to them. They were very sarcastic and even blasphemed God. When Jian could not stand anymore, he raised his voice and said 'Stop it! If you've got the guts, speak it out! Have I done you any wrong that you blaspheme my God like that?' The two men did not dare say another word. They just put their heads down and kept on working.

Jian attended meetings regularly. One day, he and his wife were arrested in a meeting and taken to the 'learning classes'. Their five children were left at home with no one to look after them. Ten days later, all those convicted of stealing, gambling and fighting were released except Jian and his wife. Because they refused to deny Jesus, they were kept in custody. Finally, there was no more food left in the house. The children kept coming to the 'learning classes' and cried outside. That really cut the Chengs' hearts. Worse still, the party leaders kept threatening them. So in the end, Jian denied Jesus and signed his name.

After they got home, they felt very sorry. They could neither eat nor sleep for a few days. Then they knelt down and wept before the Lord. 'Lord, we have been unfaithful, we don't know if you still love us or not. If you do, please let us be sick within ten days.' After they prayed that prayer, they wept even more bitterly.

259

Three days later, the whole family became very sick. The party leader saw that Jian's family had not been to the fields to work for a few days, and they came to find out the reason. Jian told him, 'Because you forced me to deny Jesus and sign my name, we have become sick, and the Lord is going to forsake us too. Give the "confession letter" back to us, or else we'll die. From now on, my whole family will not just believe on the Lord Jesus, we'll dedicate our house to the Lord as well. We will have meetings in our home.'

After Jian thus repented, he began to sweat and totally recovered. A couple of days later, the whole family recovered. They were thrilled and praised the Lord.

The Lord had specially chosen that family and their home became a very good meeting place. They had believers coming to their home almost every day. The authorities became very concerned. They always sent people to interfere and threaten them. But Jian's whole family prayed together. They committed everything to the Lord's hand and did not worry at all.

Three months later, Jian received his call as a preacher. From that time, he was always out preaching the Gospel and ministering to people. Jian was very eloquent and persuasive in his preaching. Above all he had a heart for souls. He always urged people with tears to repent and turn to the Lord. And many people came to Christ as a result of his preaching. One day, Jian heard that a servant of the Lord, Brother Ming, who lived up on the hill, was in prison for the sake of the Gospel. He had been sentenced to seven years imprisonment in 1974. Jian prayed for brother Ming and his family earnestly.

On January 23, 1975, Jian's wife told her husband to take some rice to sell in the street. With the money he made, he could buy some meat and vegetables for the New Year. So off he went. Jian made six yuan with the rice he sold. Then he thought of Brother Ming's family and was moved with compassion. He decided to pay them a visit.

Jian only knew that Brother Ming lived on the hill, but he did not know the exact location, and he knew it would be unwise to ask around. He started off at noon and it took him six hours to get to the foot of the hill. It was already getting dark and there were bushes and thorns on the way. It was very difficult indeed. Nevertheless, Jian pressed on.

Late in the evening, Jian could see some light on the top of the hill. Jian walked on in the direction of the light. It was almost midnight when he finally got to the house. He knocked on the door and an old man opened it. When he saw Jian, he was very surprised. The old lady inside invited Jian in.

They all sat by the fire and the old man asked Jian where he was from and why he had come so late at night. Jian looked around and saw a young woman beside the old couple, but he did not see any children. He began to wonder and asked, 'Is this the Zhang family?'

'Yes,' the old lady answered politely.

'How many people are there in this family then?'

'All together five.'

'Who are the other two?'

'One is my little grandson; he is turning one year old. He is asleep now. The other one is my son. He is in the "labour camp" for the sake of the Gospel. And this is my daughter-in-law.'

When Jian heard that, he could not help but cry, 'Lord, at last, you've taken me to Brother Ming's house.' Ming's parents and his wife were very surprised. Jian told them why he came and what happened on the way. Jian took four yuan out and put them in the old lady's hand and said, 'Take this and buy something for the New Year.' As soon as he finished, he got up and started to leave. The Zhangs could not make him stay. So they walked him to the door with tears in their eyes.

When Jian got home, his wife asked him, 'Where have you been? Did you get anything for the New Year?' Jian told his wife all that had happened and she began to cry. It was not until January 28 that Jian went and bought some lard for the New Year with the two yuan he had left.

The night Jian got back from brother Ming's house, he had a meeting in his home. He told all the brothers and sisters about Ming's family and said, 'We would rather eat less so that we can support Ming's family.' They were all very moved. On January 28, a group of brothers and sisters went to visit Brother Ming's family. They took with them rice, flour, lard, salt and vinegar. When they got to Ming's house, they all wept. When they left, some of them even left their coats with the Zhangs. That was the first time in years that the Zhangs could have a happy New Year. But Jian had an unfulfilled desire. It was to visit Brother Ming who was in the labour camp for the sake of Christ.

It was a beautiful day in the spring of 1976. Ming was working in the orchard. When he lifted up his eyes he saw that the fruit trees were budding. He felt very sad. He thought of the churches in city 'F' and in province 'J'; he thought of the brothers and sisters who were in prison; he thought of his parents, his wife and his son. He could not help but weep.

Then a guard came to tell him that he had a visitor. So Ming went to the reception room. When Ming walked in, a man came up to him, shook Ming's hand and said very affectionately, 'Brother Ming, I'm Cheng Jian. So nice to see you. I've always wanted to come.'

Ming had heard about Jian from his family and other brothers and sisters how zealous he was for the Lord. Now he had come a long way to see him and Ming was very moved, so he took Jian to the orchard. Jian told Ming how the Church was doing and about the first time he had been to see Ming's family. They both wept.

Before he left, Jian gave Ming 50 cents out of a small bag. Ming did not understand why so Jian told him: 'On my way here to see you, I met a little sister. She is in her teens. Her family and her parents are not believers and she often gets punished for attending meetings. She always prays for the Church and for those who are in prison for the sake of the Gospel. She longs to come and visit you, but because of her family, and financial reasons, she still cannot come. So she told me to give this to you which she has saved.'

When Ming heard that, he burst into tears and said, 'I can't take this. Brother, take this money and buy a handkerchief for our little sister. Tell her to use the handkerchief to wipe her tears every time she prays and weeps.' On his way back, Jian did as Ming told him. He bought a handkerchief with the money for the little sister. So the little sister prayed even more earnestly and she used the handkerchief to wipe her tears.

Jian always went to visit Ming's family with the brothers and sisters. He always went there to help during the harvest time and to comfort Ming's family during the festivals. Ming's wife was so touched that she finally accepted the Lord. So there was revival in Ming's family even before he came out of prison.

Chapter 3

Ye Shall Indeed Drink Of the Cup That I Drink Of
(Mark 10:39)

One spring night in 1978, while Jian was preaching in a village not far from his home, he was arrested together with about 80 believers. They were locked up in a room in the Production Brigade office. People from the village gathered round outside the office and spoke against them using abusive and foul language. So Jian led the believers in the song:

> 'Jesus came to Gethsemane;
> the soldiers came to arrest him;
> Judas came and kissed the Lord ...'

After they had sung just a few verses, they began to weep. They wept as they sang for about one and a half hours. The more they sang, the louder they became.

Before dawn, a 13-year-old-girl came up to Jian and said, 'Uncle, I attended the meeting when I was on my way home from school. Now I have been arrested. If I can't get out today, my Dad will beat me up, and I'll be expelled from school as well.' As soon as she finished, she lifted up her voice and wept aloud.

The door was locked and bolted with metal bars on the outside. In spite of his strength Jian was not able to not open it. The little girl wept even louder, and Jian became even more anxious. Then he looked around. There were about 30 chairs in the room. He thought to himself, 'Perhaps I could knock the door open with these chairs.'

So he picked up a chair and was about to smash the door with it when, all of a sudden, one of the brothers said, 'Strange! The door is open!' They were all thrilled and blessed the Lord, then rushed out of the room. Jian was going to stay because some-one had to accept responsibility for what had happened, and a few brothers and sisters insisted on staying with him too. At that moment, a doctor came by. He was quite famous in that area. When he saw what happened, he was very moved and said, 'You'd better run as well. Who would sit here and wait for punishment? Besides, believing in Jesus is no big crime. Why stay? Run!' So they all ran. When they left the brigade office, it was already dawn.

Early that morning, the Production Brigade had an emer-gency meeting on what to do with the Christians. The final decision was that the Christians would have to pay for movies for the whole year for that village as a penalty.

When they got to the place where the Christians were being kept in custody, they were shocked to find the door open with nobody inside. Only two people had the key to that door: One was the secretary and the other one was the accountant. So the secretary went with a group of people to the accountant's house. They questioned the accountant's wife as to who it was that opened the door and let the Christians go free.

'It wasn't us. We didn't open the door for them. We are innocent,' the accountant's wife screamed. She grabbed the secretary's coat and dragged him outside to swear by heaven that they were innocent. The secretary did not know what to do. He needed help from the other party officials to free himself from her.

So they all went back to the office. They were exhausted and said to each another, 'What shall we do with these Christians? "Learning classes" are of no use and they are not afraid of flogging and punishment either. The only way is to prosecute them.' They came up with the conclusion that If Christians were arrested in a meeting, they would have to be fined and flogged, and 'merits' would be deducted from them as well.

In July the same year, Jian was made to do voluntary work

for 35 days. And his merits were deducted from the production team as well. Jian was very upset. He prayed to the Lord very earnestly. The Lord spoke to him, *'I know your difficulties ...'* He was comforted and peace filled his heart. Then he heard a voice clearly saying in his heart, 'April 12.' Jian said, 'Lord, I praise you. No matter what happens that day, I'm prepared. I delight to do your will.'

Time passed quickly. It was soon April 12 the following year. When evening came, Jian had a meeting with his co-workers. While he was standing up reading the Word, officers from the PSB came. They beat and kicked him. Jian fell on the floor bleeding. They then took him to the PSB.

On their way to the PSB, Jian's shoes often got stepped on, so he had to bend down to fix them. When the PSB chief saw that, he shouted, 'What are you doing?' Although he knew that Jian was bending down to fix his shoes, he ordered that Jian's shoes be taken off. The road they were walking on was a new one, covered with small stones which were very sharp. It was very painful to walk on them and Jian nearly fainted. Then he thought about the Lord: On His way to Golgotha, He even had to carry a cross. Jian said to the Lord, 'Lord, though the road I'm treading is difficult, it cannot be compared to the one you trod. Though the cup I drink is bitter, still it cannot be compared to the one you drank.' As soon as he finished praying, the stones under his feet became very soft. Jian leapt for joy and shouted, 'Hallelujah!'

They finally got to the PSB where Jian was interrogated. He did not say a word no matter what they asked him. The PSB chief was enraged and ordered him to be flogged. At that time, five sisters came, the eldest one was only 19. They had been with Jian in the meeting that night and had followed him all the way. When they saw Jian being beaten, they cried, 'It was us who asked him to preach. What crime has he committed? If you want to beat him, you might as well beat us.'

So they took Jian to another room and locked the door. They tied his hands behind his back and hanged him on a roof beam. But the roof was too low and Jian's feet could still touch the floor. So they thought of a more cruel way of making Jian suffer. They tied another beam on Jian's wrist and then tied a big stone onto the beam. It was agonizing; Jian almost fainted. He kept on praying and asked the Lord to deliver him. Finally he fainted.

When he regained consciousness, it was dawn. Jian found that he was in the same damp, dark room and there were a lot of mosquitoes around. He thought about his own country and how they rebelled against God; he thought about the brothers and sisters who were in prison for the Lord's sake; he thought about the Church and how desolate it was; he thought about the numerous believers who had fallen, he could not help but weep and wail. Two days later, Jian was forced to work. He had to carry loads of sand to cover the road. But his wounded body was so weak that he fainted.

[faint mirror-image text bleeding through from previous page]

Chapter 4

Only be Thou Strong and Very Courageous

(Joshua 1:7)

It was a cold winter night in 1979; Ming, who just came out of prison, was speaking at a meeting in a certain village. Jian was there too; he was chairing the meeting. The place was packed. When Jian walked in, he saw a lot of people still chatting and he was quite surprised. He asked one of the sisters, 'What's the matter? Why aren't they singing?' The sister replied, whispering, 'There is a party official sitting in the front.' Jian went and sat next to him. He thought to himself, 'If he stands up to disturb the meeting, I'll grab hold of him.'

Then Jian stood up and led the others in the chorus:

> *'So may all your enemies perish, O LORD!*
> *But may they who love you be like the sun when it rises in*
> *its strength.'*   Judges 5:31

When they finished singing, Jian led them in prayer. Then he said, 'Now we'll hand the rest of the time over to the Lord's servant, Ming.' So Ming stood up, walked to the front and started preaching. He spoke on the second coming of the Lord and the signs of the end times. When they were listening attentively to Ming's sermon, the party official suddenly stood up and said, 'Stop! Come with me!' He grabbed hold of Ming's coat and tried to drag him along. At that very moment, Jian ran over to him and grabbed hold of him with all his might. Jian held him so tight that he could hardly move.

In the meantime, Ming had escaped. The man became even more mad; he yelled at Jian, 'I know what you do!'

Jian retorted, 'I know what you do too! I know your motives!'

'I know your motives too!' Jian continued, 'You always persecute we Christians; that's about all you do. You always come and interrupt our meetings but we never interrupt yours. What kind of policy is this?'

'I'm a party official; you must listen to me.'

'No, we won't listen to you; we'll only listen to the Lord.'

After Ming had gone out of sight, Jian let go of the party official. He then led the others in chorus again. After that, he closed the meeting.

They all went home; nobody paid any attention to the party official. He was mad and he said to himself, 'You wait and see!'

The Production Brigade brought charges against the Christians before the County PSB the following day. Not many days later, the party official came with a group of soldiers to Jian's house. He patted Jian's shoulder and laughed, 'I want to invite you to tea today; please come with me.' Then he turned to the soldiers, 'Bind him!' Then Jian was taken to the Production Brigade office; when the party official's chief saw him, he yelled at Jian, 'Are you that damn guy called Jian?'

Jian did not take any notice of him. The official got mad and struck Jian's forehead. 'You damn thing, our country is so strong and prosperous; people are living a very sweet life; nobody is afflicted. How dare you attack our country?' Jian was puzzled. He did not know what he meant. The officer slapped Jian's face and said, 'Stop pretending! You were the one who led in prayer at a meeting in Guo village.'

'Yes,' Jian answered.

'After you prayed, you said, "We'll hand the rest of the time over to the afflicted."' (The word 'servant' and 'the afflicted' sound similar.)

'No, I didn't.'

'How dare you! When we have all the evidence; you'll see.'

The Party official came over and struck Jian's head with his fist. 'I heard you say that with my own ears.'

Then Jian realized what he meant; he said, 'Oh, I see. I said,

"We'll hand the time over to the Lord's 'servant', not 'the afflicted'." You misheard what I said.'

The chief had a lot of experience in dealing with Christians, and he did have some knowledge of the terms used by them. After Jian explained, he began to understand. So he said, 'OK. Comrade X has misheard you. But what is that servant's name then?' Jian responded, 'What name? A servant is a servant. A servant's name is servant. What other name does he have?'

The chief was very disappointed; he thought Jian was just a country yokel. 'You fool! You don't even know what the Lord's servant is. What kind of a preacher are you?' So he gave up and did not pursue the matter any further. But he hated God and Christians, so he started to blaspheme God and the virgin birth of Jesus.

Jian was enraged; he stood up and banged the table. He shouted at the chief, 'Shut up! Stop blaspheming my God! You said I know nothing. But what do you know then? You don't even know the policies of the Party.'

The chief blushed; he slapped Jian's face. 'OK. Tell me what you do know.' Abuses and curses followed, but Jian was a funny man; in the midst of all that, he stood there and fell asleep. When the chief saw this, he became even more angry. He slapped Jian's face again, trod on his foot and scolded him even more severely. Jian just stood there and fell asleep again. Eventually he was set free.

On another snowy day in the winter of 1978, Jian woke up very early in the morning to pray in the snow. He thought to himself, 'What a good opportunity to go out to preach the Gospel.' Normally, if he wanted to go out to preach the Gospel, he would have to get permission from the production team to have a few days off. Because it was snowing he did not have to do that; he could just go. When Jian went back to the house to get his Bible, his son called him. 'Dad, can I have a word with you?'

'Sure. What is it?'

'When you go out this time, could you get us a pressure pump?'

'What for?'

'Because you and Mum always get caught and are put in

prison, and we are very small. When we go out to get water, we always get bullied. It is difficult! If you can get us a pressure pump, we can dig a well in front of our house. So that next time when you are caught, we can still have water to drink.'

Jian was moved to tears; he said in his heart, 'Lord, thank you. Even the children know what persecution and hardship are.' Jian went to town; he managed to get a pressure pump. Now the authorities knew that Jian was an influential person and he would not bow to pressure, so they thought of some tricks. The County Government sent Jian a letter inviting him to attend a County meeting and be a committee member as well. When the Production Brigade got the letter, they were envious: 'What? Inviting these Christians to a County meeting?!' They had no choice but to follow instructions. So they sent two party officials to deliver the letter to Jian.

When they got to Jian's house; they were very polite. 'It is our honour to have you attend the County meeting; you must do your best and tell them how well we have done.' Jian took the letter, read it and put it aside and said, 'I'm only a farmer, how can I be a committee member?'

They came to Jian three to four times, but Jian still did not take any notice of them. Finally, the County Government office called up the Production Brigade telling them they must get Jian to the County meeting. But Jian still would not go. The authorities were incensed and sent an officer to see Jian in person.

The Production Brigade sent for Jian but Jian refused to go. He said, 'I'm having some furniture made, I have to attend to the workman, so I can't go.' The party official was indignant.

'They have sent an officer specially to see you and you still won't go. You ...'

Jian continued, 'If it is something urgent, tell him to come to my house.' The Party official did not know what to do, so he left.

Then he came with the officer to Jian's house. Jian stood up and let the officer sit on his broken bed. The officer was rather displeased and he could not speak for quite a while. Then Jian spoke to him, as if addressing an ordinary person, 'What do you want me for?' The officer stared at Jian and asked him, 'Have you received the "Ten No's" we gave you?'

'No,' Jian replied.

The Party official cut in, 'We have got the notice. But we have been very busy; we still haven't given it to him yet.'

'Though I have not received it yet; I have heard about it. Is it the one that says: No youth under 18 can become a Christian?'

'Yes.'

'No praying for the sick? No casting out of demons?'

'Yes, exactly.'

'I don't care how many "No's" are there; just take the first one, I can't accept it.'

'You dare to object?'

'No, it's not objection. Let me ask you: I have five children; the eldest one is only 18. We have meetings five evenings a week. It's rainy in spring, windy in autumn and cold in winter. Could I leave my children outside and wait until the meeting finishes? If you were me, would you do such a thing?'

The officer was dumbfounded, so he changed the subject. And he asked Jian, 'Why didn't you go to the County meeting then?'

'I cannot accept your "Ten No's" and that's why I didn't go.'

'It wasn't us who set them up; they were written by a pastor in town. He knows the Bible better than you.'

'Does he believe in Jesus?'

'Of course he does. How can he be a pastor if he doesn't believe in Jesus?'

'Well, I don't think he believes in Jesus. There are only "Ten Commandments" in the Bible; there is no such thing as "Ten No's". I strongly object to this kind of religious hypocrisy.'

'I won't argue with you. The reason why I'm here today is to invite you to join our Three-Self Patriotic Church, to assist us in our work.'

'There is no such thing as Three-Self Patriotic Church in the Bible, so I'm not going to go.'

'Joining us doesn't mean that you can't pray or meet together. So why don't you listen to us?'

'We only listen to God, not to man.'

The officer became furious and he said, 'If you don't join our religious organization, all the meetings held in your house will become illegal and they will have to be stopped.'

'No, we won't stop. The Bible tells us not to stop meeting together.'

'If you don't stop, then you'll be responsible for all the crimes in the village.'

'If it is for security reasons, you will have to stop showing all the movies and plays. We will stop only if they are stopped.' The officer became so mad that he could not speak, so he left.

Ten days later, the officer summoned Jian to the Production Brigade office. He said, 'I've told you for the last time that without our permission, all your meetings are illegal. Why don't you listen and stop meeting?'

Jian laughed, 'Have you forgotten our agreement? We'll stop only if all the other activities in the village are stopped first. It's you who broke the agreement, not me. How can you blame me for that?'

The officer gnashed his teeth and said, 'The Communist will outdo you in the end. You wait and see!'

'Well, if you are so unreasonable I think I'd better leave.'

'You'll have to bear the consequences.'

'My God will bear the consequences,' Jian answered loudly. Jian then walked out of the office; he did not even turn his head. They finally brought Jian's case to the PSB in city 'B'.

Chapter 5

Of Whom the World Was Not Worthy
(Hebrews 11:38)

One day, Jian heard a very clear voice saying in his heart, 'You must leave home within three days.' On the same night, while Jian was preaching, the Lord spoke to him again, 'Arrange for someone to take over your work; pack up and go as soon as possible.'

After the meeting, Jian called for all the co-workers and met with them. When they had made all the arrangements, they committed Jian to the Lord and wept. After that, they all departed. When Jian got home, he packed up a few things: a Bible and a few notebooks. Then his wife and children walked him to the door. It was almost dawn when Jian left.

Three days later, a PSB car stopped outside Jian's house. A few security men in uniform and a group of soldiers went into Jian's house. They ransacked his house but still could not find Jian. So they interrogated his wife and children but they all said they did not know where Jian was. Then they turned to Jian's little daughter who was only 13. They pulled her ear and asked her, 'Where is your Dad?' She answered, 'I don't know.'

They slapped her on her face; her nose and her mouth started to bleed. One of them wanted to tie her up, but she was very swift and ran out of the house before they could grab hold of her. They chased after her, and when one of the men was about to reach her, she jumped into a ditch. The water was quite deep and dirty, so the men did not bother and left.

From that day, Jian lived like a fugitive for 21 months. Brother Ming, Sister Bai and a few others were with him too. They always spent the night in the hills, in the wilderness, in the bushes and in the fields. They had to suffer the cold and the wind and were bitten by mosquitoes. They would sneak into the houses of the believers before dawn. And the Lord always delivered them from the hands of their enemies. They played 'Hide and Seek' with them. Whenever they had the opportunity, they preached the Gospel and exhorted the brethren to serve the Lord with all fervour.

At one time, the security police really chased them hard; they could hardly breathe. So they went to a town called He Ping in Province 'R'. The security was very tight there so the brethren did not even dare to receive them. They had nowhere to go, so they went to a stable. There was animal waste everywhere; they could hardly find a place to stand. At last, they found some straw. They crouched down and slept there. It became very cold towards dawn; they were shivering. So they decided to go out and jog to beat the cold. While they were jogging on the road, they met Brother Ming and Brother Yun. So they jogged together and left Province 'R.'

When they got to a place called Liu Shan, Jian wanted to visit a relative there and to find out how his family was. Ming knew that this relative had suffered much because of Jian, so he warned Jian to come back early and not to spend the night there. When Jian got to his relative's house, his relative received him very warmly. He would not let him go, so Jian stayed. In the middle of the night when Jian just got to sleep, people from the PSB came. They surrounded the house and searched from room to room. There were altogether four rooms in the house. When they were searching in the third room, Jian became very anxious. So he committed himself into the Lord's hand.

Then he noticed there was a trunk beside the bed. So he lifted the lid, took out the bedding and put it onto the bed. He then crawled inside and pulled the lid down. As soon as Jian had hidden himself, the security police came in. They waved their torches about and searched everywhere. One of the men even hit the lid of the trunk with a staff. Jian was worried that he would open the lid, but he did not. After a while, they all left.

After the security police had gone, Jian's relatives came to look for him. They searched every room and everywhere but they still could not find him. Jian did not know it was them; he thought it was the security police. So he did not dare move. The old lady became worried and said, 'Where is he?' Jian recognized her voice, so he said, 'I'm here. Have they gone?' And he stood up.

When they saw him, they were so pleased and praised God. 'Well, they're really searching for us; I'd better go and tell them.' So Jian ran about 30 kilometers and finally got to the place where Ming and the others were staying. They all ran to the corn fields to hide and spent the night there.

One night, Jian went back home and stayed there for three days. During the day, his wife and children went out to the fields to work and the door was locked. Whenever he sneezed or coughed, he had to do it under his quilt; he felt very lonely. Satan came to attack him on the third night. While he was sleeping, a big rat bit him on his wrist. One of his tendons was injured and he bled profusely. The bleeding would not stop. His whole family knelt down and cried out to God; suddenly, the bleeding stopped. But his right arm was still swollen and it was very painful.

Jian then went back to Ming and the others. He went to many places. Wherever he went, he established churches and also tried to avoid the PSB.

Chapter 6

They Were Counted Worthy to Suffer Shame for His Name

(Acts 5:41)

Jian, Ming, Yun and a few others held a ministry-training seminar in January 1983. That very night, Jian went to the backyard; he knelt down on the snow to pray (this incident was mentioned at the beginning of Part Two, 'The Heavenly Man'). The Lord showed him clearly that within three days, some of them would be arrested.

On the third morning, when they were meeting together, Jian stood up and said: 'Some of us will be arrested today for the Lord's sake; let us pray earnestly for them.' On the same night, Jian, Yun and a few others – altogether five of them were arrested on their way home after the meeting.

The security police struck Jian with a club, but quite miraculously, he did not feel any pain at all. When they saw that clubbing did not have any effect on Jian, they pushed him down on the floor and tied his hands behind his back. Since Jian had been bitten by a rat, he had always been worried that if he got caught and bound, his arm might become handicapped.

Miraculously, Jian's right arm, which was hurting until then, did not hurt any more after he was bound.

'Where are you from?' they asked him.

'I am from city "F". I was just passing by. When I saw that there was a meeting, I just went in,' Jian answered.

'Where was the meeting held? Take us there then,' they demanded of him.

So Jian took them to a primary school and stopped outside.

277

'OK. This is the place.' The security police and the soldiers barged inside. A group of teachers were preparing for their lessons; when they saw them come in, one of them stood up and asked, 'What are you doing here?'

The police were very embarrassed; so they struck Jian even more. 'Come on, where is the meeting place? If you don't tell us, we'll kill you.' Jian wanted the brethren to know that people from the PSB had come, so he raised his voice, 'Why do you beat me like that? I've forgotten where they met.'

At the same time, Yun was being brought over under police escort. He also shouted, 'I'm from heaven; I don't know where they met.' The brothers and sisters at the meeting place heard Jian's and Yun's voice, so they moved to another place immediately. The security police knew they had been tricked and they were enraged. They said, 'Come on, let's go. When we get to the office, you'll see.' They pushed Jian onto the truck. Because Jian's hands were bound, he slipped and fell onto the snow. So the guards picked him up and threw him onto the truck. His head hit the truck, and he fainted. When the other brothers and sisters saw that, they were very sad and wept; they did not dare to say a word.

They took Jian and three other brothers to the Shi Lin Police Station. When they got there, Yun was already there; they all had handcuffs on. The five of them were shivering with cold, so they knelt down to pray, and they prayed very earnestly.

Early the following morning, they were taken to the court-yard to sweep the snow. After that, Jian, Yun and another brother were taken to the detention prison. There were already eight people there. When the guard saw the two new-comers, he put his hands on his waist and stared at them. He yelled, 'Get over there!' Jian and Yun obeyed, then he said, 'Now I'll give you something to do – "fishing" and "riding the motor-bike".'

The so-called 'fishing' was a very cruel kind of punishment. The prisoner had to put a straw in his mouth and dip it into a bucket of urine. He then had to blow bubbles inside until the urine was all over his face. The guard would just laugh and taunt, 'Have you got anything?' The second kind of punishment 'riding the motor-bike' was like this: The prisoner had to half squat, with his two hands stretching forth. He had to make the sound of a train.

Whoever could not do it or stopped doing it would be punished severely. Oh! How many of God's faithful servants were insulted and ill-treated there. The world was really not worthy of them. The prison guard ordered the other prisoners to beat Yun. After Yun had been beaten, he fell on the floor. The other prisoners even stepped on him. His mouth was bleeding; he was almost dying.

At first, Jian and Yun pretended that they did not know each other. But when Jian saw that Yun was beaten like that, he could not pretend any longer. He went over to Yun, held him and wept. He asked the Lord to comfort and protect Yun, and he wiped away the blood that was coming out of his mouth.

After a few days, the other prisoners saw that Jian was so warm and approachable, they began to like him and they asked him to sing them a song. So Jian began to sing and he also shared the Gospel with them, while Yun prayed earnestly for them. They did that for three successive days. On the fourth day, Jian started to sing after he got up:

> *'Today is a beautiful day;*
> *it's the day that the Lord has made;*
> *He causes me to feast in the presence of my enemies.*
> *The Lord is with me today.'*

The other prisoners listened attentively; they seemed to understand what Jian was singing about. After breakfast, the PSB van came to take Jian away. The other prisoners were very surprised, they said to each other, 'Wow! This man is really something; he sang about a beautiful day this morning and now he is released!' They began to think about what Jian had shared with them in those few days and some of them accepted the Lord.

Meanwhile the security police put handcuffs and fetters on Jian and tied him to the seat in the van. They had not got very far when suddenly the van broke down and stopped. The security chief yelled at Jian, 'Don't you run away.'

Jian laughed, 'Are you kidding? I have handcuffs and fetters on and I'm tied to the seat, how can I run away?'

The chief was furious and said, 'Stop laughing! We have

spent a few thousand yuan just to catch you and now the van is broken down; you have to pay for everything.'

Jian said with a smile, 'I didn't ask you to do that. It's not my fault.' The chief picked up a metal rod and threw it at Jian. Jian tilted his head immediately but he still could not avoid it. It brushed past his forehead and his forehead was slightly injured and it began to bleed.

At that time, a lot of people crowded around them. Some scolded Jian and spat on him but some pointed their fingers at the security police and said they were too inhuman. Acts 5:41 came to Jian's mind: *'rejoicing because they had been counted worthy to suffer shame for the Name.'* So Jian smiled. The people around were very amazed and said, 'What kind of a man is this?' With so many eyes watching, the chief did not know what to do. So as soon as the van was fixed, they left at once.

The van came to the prison and stopped outside the prison door. The security guards dragged Jian down from the van and the chief asked him, 'Do you know this place?'

'No.'

'No? This is the famous city "F" prison. And this is your place.'

'My place? Ha, ha!'

'Don't you run away! If you run away, you'll die here.'

The atmosphere was very tense inside the prison; the new-comers hardly even dared to breathe. Jian was searched thoroughly; both his belt and his shoe-laces were taken away. Jian was taken to a certain room where an old prisoner said to him very seriously, 'Don't you believe what they say; you mustn't tell them the truth.'

Jian smiled, 'Thank you for your concern. I believe in Jesus; there is nothing to hide. Besides, my Lord will take care of me.'

Jian was interrogated that afternoon. They questioned him about the Church in district 'B'. Jian was bold and courageous; he used the wisdom that the Holy Spirit gave him when he answered the questions. They stripped Jian of his clothes and whipped him. He gritted his teeth and did not make a sound.

Those crazy security guards used all kinds of methods to torture Jian. When they used a hot iron to brand his body, Jian could not bear it. He screamed, 'Father! Deliver your child!'

Then he fainted. A bucket of cold water was poured over him; Jian regained consciousness. Then it was interrogation and torture again. That was repeated five or six times; Jian was seriously wounded.

Seven months passed. One night, the Lord showed Jian: When the trees begin to bud, you will leave this place. The winter was gone; spring had come. Jian looked out of the window everyday to see if the trees had budded. It was a beautiful day; morning had just dawned and the sun was shining. Jian had been kneeling down in the prison room praying for a few hours. When he opened his eyes and saw the beautiful sunshine, he leapt, clapped his hands and praised the Lord. Suddenly, he saw a twig hanging at the window and it had begun to bud.

He said to the Lord with tears in his eyes, 'Lord, I praise you. Though I don't know what lies ahead, I commit everything into your hands. Keep me, Lord.' The following day, Jian was sentenced to two years imprisonment for disrupting public security.

Jian was taken to the Xin Yang Labour Camp. It was the most notorious labour camp in the province. Prisoners received the most cruel kind of treatment there. Each prisoner was given only one bowl of rice a day and they had to do over ten hours heavy labour every day. That was why all the prisoners were very skinny. If anybody ever dared to resist, they were whipped, beaten and tortured.

Chapter 7

He ... Break, and Gave to the Disciples and They Did Eat

(Luke 9:16, 17)

The more you refine gold, the purer it becomes. Though Jian was getting weaker and weaker physically every day, his heart was renewed day by day and he was getting closer and closer to God. Jian would not miss a single chance to love people and save souls.

There were about 20 people in the same room with him. He was cheerful and approachable, and the other prisoners looked up to him as to a father. Because of his pleasant personality, a lot of the prisoners accepted the Lord.

Two years passed. Just before Jian was released, he was called in. They said to him, 'People usually change after they have been here. Now you have been here for two years, have you changed at all?'

Jian answered laughingly, 'Jesus lives in my heart; it doesn't matter how long I have been here, ten years or 20 years, I still will not change. If you kill me, Jesus will take me to heaven.' The man became very angry; he pointed his finger at Jian's nose and said, 'If I ever catch you again, I'll put you to death.' Then he yelled, 'Get out of here!' Jian left there joyfully.

Jian's family had suffered a lot of insults and persecutions because of the Lord. They always got less and the worst kind of grains. But the Bible tells us: *'Better the little that the righteous have than the wealth of the many wicked.'* The Word of God is true. There was a shortage of food; life was very difficult for everybody. But Jian's family had always had enough to eat. God was really merciful.

One spring, just three months before the harvest, Jian's family had only half a basket of dried sweet potatoes left. Normally, that would only last for two days. Jian took some to grind into flour and quite miraculously, there was an unending supply of sweet potatoes. Jian's whole family knelt down and praised the Lord with tears in their eyes.

One day, a believer in Jian's village came to him and said, 'Brother, we have six people in my family. We only have about 30 kilograms of corn left; it will only last us for about half a month. We still have three more months before the harvest. Do you know of anybody whom we can borrow money or cereal from?' Jian answered, 'Just keep trusting the Lord; He will help you!' So that believer went home. He took seven and a half kilograms of corn out every five days and ground them into powder. He kept doing that for three months and there was still 15 kilograms left!

Jian once went to Province 'M' to preach the Gospel there. During one of the meetings, a woman who was in her thirties came with her son in her arms. He was already dead. Jian laid his hands on him and shouted, 'In the Name of the Lord Jesus, I command you to rise up!' Immediately, the boy opened his eyes and rose.

At another time, Jian was conducting a baptismal service by the river in the same province. A teenage boy who was dumb since birth shouted 'Hallelujah! Praise the Lord!' as he came out of the water.

Once a brother surnamed Zhang was caught. The authorities summoned a lot of people to see him tortured. They wanted to use that as a deterrent to stop people from believing in Jesus. They hanged him upside down; they struck him and flogged him. He cried unto the Lord, 'Lord, Peter was hanged upside down for You, but I'm not worthy!'

When the other brothers and sisters saw that, they wept bitterly. Even some of the non-believers wept as well. However, those who persecuted the Christians most severely all had a very bitter end. There was an officer who used to be in the army. He hated the Christians. Once when Jian was arrested, he tied Jian up, put him on the floor, stepped on his back and kicked him. And he said, 'I'm not stepping on you, I'm stepping on your Lord; I'm not binding you, I'm binding your Lord. I'll see what your God can do to me!' Then he took Jian to parade in the street. He kept beating Jian while he was speaking, 'Where is your Lord? Why doesn't he come and deliver you? Why doesn't he come and compete with me?' All of a sudden, a rabid dog came out of a lane and bit his leg. Then his wound became festered and his stomach was swollen. Within two months he died a terrible death.

But there was revival in the surrounding villages. The Lord performed many wonders and miracles through Jian and added to their number daily those who were being saved.

The fire of the Gospel kept spreading and spreading ...

PART EIGHT

Maturing of the Seed Sown in Blood and Tears

Chapter 1
The Difficulty of Reaching China
(1807–1899)

China, spread over 9.6 million square kilometers of diverse terrain, holds a quarter of the world's population. Its vast territory abounds in natural wealth and it boasts one of the oldest civilizations. For hundreds of years, it has been like a magnet, drawing the hearts of many missionaries. But it has not been easy to bring the Gospel of Christ to China because of deep-rooted superstition, ancestor worship and idolatry. Besides, China has always been very closed to the outside world; most of her people are either anti-foreigners or they are afraid of foreigners. Christianity has always been considered the 'foreign devil's' religion.

In 1573, the Pope sent a team of 40 people to China. But the door to China stayed shut and they could not enter. Standing at the border they cried, 'Oh rock, oh rock, when will you open?'

In later years many faithful servants of God, having no concern for personal gain or loss and who were willing to make any sacrifice, brought the Gospel of Grace to China. They not only offered their property and time to the Chinese, but they even sacrificed their very lives. Theirs was a moving testimony of blood and tears. Their lives left an indelible legacy in the history of the Church in China.

The Nestorian Christians first came to China in the sixth century during the Tang dynasty. Christianity then gradually faded but re-emerged towards the end of the thirteenth century, during the Yuan dynasty.

In the fifteenth century, Matteo Ricci and others brought Catholicism to China.

In 1807, Robert Morrison landed on her shores; he was the first Protestant missionary to China. He toiled for seven years and saw only one person come to the Lord. After another seven years of hard work, another Chinese accepted the Lord. This second convert was Liang Fa of Canton who later became the first pastor of the Chinese Church.

Robert Morrison remained in China for altogether 27 years and in that period he led 10 people to the Lord. He finished translating both the Old and New Testaments into Chinese and compiled a dictionary. Although he only ministered in Canton and Macau in those 27 years, he had accomplished much. He laid down his life for the Lord and for the Chinese and he also laid the groundwork for future missionary work. In 1834, Robert Morrison completed his course and was taken to glory.

Sadly, it was to be only several years after his death that China finally opened up. Between 1842 and 1858, there were more than 200 missionaries from 20 different organizations working in China. However, they were confined to the five treaty ports only; the heart of China remained out of bounds.

In 1852, an Englishman, Hudson Taylor, ventured to China alone. He was determined to bring the Gospel to inland China. Later, he was to return to England to recruit 22 missionaries who went to China with him in 1866, and together they set up the China Inland Mission. They picked Hangzhou as their base and travelled as far as Jiangsu, Anhui, Jiangxi and other provinces to preach the Gospel. The fire of the Gospel spread to many cities and villages. Because of Taylor's diligence, many Chinese churches were established inland.

The testimony of an English missionary in Zhejiang Province

There was a young Englishman called Pastor Cao (this was his Chinese name; his original English name could not be traced) who was lame in the left leg. He had a great burden for China. In 1866, he went to city 'H' in Zhejiang province by himself. There he found a very superstitious people who worshipped ancestors and idols and who had never heard of the Lord Jesus

Christ. Neither had they seen a foreigner before. So when they saw Pastor Cao, they were very afraid; they thought he was a monster!

Pastor Cao wanted most of all to be with the people but everybody avoided him. It grieved him terribly. He soon came by a river. His thoughts turned towards his family, his home church and the brothers and sisters. Then he cried out to the Lord: 'When can I lead these ignorant people to You? O Lord, have mercy upon them!'

He sat on a rock by the river and began to pray. When the sun dropped below the horizon it took the warmth with it, leaving Pastor Cao shivering in the nippy evening air. He sought shelter in a building nearby. To his amazement, he found many people inside, most of them beggars. Cao spent the night with them.

In the morning, Cao was rudely awakened by garbage 'missiles' hurled by the beggars. Some of his 'bed mates' had turned vicious, so Cao had no choice but to leave.

'Lord, forgive them for they do not know You!' he prayed.

At that time, it seemed as if there was a burning fire shut up in his bones, and he could not hold it in (Jeremiah 20:9). He preached the Lord Jesus and gave out Gospel tracts in the streets everyday. He wept and asked the Lord to soften the hearts of these people.

At night, he returned to the same building to sleep with the beggars and hooligans. Whenever the beggars fell ill, Cao always bought food and medicine for them. Gradually, they began to accept him. However, when he began to share the Gospel with them, they would sneer at him.

'Where is your God? If He is a good God, why do you have to live here? Why doesn't He give you a nice house to live in?'

After some time, Cao left his companions and went to the villages. He thought the village people might be simpler and more open to the Gospel. When he arrived at a village, he caused quite a stir because the villagers had never seen a foreigner before. Cao began to sing. The people stopped whatever they were doing and listened. Then Cao began to preach the Gospel. Without warning, the children pelted him with stones. He fled to another village where he met with the same reception.

Cao really had a heart for the Lord and for the Chinese. He limped from one village to another, living in abandoned temples and pagodas. He laboured for the Lord unceasingly, preaching the Gospel of Christ. He bore shame and scorn and never gave up.

Three years went by; Cao had used up all his money and not even one person had come to the Lord. He was very dejected and decided to leave city 'H'. However, he was determined to return.

A real soldier of Christ will never turn back. Cao was not abandoning his vision. He was simply rallying his forces knowing in his heart that the Lord had given him the land already.

Years later, Cao returned with a wife and a lot of Bibles. The Lord gave him favour with the British Embassy in city 'H', which helped him to set up the city's first church.

Now there was a church and a pastor (Cao himself), but there was no sheep! Cao and his wife prayed earnestly every morning. Then Cao had a wonderful idea.

One Sunday morning, Cao met a water-carrier outside his church (in those days there was no running water and people had to buy water). He was carrying two buckets of water hanging from a pole balanced on his shoulders. Cao bought some water from him and invited him into the church. He poured him some tea, asking at the same time, 'How much do you earn a day?'

'50 cents,' the water-carrier replied.

'From now on, we'll buy water from you. You don't have to work on Sundays, just come to church and after that you may have lunch with us. And I'll pay you one yuan a day. How's that?'

The water-carrier later became the first convert and became a pillar of the church. The second convert was a firewood vendor. And then a barber.

That was how the church in city 'H' began. 'He who sows in tears shall reap in joy.' Cao was beginning to reap the harvest at last; his years of labour were not in vain.

After that, his church in England sent out a few more missionaries to city 'H' to assist Cao in the work.

The Lord was with them and the church grew very quickly and the fire of the Gospel spread to other counties. As a result, a church was being built in a village in county 'C' near city 'H'. A pastor and his wife were sent to work there and the Lord blessed their work tremendously.

One day, a man whose occupation was to castrate pigs, came to the village. His name was Aquan (pronounced Ah-Chuan) and he was a rather violent fellow. He had castrated a few pigs before he went to this pastor's house. Now, the pastor also kept pigs. When Aquan finished castrating the clergyman's pigs, the pastor gave him 30 cents, to which Aquan exclaimed, 'What? Only 30?'

'Well, that's the standard rate and that's what the others paid you, isn't it?'

'True, that's what I charged them. But because you're a foreigner, you have to pay 60.'

The pastor went into his room and locked the door behind him. Aquan followed him to the door. He heard the pastor praying inside, so he paused and listened.

The pastor was praying, 'Lord, have mercy upon Aquan. Forgive him his sins and cause him to accept Your love and be reconciled to You. Bless his family too.'

Aquan was very surprised and he banged on the door. The pastor opened it.

'I tried to bully you just now, yet you didn't ask your God to kill me. But you asked Him to bless me instead. Why? I don't understand,' Aquan demanded.

The pastor was greatly relieved. He then pleaded with Aquan, 'Uncle Aquan, our God is different. He is a God of love. Men only love those who love them. But our God loves all men and sinners, including you and me. He loves us so much that He even sent His only begotten Son to die on the cross for us, to save us from sin and death ...'

The pastor's words were like a two-edged sword piercing through Aquan's heart. Within an hour, he surrendered.

Aquan became a dedicated Christian and he prayed continually. This made his wife very angry. One day, while Aquan was praying on his knees, his wife took a hot iron rod and burned the soles of his feet. Aquan fainted and his wife thought he was dying. When he regained consciousness, he said to his wife, 'If you want me to be well, you have to confess your sins to the Lord.' Aquan then led her through the sinner's prayer and the Lord healed Aquan.

Later, Aquan felt called to full-time ministry. The power of the Holy Spirit came upon him, and signs and wonders followed him. He worked in the mountain districts in counties 'D' and 'E' and the Lord was with him. Even the sorcerers and monks turned to the Lord.

The Lord's work was prospering in counties 'C', 'D' and 'E'. And churches were built in different counties of city 'H'.

It is a general rule that where there is growth, there is persecution. The more the Church grows, the more severe the persecution.

Chapter 2

The Blood and Tears of the Saints
(1900–1966)

With the setting up of the China Inland Mission, the believers went through many periods of widespread persecution, the most severe of these being the Boxer Rebellion in 1900. The property of Christians were confiscated and many missionaries were killed.

In Taiyuan, Shanxi Province, 60 missionaries were killed in one afternoon, a four-year-old boy among them. In Jinzhou, Liaoning Province, 54 people were martyred. It was estimated that a total of 188 missionaries and 5,000 believers were killed. The land cried out with the tears and blood of the saints. Oh, when will the seed spring forth?

Although Pastor Cao escaped persecution because of the protection of the British Embassy, he died several years later.

In county 'C' there was a man called Elder Dai in his sixties. He loved the sheep more than his own life. When the bandits came, all the other believers ran for their lives except Elder Dai. The bandits took Elder Dai to a temple. Their leader commanded Elder Dai to kneel down. But he refused and said, 'I will not bow down to anybody or any idols except Jesus.'

The bandit chief then ordered him to be beaten. Elder Dai fainted. When he came to, the bandit chief offered, 'I'll release you only if you will bow to me and Buddha and deny Jesus.'

'You can do whatever you like but I will never deny Jesus,' was Elder Dai's answer.

The bandit chief took out his knife and, under the smiling gaze of Gwanyin, the Goddess of Mercy, cut off his head.

The Qing government incited the 'Boxers' to persecute the church and to murder missionaries and Chinese believers. This drew international criticism and indignation. Under pressure from western governments, the Chinese government was forced to put an end to the Boxer Rebellion.

Eventually, the dark clouds blew over and the sun shone again. The martyrs did not die in vain. The blood and tears of the saints soon bore fruit. In every generation and wherever the saints have shed their blood, revival often breaks out. This principle is oft repeated in the 2,000 years of church history!

Between the end of the Boxer Rebellion and 1911, about 5,000 missionaries flocked to China and God had also raised about 7,700 Chinese pastors and ministers. By then, there were about 607,000 believers and 2,900 churches. Praise the Lord for His mighty work!

The period 1911 to 1919 were the golden years for missionary work in China. Many internationally-known preachers from all over the world visited China. Rev. Ding Limei started the 'Chinese Students Dedication' Crusade in all the universities. There was also the 'China for the Lord' Crusade in 1918, calling upon Christians from all over the nation to preach the Gospel.

From 1919 to 1927, China developed as a nation, after which church growth began to slow down till the forties. In 1940, civil war broke out and it lasted ten years. But God had not forgotten China, He raised many faithful servants for Himself and the Church continued to grow.

Between 1950 and 1958, the Church in China went through a period of uncertainty, chaos and persecution. Although the new communist government guaranteed freedom of religion according to the new Constitution, in reality it was quite the opposite. All overseas missionaries were thrown out of the country. The revolutionary authorities started the 'Three-Self Patriotic Movement' and set up the so-called 'Three-Self Churches' (Self-governing, self-supporting, and self-propagating).

In order to curry favour with the new regime, many pastors, preachers and ministers began to accuse and attack one another (Matthew 24:10–12).

'We were deceived by the overseas missionaries,' they cried.

'What they taught was imperialism.'

'So-and-so is anti-revolutionary; so-and-so is a spy; he has attacked the Party ...'

Some even denied their faith and cursed Jesus publicly. These people were pastors and preachers who had preached the Gospel in Jesus' name and performed many miracles. It was really a tragedy that they had come to this!

Those who would not bow to the authorities and were faithful till death were classified as 'counter-revolutionaries' and 'secret agents.' They were duly deported to the remote northeast and northwest of China to be 'reformed through labour.' Many of the older servants of the Lord never returned. They died of cold and hunger.

There was a couple from Shanghai who were both university graduates. The husband's name was John, and he and his wife were on fire for the Lord. They went to Xinjiang Province in the northwest to preach the gospel. And because they refused to join the 'Three-Self Church', they were 'struggled against' day and night. John and his wife were both put in prison where his wife eventually died.

He was so grieved over his wife's death that he lost his will to live. But the Lord comforted him with 2 Corinthians 4:16–18. John was released in 1984; he was over 70 years old then.

Other servants of the Lord were sent to the villages in their own home districts to do hard labour. There was no exception; they were also 'struggled against' all the time.

But the traitors of the faith donned their masks and emerged as leaders of the church. They called themselves pastors and teachers but they were not.

Sunday worship became a ritual. Instead of teaching from the Bible, they taught from 'Tien Feng' (Heavenly Wind) which was the publication of the official church. As a result, fewer and fewer people attended church. In 1958, they sold the churches to the government and the government turned them into factories, warehouses and canteens.

By now, all the churches in China had been closed. You could no longer hear people preaching the Gospel or praising God openly and this went on until 1966. The atheistic government thought that the Church in China had died. They did not know that God had kept for Himself His faithful servants who had not bowed to Baal (1 Kings 19:18). These servants of the Lord fasted and prayed day and night for the Church.

Jesus did not shed His blood in vain; the foreign missionaries did not shed their blood in vain; neither did the saints in China shed their blood in vain. The seed they sowed would certainly spring forth one day! Even before the Cultural Revolution got into full swing, many believers had already set up home meetings. In 1966, the unprecedented Cultural Revolution was unleashed. It was to cause untold damage both politically and financially. The Chinese people suffered terribly at the hands of the 'Gang of Four.'

Ever since the 'liberation' of China in 1949, every political purge or movement meant persecution for the Church. Ten years of the Cultural Revolution could be said to be China's, and the Church's, darkest hour. The Red Guards unleashed by Chairman Mao went on a rampage throughout the nation, ransacking homes and stamping out all superstitious and old ideas. Believers' homes were especially not spared. The young guards burned all their Bibles and Christian literature. They interrogated the Christians, beat them up and forced them to deny their faith. Then they put tall hats on them and paraded them through the streets to be 'struggled against.'

Those from the Three-Self Patriotic Movement Committee did not get off scott-free either. They received similar treatment but the difference was they would deny their faith immediately.

To please Chairman Mao, the Gang of Four passed an edict requiring everyone to bow to the Chairman's image. This was Satan's tool against the Christians. Many of the saints lost their homes and even their lives simply because they would not bow to Mao.

There was a brother from Shanghai called Liu who was a scientist. He was beaten and 'struggled against' everyday for refusing to bow to the chairman's picture. When Brother Liu could not bear it any more he ran away, with the authorities in hot pursuit.

A brother in city 'X' received brother Liu into his home and was sentenced to more than ten years imprisonment. Another servant of the Lord was given a 20-year term in prison also for receiving him. An old brother, also from city 'X' was arrested by the Public Security Bureau (PSB) and interrogated for the same 'crime.' When he refused to divulge the whereabouts of Brother Liu, he was tortured to death. When Brother Liu was finally caught, he persevered till the end and did not yield. He was martyred.

At that time, the man who was plotting to take over the government, Marshal Lin Biao, was very pleased; he thought the whole of China had at last become 'red' and the Christians had been eliminated. But the Chinese Church was just like a ball, the harder you hit it, the higher it bounces. It was like a volcano about to erupt, and nothing could stand in its way!

Chapter 3

The Flaming Torch (1976–1983)

It was 1967 and the Cultural Revolution had just begun. The following story was set in a small mountain village named 'Lishan.' The cluster of a little more than 100 households nestled in the valley, 20 kilometers from the site where Daibuo was martyred. Every Friday evening, the sound of weeping and prayers could be heard from the upper room of a house deep in the bamboo forest. There, five brothers and sisters from several other small villages in that area gathered together.

Among them were two brothers who had recently been called to the ministry. They were greatly burdened that the atheistic rulers in China had tried to eliminate the Church by persecution, reducing it to a remnant. They shared the same vision and burden and the Spirit of the Lord had brought them together. They determined they would meet in this place every Friday to pray and fast for the nation, the one billion lost souls and the Church. Regardless of the circumstances, or how busy they were on the farm or the weather, not one of them ever missed this meeting.

In different cities and districts, God raised His army of prayer warriors. They faithfully prayed unceasingly, fervently, with great intensity and in one spirit. After several months the fires of the Holy Spirit began to burn in each district. In 'H' city, the Holy Spirit came down upon a group of intercessors and filled them, and they began to speak in tongues, praising God.

Soon, the tiny upper room in which the five had their prayer meetings was no longer adequate as they were joined by more and more intercessors. The Lord worked through this group of people mightily and many were the miracles and signs and wonders as they preached in the neighbouring villages. Many sick people were also healed.

There was a small child who had smallpox in Lishan Village and his life hung in the balance. The doctor simply took one look at the boy, who was barely breathing, and shook his head hopelessly.

'There is nothing I can do ...'

Then he just walked away.

However, a young believer got up, laid his hands on the child and the boy immediately got up and began to play!

There were only a handful of Christians in this village at first. But eventually all the villagers believed in Jesus. After that, nobody was interested in taking part in commune plays or other entertainment. On the hillsides, the shepherd boys sang and danced before the Lord. In the fields, the labourers praised God aloud as they worked. The village women who usually gathered by the stream to do their laundry ceased arguing and sang from the depths of their hearts. The whole village was full of the harmony of praise. It truly was as if 'the angels were singing with men and the harmony of heaven prevailed.' Superstition, evil spirits and sin in the village soon became a thing of the past.

The number of believers increased by leaps and bounds, as neighbouring villages turned to Jesus. Before long, there were more than 300 Christians and they quickly outgrew the meeting place. So from one meeting place the believers split into two then three, four, five meeting points. The Holy Spirit swept throughout 'C' district and 'H' city and soon revival broke out also in the other districts.

Persecution in Lishan Village

Before long, a wave of persecution began. The commune authorities, seeing the numbers of believers increase daily, were alarmed and did not know what to do. They commanded the brigade secretary of Lishan village to put a stop to all the activities of the church. For several consecutive week's the brigade secretary would go to the meetings to break up the gathering by force.

How could the brothers and sisters ever agree to stop meeting together? The secretary was so furious that he smashed to pieces all the stools, tables, and windows as well as beat up the believers with his fists. But the Christians ignored him and continued to sing and pray.

Several times, the cadres from the commune accompanied the secretary on these missions. But the amazing thing was that instead of suppressing the Christians' activities, they only served to incite the believers to become more fervent and zealous! Therefore, the number of believers increased even more!

The village authorities were rather helpless. All they could do was to report to the commune authorities and request them to send reinforcements to help suppress the Christians. The county government, therefore, whipped together a group of several dozen workers and sent them to the Lishan village commune. First, they sent a threatening letter to the church there. It said, 'If you gather again for a meeting this Sunday, you are truly good Chinese.'

On Friday evening, a brother read the letter out loud before the fellowship of believers. Then in a low but firm voice he said, 'Brothers and sisters, it is possible the Work Unit will come this Sunday. Should we stop meeting?'

Everyone responded without hesitation and in unison, 'We cannot cease meeting.'

Several believers stood up and said, 'If we don't allow ourselves to be refined in these small storms, then how will we stand when great persecution comes?'

These brethren then led everyone in praise and prayer. They were all filled and encouraged in faith. The meeting continued until the early morning hours.

On Sunday, the brothers and sisters made their way to the meeting place, getting there earlier than usual. There was already a very large crowd and every inch of the house and the courtyard were crammed with people. Some four hundred and fifty people sang and prayed in one accord, their voices rising up to the clouds as they praised and worshipped for more than two hours.

After several hours of preaching, a lad of about seven or eight years old ran frantically through the crowd, his head drenched with sweat. He shoved his way to the preacher and tugged urgently on his coat. He ran so hard that he lost his shoes, injured his toe and now blood was oozing out.

He shouted frenziedly, 'Papa, run quickly! The People's militia are coming ...'

Three young co-workers shot up from their seats and comforted the crowd. 'Brothers and sisters, be not afraid, for the Lord is in our midst. Let us first praise Him!'

Then they all stood up and sang, 'Oh Lord who sits in the heavens, I lift my eyes up to you ...'

The Work Unit cadres looked smug, having brought with them a large group of the People's militia armed with guns and real bullets. They immediately surrounded the meeting place. The brothers and sisters, however, were not afraid but continued to sing with even greater fervency. The shouts and curses of the soldiers were completely drowned out by their singing.

Now, we do not know if it was due to anger or fear, but the armed men turned pale. Under the command of their supervisor, a group of them rushed to the platform and tied up three of the brethren. Then they beat a hasty retreat.

The believers wept as the three brothers were taken away to the commune offices where a crowd had gathered at the gate. Their captors shaved their heads and painted a red cross on top. They also used red, blue and black ink to paint their faces and then forced them to sit on the edge of a bucket filled with human faeces.

The crowd of onlookers were entertained by the spectacle, and they clapped their hands and laughed scornfully, 'Ha, ha! These are the leaders of the Jesus followers. Where is your God? Why doesn't He come to save you?'

Some simply shook their heads and sighed, 'How pitiful, how could these three young men be harmed by superstition to such a degree?'

Others hurled stones and orange peel, or spat on them. There were some, though, who commented, 'They are a good example. I truly admire their courage as they hold steadfast to their faith. It is evident there is a God, otherwise how could they gladly suffer reproach like this!'

At night, they were put in a small room and for three days they were not allowed to eat or drink water. Many of the believers brought food and fruit when they visited them, but they were driven away by the soldiers. After three days, the Work Unit prepared a meal for them. When the three brothers had received their bowls of rice, one of the cadres glared at them and said, 'This evening let's see if you have the nerve to pray for your meal before me. If so, I will know you are true Christians.'

When the first brother held up his rice bowl with both hands to give thanks, he was slapped with such force that it knocked him to the ground and his rice spilled all over him. All eyes were then glued to the other two believers.

The second brother also lifted his rice bowl without hesitancy, to say grace. Suddenly, he was struck on the chest with a fist. Everything went black as he slumped on the table.

'Lord, help me to glorify you,' was the third brother's cry. He took up his bowl unflinchingly and prayed out loud.

The men from the local work brigade were furious and one of them prepared to pour hot water from the thermos flask on the table on that brother's head. The commune secretary intervened, however, and said, 'If you do this it will result in a loss of life. These three men are hard workers in the brigade, only they are too superstitious and too stubborn.'

The following week, there was no decline in the numbers meeting in Lishan village. The Work Unit, with the aid of the People's militia, arrested three more brethren. And the week after, they arrested several believers. But this did not put out the fires of the Gospel. On the contrary, it burned all the more and spread quickly to 'C' district.

This alarmed the Work Unit but it was helpless to do anything. The Unit comprised cadres from several government units in that county. They include the Public Security Bureau, the United Front Department, Transportation Bureau and Taxation Bureau.

At first, they were confident that they could solve this 'problem' of the local church. They had thought that it would be very simple operation and that they could achieve their objectives within a week. In two months, however, not only

301

did they fail to suppress the church, but they contributed to church growth!

In the end, they devised a method in which they moved to Lishan village to visit each family and break them up with Marxist propaganda. But on entering the village, they heard the sound of singing everywhere. When they got down to work, many children would follow them closely, singing songs of praise. No amount of scolding or threats could stop them. They continued singing boldly without ceasing. The communists were so frustrated they did not know whether to laugh or to cry. Their plans thwarted, they had no choice but to leave the village.

Persecution spreads throughout the province

The authorities issued similar notices to another village in 'C' district ordering them to stop their meetings, but the believers refused to comply. One Sunday morning, while the Christians were praying, the commune cadres arrived with the People's militia. The armed soldiers fired several shots into the air before rushing into the meeting place.

They tied up the sister who was leading prayer. But another sister would stand up to lead the believers in prayer, and they would arrest her as well. But more sisters would take the lead until the soldiers had them all bound one by one. The sisters were then taken to the commune where they were meted different punishment.

The old 'aunty' of the family hosting the prayer meeting was forced to kneel on a heap of broken ceramic tiles with a bamboo pole placed on the back of her legs. Two men would then stand on each end of the pole. It was too much for the old lady, who soon passed out.

The next day, old 'aunty' sent back a message through the believer who brought her food that the meetings must go on, regardless of what had happened.

In another case, a young brother was about to graduate from a teacher's college, but the night before his graduation he was found preaching in a meeting. He was duly expelled. When he returned home he was arrested, cruelly beaten and suspended from the ceiling of the bathroom for the entire night.

Prayer causes an earthquake

In the fall of 1973, the church in Lishan had a baptismal service. There was a large number who were to receive baptism. The brethren, realising that such a gathering was not like their usual meetings, was acutely aware of the need to be cautious lest the authorities find out about it and came to break it up. Therefore, they notified the baptismal candidates to gather in Lishan village at different places after dark to rest and they would begin the meeting and baptism at midnight.

Now, the commune authorities got wind of this baptism service and had already organized several dozen people to hide in a house behind the meeting place. They had prepared a lot of animal manure which they would begin to dump into the small stream upstream from where the baptism was to be held, once the Christians began their meeting. They had also prepared a store of stones to throw at the believers.

But the brethren knew of their plan, and they immediately rounded up the co-workers and brethren who had a real burden for the church to kneel and pray fervently unto the Lord.

'Lord, have you not been given all power in heaven and earth? You blinded the eyes of those wicked people in Sodom. Lord, we ask you today to use your unlimited power to perform miracles and deliver us.'

As they were praying, the power of the Lord came upon them and they were all filled with the Holy Spirit, speaking in tongues and praising the greatness of God. All the believers felt that they should immediately begin the service so they started singing and praising God. There were about 400 to 500 people gathered there, and they sang with much exuberance, making a joyful sound that could be heard everywhere.

The Holy Spirit fell as the latter rain, they were all filled with the Holy Spirit and everyone felt as if they were on the mountains and in the clouds! They were before the very throne of the Lord worshipping Him face to face. It was truly heaven on earth!

'Be faithful, be faithful, proclaim this message everywhere; be faithful in that which has been committed to you, be faithful to your glorious King ...'

The brothers and sisters sang this majestic battle song over and over. Suddenly, the place began to shake and dust began to fall from the ceiling. Then the houses in the village all began to rattle and even the hills rumbled and shook.

Several sisters were in their homes washing bowls when they felt the ground beneath them shake. Windows and doors shuddered and crockery rattled. Their hearts also shook! They immediately sped to the meeting place where they 'ascended to the mountains and entered the clouds' in worship.

The worship went on for another two hours. Then a brother was asked to speak, but he declined saying, 'I have believed in the Lord for more than 50 years, but never have I seen a meeting like this. How can I stand up to speak?'

Finally, a local brother was moved to speak for over 40 minutes and then he led the crowd to a deep pool beside a small stream where 78 brothers and sisters were baptized.

What about the 90 workers hired by the authorities to break up this baptismal service? When they heard the sound of singing that shook heaven and earth and which reverberated throughout the whole village, shaking the very ground they were standing on, they took off in fright! How amazing! What a wonderful work of God!

A dying woman is instantly healed

There was a village in a certain district in Zhejiang Province where there was not one Christian. A woman who had an incurable disease after giving birth to a child was on the brink of death. When the doctor came and examined her, his diagnosis was, 'She will die immediately.' So he forced her family to move her to a room where they keep the dead. However, as she lay dying, she came to and called out, 'Jesus save me!' Not long after, this woman was completely healed. This miracle shook the neighbouring villages.

God heals an old man

In another house lay an old man who for years suffered a serious leg infection, scorned even by his family and all the villagers. Blood dripped continually from the open sores, which itched and were very painful. He was unable to rest day or night. Not only did other people avoid him, but his own children wished he would die.

When he heard the testimony of the dying woman, he was so moved that he didn't sleep a wink all night. The next morning, he begged his two nephews to take him to the woman's house.

With tears in his eyes he said to her, 'Auntie, I heard that as you were about to die, a doctor named Jesus came to bring you back to life. Where is this doctor now? Please call him to heal this pitiful man!'

The woman laughed and said, 'Jesus is not a doctor who carries a medicine box, and I can't really tell you much about him. I only know that when I called out his name, I was healed! Today I can call on the name of Jesus!'

She then cried out, 'Jesus, you saved me in the past. Now I ask you to come immediately and have pity on this old man!'

After crying out thus several times, the bleeding from the sores stopped. Within two days, he was completely healed. As a result, many people came to know that Jesus could heal the sick and cast out demons, and that when they called out, 'Jesus, save me!' their diseases would disappear.

However, they regarded the name of Jesus as a secret to be shared with only relatives and close friends. Even so, the name of Jesus was eventually proclaimed in every district and the neighbouring provinces.

A drowned child comes to life

One day, one of the believers' four-year-old son drowned in a river. The brethren recovered the body and laid it in the middle room of his house. Then they all knelt down and prayed with authority.

'Jesus, save this child! We have seen you heal so many sick people and we deeply believe you can bring this dead child back to life.'

They did not have much understanding of the Word of God but they simply trusted in the miraculous power of the Lord. They cried out to the Lord on their knees.

Suddenly, a witch who lived nearby shrieked: 'Your Jesus has come! Quickly, come and see!'

The roomful of believers immediately opened wide their eyes and saw the child sitting up, but they did not see Jesus.

Then the witch said to them, 'When you shouted loudly "Jesus," a man whose whole body shone brightly, dressed in light, with a face of great love came in. He placed his hand on the child's head, and the child got up.

'Your Jesus is truly amazing. He is in fact the true God, the living God. From today I renounce my previous beliefs and I now believe in your Jesus.'

She then asked several brothers and sisters to go with her to her house to destroy her idols, incense altar and all the artifacts used in her superstitious worship.

Persecution and revival

Between 1955 and 1975, great persecution came to the Church in China. During the first six months of 1976, Wang Hongwen (the leader of the Gang of Four) ordered a large group of Christians to be killed. But by the time this document reached the local county government, the Gang of Four had already fallen from power. From that time to 1980, persecution of the church eased.

Many servants of God who had been imprisoned for up to 20 years were released. Great revival came to several of China's provinces. The churches near city 'H' in Zhejiang province began to prosper greatly. The leaders of more than ten counties met regularly four times a year. They would share information about the work of the Holy Spirit and plan how to preach the Gospel in other unreached fields. The churches were thus greatly encouraged.

In 1980, the Three-Self Patriotic Movement Committee was revived once again. Those whom the true believers considered 'demons, monsters, false teachers and traitors' were used by the communist government. These men were placed in positions in the official church as chairman, secretary, pastors and teachers of the Three-Self Patriotic Movement Committee. The church was forced to follow their leadership.

There was a group of believers who had been baptized in the Holy Spirit and had even suffered for the Lord. They knew that this movement was imposed on them by the government. However, due to fear of the absolute power of the Three-Self Church and other reasons, they joined it. Some even taught in the government-controlled Bible seminaries. The government's strategy was to control the seminaries and thereby destroy the Church.

The Three-Self Patriotic Committee of every province and county published regulations entitled 'Ten Prohibitions, Eight Prohibitions or Fifteen Prohibitions'. The following are some of these prohibitions:

1. It is prohibited to preach outside the Three-Self Church.
2. Believers are forbidden to use fasting, prayer, healing the sick and casting out demons to draw new converts.
3. Do not fellowship with other TSPM church workers. Approval must be given by the official TSPM committee before workers can be recruited.
4. No person under the age of eighteen is allowed to join the church.
5. No one is allowed to receive water baptism without TSPM approval.
6. The gifts of the Holy Spirit are not allowed to be operated in meetings.
7. It is prohibited to preach on the Book of Revelation, Daniel, Matthew 24 and the coming of Christ.
8. No private Bible study meetings are allowed.

It was sad that so many churches that sprang up during the Cultural Revolution eventually came under the control of the Three-Self Church. Many believers and co-workers who did not understand the truth thought that the days of persecution had ended. During the years of darkness and storm, they had yearned for a free and peaceful environment. However, little did they realize that this 'free environment' would be much worse than the cruel persecutions of the past.

Thank God that He raised up a faithful remnant to be his witnesses in every dark generation. The Lord calls them 'stars on a dark night' and 'light for the traveller.'

God raised up a group of strong, brave brothers in each place who exposed the false teachers and the true motives of the Three-Self Patriotic Movement. Thus, the brothers and sisters understood better. They left the Three-Self Church and established many home fellowships. Although they lacked theological knowledge, they had great power. The work of the Gospel prospered and the number of believers continually increased.

These false teachers were greatly disturbed. They realised that their threats and promises were ineffective, so they reported to their superiors asking for help. They were determined to destroy the Lord's servants so that they would never rise again.

From 1983, constant persecution came from the government. The authorities wanted to force the 'underground' churches (house churches) to become visible churches (Three-Self churches) so that they could have total control.

A group of men from the TSPM church in 'X' county declared, 'Resolutely demand the People's Government severely punish those opposed to the Three-Self.'

There were many believers in 'X' county. None of the homes were large enough for their meetings. So the believers collected an offering and built a church, each person contributing in the construction. As the building neared completion, they forgot their hard labour and their hearts leapt with joy.

Then an unexpected thing happened. The chairman of the Three-Self Patriotic Committee, who betrayed the Lord, arrived with a group of unbelievers to destroy the church building. When a 70-year-old man, who had given his life savings and worked hard on the construction of the church, saw it being destroyed, he was heartbroken. He stood on the side and wept.

The TSPM chairman spotted the old brother and promptly reported him to the Public Security officials who grabbed him and broke his arms. He passed out from the pain and collapsed on the ground.

The authorities set up 'learning classes' in many places and forced those who were not willing to attend the 'Three-Self', to attend these classes. In many cases, they accused faithful servants of the Lord of being members of the 'Yellers Sect' and duly arrested them.

However, this was like pouring oil on fire, for it caused house churches to spring up everywhere and nothing could stop this explosion. A large group of preachers rose to the need. The charismatic movement spread in many parts of China and the ministry of preaching the Gospel was accelerated. The Gospel began to flow throughout China like a torrential river.

Chapter 4

The Gospel Torrent (1983–1991)

1. The Prelude to the Gospel Torrent

The work of the Gospel up till then could be compared to a small but intense fire. The enemy tried to put it out but his plans backfired. Instead, the revival flame spread like wildfire, fanned by a zeal that was impossible to extinguish.

Thus, the Gospel penetrated several inland provinces like Anhui and Henan, where the number of believers in many counties surpassed 100,000. Very few believers, particularly those in Henan province, were deceived by the Three-Self.

In 1983, in 'X' district of Henan Province, the authorities executed two believers, sentenced one to a life term, and gave several dozen other Christians long prison sentences.

Dark clouds hovered over Henan. Sorrow, grief and pain filled the hearts of the believers. The main co-workers were in prison and the remainder travelled all day and all night to visit and strengthen the sheep. With tears they prayed, 'Lord, in order to bring revival to the Henan churches we are willing to be executed under 'XX' bridge (the local execution ground).'

Some knelt on the snow-covered ground and cried out to the Lord while others sat on their bicycles, weeping and praying till they fell off.

What became of those brothers and sisters who were thrown into prison? Injustice was evident everywhere in that kind of environment and God's children cried out to the Lord. There was much weeping and mourning. The saints paid dearly with their lives. But God is not deaf, neither are His arms shortened.

God shook the prisons and worked mightily through His

beloved children who were imprisoned. In one women's prison, one-third of the thousand over inmates accepted the Lord and every single prisoner heard about Jesus.

In Henan, a large group of young believers dedicated their lives to serving Him. They were all willing to sacrifice for the Lord. This brought a fresh wave of revival.

Before the dozen or so brothers and sisters set out to preach the Gospel they knelt down to pray.

'Lord, we don't ask you to bring us home in peace, but to bring us home in chains so that we can share in your suffering,' was the fervent cry from their hearts.

After a time in the ministry, they did in fact return home in chains as they were taken in by the local PSB.

Although there were many believers in Henan and Anhui, these had not yet been baptised in the Holy Spirit and had a limited knowledge of the Bible. They lacked power and were not satisfied with the fruits of their spiritual labour.

At the end of 1985, a pastor went to Henan to conduct a meeting for co-workers from several dozen districts. He taught on the baptism of the Holy Spirit and urged them to seek after this experience with one heart. But contrary to his expectations, the Christians shrank back as most of the co-workers had previously seen those so-called 'spirit-filled' believers demonstrate strange manifestations. They were afraid they would be filled with evil spirits. One by one, they left the meeting and that pastor returned home deeply disappointed.

In the winter of 1987, a splinter group broke away from the preachers. This split initially hindered their outreach ministry, but Romans 8:28 says, *'all things work together for good to those who love God, to those who are called according to His purpose.'*

For after they left, the hindrances to the work of the Holy Spirit was also removed, as this group was adamantly against the baptism of the Spirit. This prepared the way for the work of the Holy Spirit.

In July, 1988, a pastor who had a great burden for China and who loved the Chinese with his whole heart came to Henan. He fervently preached to the co-workers the message of the filling of the Holy Spirit and some of the workers opened their hearts. They experienced a heavenly outpouring.

Three months later, this pastor once again returned to the area. This time he emphasized to the co-workers, 'If you are to complete the work the Lord has given you, you must absolutely receive the power of the Holy Spirit.'

The Lord melted their hearts and seventy percent of them were baptized in the Holy Spirit!

This pastor had an intense love for the Lord and the Chinese. For the sake of the work of the Gospel in China and the hundreds of millions of lost souls, and in spite of many dangers, this pastor made repeated trips to inland China to lead them to seek after the baptism of the Holy Spirit.

By the end of 1989, more than eighty percent of the co-workers and believers had been filled with the Spirit and all spoke in tongues! Thus was the foundation laid for the extensive evangelical work that was soon to begin.

This pastor also led the Henan churches into true worship and praise. This was a revolutionary change from the traditional, dead, formal, silent type of worship.

He travelled to the backward rural areas of Anhui, Shaanxi, Sichuan and several southeastern provinces to take the torch of the Holy Spirit throughout China and lead the Chinese churches into a new realm of praise and worship. Not only did he dedicate himself wholly to the Gospel work in China, but he also offered his son and daughter to the Lord.

He would consistently fast forty days or longer for the sake of the church in China and the one billion lost souls. While on such fasts he still continued to bring in large bags full of Bibles and teaching materials and would persistently preach the Gospel.

During one co-workers' meeting, he told the brethren enthusiastically, 'I am not only willing to offer my body, time and family for the ministry in China, I am prepared to be a martyr for the Lord in China.'

In the winter of 1990, he was led to minister in northwest China. He had heard about the persecution in Sichuan but he planned to visit the brethren anyway. Other co-workers urged him not to go, lest he would be arrested.

But he said joyfully, 'The Lord said I had to be prepared to die for Him. It would be a privilege if I could shed my blood or suffer in the most populous province of China.'

The co-workers all wept silently.

His were not empty words, for during more than ten years of labour his love and works proved he had such a heart. He continues to earnestly cultivate the field and today sees the fruit of years of hard labour.

2. Missionaries from Zhejiang

The church in Zhejiang was catching up. Since the establishment of the Three-Self Church, the church in 'C' county had gone through all kinds of trials. There was persecution on the outside and division on the inside. Like the church in Henan, a small group of people broke away from them. Although it was a painful experience, nevertheless the church was cleansed and it helped to prepare the way for future missionary work.

In 1986, when it was relatively easy to make money because of the open door policy, a group of brothers left their homes instead and went to the mission field, as far as Inner Mongolia, Ningxia, Yunnan and Shanxi.

The church in 'C' county strongly emphasized prayer. Each time they planned a missionary trip they would hold all-night prayer meetings and morning prayer meetings before setting out.

In the winter of 1987, several brothers went to the rural areas of Shanxi to preach the Gospel. The Lord was with them and signs and wonders followed them. They led many to the Lord and planted a church there.

When it came time for the brothers to leave for other counties, it began to snow heavily. More than 30 brothers and sisters climbed the snow-covered mountains to escort them to the railway station. They gathered around the brothers and wept.

'Brothers, please don't leave us! Stay with us and shepherd us,' they pleaded desperately.

The younger ones added, 'Uncles, if you leave us now, who is going to take care of us?'

'Uncles, when are you coming back to see us again?'

But before they could finish speaking, the tears started to flow and they were unable to continue.

When the other train passengers saw them, they were very touched and they commented, 'I have never seen people so close like you, you must be blood brothers and sisters!'

Then, turning to the preachers, they added, 'Since your family wants you to stay, why don't you stay?'

However, the brothers boarded the train, and the other believers clung to them tightly. When the train began to move, the brothers and sisters ran after it; the preachers on board leaned out of the train windows and kept waving till they lost sight of them.

In the carriage, the missionaries were weeping. They said to the Lord, 'Lord, there are many young lambs that need a shepherd. Raise up people after Your own heart to do this.' The Lord had prepared the hearts of the people, now we just need workers to sow and water the young seedlings.

Between 1987 and 1990, the main theme for the annual conference for co-workers in 'C' county was: 'Reach out and Preach the Gospel'. Therefore, at the beginning of every year, groups of co-workers were sent out to other provinces to plant churches.

As it was written: *'Those who sow in tears will reap with songs of joy. He who goes out weeping, carrying seeds to sow, will return with songs of joy, carrying sheaves with him.'* (Psalm 126:5–6)

These were uneducated, unlearned people; some of them had only been to school for one or two years. At the beginning, they could not even speak fluent Mandarin. But they had a fervent heart; wherever they went, they led many to the Lord.

(a) The Blooming Fujian Church

Before 1987, all the churches in Fujian were under the control of the Three-Self. There were very few believers in the north of Fujian and they were scattered all over. They were just like sheep without a shepherd.

In the spring of the following year, the church in 'C' county sent some workers to the north of Fujian. They climbed mountains and crossed rivers, looking for lost sheep, beseeching people to repent. The Lord performed many miracles through them and as a result, more than 20 meeting points were set up.

There was a Three-Self church in 'E' county in the north of Fujian. The pastors there smoked and drank wine, and cared little for the believers. They never visited the brethren neither were they willing to go to the villages or mountains.

When they heard that co-workers from 'C' county had arrived in their area to do Gospel work, they promptly reported to the authorities and asked them to stop these evangelists. So a group of government men were sent to help the pastors from the Three-Self-Church.

Together, they clamped down on home meetings. If the believers wanted to get together, they had to go to the Three-Self church in the city.

Now, most of the true believers lived in rural areas which were between ten and 100 kilometers from the city. Moreover, public transportation was scarce. To tell the Christians to go to the city was just like telling them not to believe in Jesus.

Not only did the authorities stop the home meetings by force, but they also arrested some of the home church leaders. In spite of this, the believers boldly continued to meet in their homes and the 'underground' church thus prospered beyond measure.

In a city in 'E' County, God raised a sister called Zhi, who was originally from 'C' county. She started a meeting in her home with only ten to 20 people. Sister Zhi was, however, very faithful to the Lord and she bore good testimony before the people. She was just like a light shining in the darkness and there was power emanating from her.

Before long, therefore, the number of believers increased greatly and many sick people were healed after she prayed for them. Eventually, even those from the Three-Self Church came to her meetings. Soon the church grew to such a point that she had to break it up into three house groups. Later, their Gospel work extended to the countryside.

In December, 1990, Sister Zhi returned to her home county in Zhejiang to attend the annual conference for co-workers. She was astonished to see the mighty work of the Holy Spirit and how freely the believers praised and worshipped God. She, too, received power from on high and later stirred up the ministry in 'E' county.

For several years, the church in 'C' county faithfully sent co-workers to the north of Fujian; labourers were also sent out to five other counties. God raised strong leaders in each province and the Church grew very quickly.

When the pastors from the Three-Self Churches in all the provinces of north Fujian saw how the house churches were prospering, while theirs were getting weaker and weaker, they were very jealous and they would continually report to the authorities.

In the spring of 1990, the authorities accused the Christians of being 'counter-revolutionary shouters' and more than 30 believers in every province were arrested. The officials vowed to execute two sisters because they had 'prayed people to death' (actually they did not have any evidence), while five of the key brothers were put in prison.

When the five men were thrown into cell number eight, their fellow inmates set upon them and beat them up good. The ruffians continually bullied them every day.

One of the five was Brother Yin. He had not received his call for very long, yet he was very faithful, having shown strong leadership while he was in north Fujian. He was interrogated several times and he was beaten the most.

During one of these interrogations, he was accused of all sorts of things, which his interrogator practically spit out in his face.

'Who are your contacts in Taiwan?'

'How much do you get for shouting?'

'What are the names of those from 'C' county in Zhejiang?'

'How many times have they been here?'

Brother Yin did not flinch. He was not afraid but answered boldly, 'No! I will not tell you anything! Absolutely not!'

His interrogator was furious and turned to his assistants. 'Beat him up until he tells us what we want to know.'

As they were beating him, Brother Yin passed out several times. When he came to, he felt pain throughout his body and could only grit his teeth and endure it.

His concern turned to the Church that had just begun to rise up. How would those little lambs stand in this persecution?

He struggled to his feet and grabbed hold of the prison bars.

'Lord, the shepherd has been smitten. What will the sheep do? Help the brothers and sisters to stand steadfast and I am even willing to die for you here,' he prayed out loud.

The next day, he was taken out for the trial. The judge looked him in the eye and said with contempt and hostility, 'The policy of the Party is to treat those who confess with leniency and to punish those who resist. Today is your last chance.'

Then he struck the table with his fist and said, 'You will be beaten to death.'

Upon hearing his sentence, Brother Yin calmly removed his shirt to show his already battered body and then said, 'I have nothing to confess. There is not much left of this body. Come with your electric cattle prods and bayonets.'

The judge ordered the guards to take Brother Yin back to his cell. Eventually, the PSB had to release him after six months for lack of evidence. The two sisters who were sentenced to death were also released.

Freed, Brother Yin and Sister Zhi from 'E' county, together with a dozen co-workers from north Fujian Province, attended a co-workers' meeting in 'C' county in Zhejiang Province. There was a mighty outpouring of the Holy Spirit and they returned to their home counties to conduct revival meetings.

This happened during the Chinese New Year. Most of the believers were baptized in the Holy Spirit and praise and worship reached a new level.

(b) The Rising Church in North Zhejiang Province

There were previously few believers in a certain county in north Zhejiang Province. But during the past few years the Lord moved in a mighty way and raised up many young people with evangelistic gifts and they have taken the Gospel to neighbouring provinces.

In the winter of 1989, an idol was dedicated on a high mountain in Anhui Province and countless numbers of people came to participate in the ritual. After seeking the Lord fervently about this, the churches in north Zhejiang sent several dozen co-workers to Anhui. They spread out over the area like a net to reach these ignorant people.

The preachers lined every road leading to the idol, standing under trees and beside the food vendors' stalls and in front of the temples and shrines, preaching the Gospel to those who passed by.

They employed every tactic they could think of to grab the attention of the people. The young sisters sang beautiful, moving songs while the young brothers invited the travel-weary people to sit down and rest. Others gave them illustrated Gospel tracts while some of the brothers played music on their harmonicas.

Masses of people thus gathered on the mountain peak and at the foothills. The Christians preached with great fervency and with tears urged them to separate themselves from the vanity of the world and to turn to God.

'Those who believe in Jesus can be set free and have eternal life, the sick will be healed ...' they proclaimed.

A great shaking took place just then on the mountain and its surroundings. Many repented and believed in Jesus. The crowd then stomped on the incense and joss sticks they had brought for the idols.

Just as the devil was looking forward to all these people coming to worship him, he suddenly lost their adulation. How could he accept this?

Angered, several of the leaders of this idol worshipping cult reported to the PSB. Now, there was no lack of PSB officers on that day, for they knew there would be a dedication service in which thousands would attend so the PSB were out in force to keep order and prevent crime.

Most of the believers were, therefore, picked up by the PSB for interrogation. They all gave the same answer for their activities: 'We knew that to dedicate this idol many would throw away their money and waste their energy. We came here to urge them to abandon superstition and turn to the true God ...'

The PSB, seeing that these country folk were simple and sincere and had not broken the law, released them after four days. The brethren praised the Lord loudly and went to another harvest field.

(c) The Fire of the Spirit Burns in the South Shandong Church

In the history of the Chinese church, the church in Shandong once shone like a pearl. God had raised up many servants and handmaidens whom He used greatly. However, since the establishment of the 'Three-Self' movement, the majority of the Shandong churches came under its control. There was strong resistance to influences from outside the church, and Christians from other provinces were not allowed to work in Shandong.

In the spring of 1989, God brought two co-workers from 'C' county of Zhejiang Province to south Shandong. The churches there were originally Presbyterian, so the meetings were very solemn and formal. The believers there had never experienced the work of the Holy Spirit.

When they heard about the meetings that were to be held, the workers from many counties in south Shandong met together to discuss the situation. They asked themselves, 'Should we receive these workers from Zhejiang?'

They decided to 'interview' them before making a decision.

'What is the message that you have prepared to share with us?' was their first question.

The pair from Zhejiang replied earnestly and with a humble attitude, giving an account of the revival that was taking place all over China. They painstakingly detailed the reasons for the revival, emphasizing that it was the work of the Holy Spirit.

Suddenly, a young man stood up and said aloud, 'We need the filling of the Holy Spirit. I have desired this for a long time, but didn't have the courage to say so ...'

He had barely finished when another brother jumped up and declared, 'In my heart I am so bored. The church is boring to death. We must have a revival meeting!'

It was evident that the Lord had begun to move in the hearts of these two men. The co-workers from the different counties later returned to organize a revival meeting to which more than 100 preachers came.

They all arrived the morning of the next day. At six o'clock, through the power and anointing of the Holy Spirit the two brothers from Zhejiang shared on the baptism of the Holy Spirit. They brought out many scriptures and present-day testimonies, and the other preachers were greatly moved.

In the afternoon, they taught on the relationship of praise and the baptism of the Holy Spirit, emphasizing that 'only the dead and those who go to the grave do not praise.'

Although this group of 100-odd co-workers were moved, they still were not entirely open in their hearts. The two brothers prayed most of that night for the meeting the next day.

On the third day, at the early morning prayer meeting, the Zhejiang brothers laid hands on a 13-year-old sister. Suddenly, she stood up and prayed, 'Lord, I ask you to have mercy on us!'

As soon as the words left her lips, the meeting place was shaken and each and every one began to weep loudly, some of them beating their chests and confessing their sins. Many wept bitterly for the lukewarm, backslidden, churches in south Shandong.

That morning, the Zhejiang brothers taught them how to receive the baptism of the Holy Spirit and also on praise and worship. Hallelujah! Ninety percent of them were filled with the Spirit, and began to fervently clap their hands and praise out loud. The whole meeting place was shaken as their shouts were like thunder.

Then an elder who was in charge of a home group stood up and said angrily, 'I have believed for several decades and have never seen such confusion. This is the work of evil spirits.' He left in anger.

On the last day of the Holy Spirit meetings the participants requested the two preachers to lay hands on them. As they did so several people saw a dove hovering above their hands.

One brother had been afflicted with arthritis for many years and was not able to move his hands. The preachers laid hands on him and he was immediately healed. Lifting his hands up high he began to dance and praise God. When it came time for the Zhejiang brothers to return home, they could not bear to let them go. But there was work for them to do in other areas so the Shandong brethren tearfully walked them to the bus station and said their farewells.

Following their departure, the various churches in south

Shandong responded differently to the message of praise and worship, therefore there were differences in their development.

The first situation was where they wholeheartedly accepted praise – that is, in each meeting they put great emphasis on praise and worship.

The second situation was where the church practised a little praise. Though they praised, it was not at all exuberant.

In the third situation, there was no praise at all. As the church leadership became fearful of criticism, they did not dare to praise. These churches, however, were in the minority.

Lastly, there was the situation where praise was totally opposed. There was only one church which opposed praise, and that was led by the elder who walked out of the meeting with the preachers.

Several months later one could clearly see the results of these four attitudes toward praise and worship. The Holy Spirit moved mightily in the churches that practised much praise. The work of evangelism expanded quickly and in several villages even the government officials believed. In one village, the believers grew in a few months to four-fifths of the population. Out of 600 people 400 became Christians.

In the churches that had little praise there was some growth, but not as much. The few churches that kept praise out of their services stagnated and had zero growth. As for the one church that was opposed to praise, the numbers decreased from 90 to 10 old people. The young people all left and joined the churches that were filled with the Spirit.

The believers in south Shandong urgently requested the Zhejiang Christians to return and help them. They gathered before dawn for prayer and faced the south asking the Lord to send His servants back.

Up to the spring of 1991, the churches in 'C' county in Zhejiang Province sent many workers to south Shandong to work. The one elder who was previously opposed to praise and the filling of the Holy Spirit repented before the Lord with tears. He was then filled with the Spirit and began to lead the believers in praise and worship. Therefore great revival came to the church he was leading.

When the brethren arrived in south Shandong in March,

1991, a 22-year-old paralytic was brought to the meeting. He had no parents or relatives and his hair was unkempt, absolutely filthy and smelly. He would continually stare at people and laugh at them.

The brethren laid hands on him and in the name of the Lord commanded the spirit of paralysis to leave the young man. It left at once. The next day, the believers brought a handsome, clean, young man. Nobody recognized him as the paralyzed man who was carried in the day before.

The Lord raised up a team of co-workers in south Shandong who love the Lord fervently. Signs and wonders followed them. Thus, the Gospel spread quickly. Most of the believers were young and they zealously took the Gospel to the surrounding counties and cities.

(d) The Jiangsu Churches Follow the Torrent of Revival

In the winter of 1988, several sisters from Shanghai brought a sick person to 'C' county in Zhejiang Province. They arrived smack in the middle of a revival meeting and witnessed with their own eyes the spiritual atmosphere and power of the Holy Spirit. They greatly desired to have such a revival and pleaded with the brethren to hold similar revival meetings in Shanghai.

During the first half of 1989, therefore, several brethren were invited to preach in the house churches in Shanghai. As one brother was speaking in the power of the Holy Spirit, a sick person who had been afflicted with an illness for 17 years suddenly jumped up and shouted, 'Hallelujah! My sickness is gone. Just now, as I was listening to the preaching, I suddenly felt power surging through me and I stood up. Hallelujah!' This shook the whole meeting place.

As the second brother was speaking, the whole church saw light emanating from him and every single person there was filled with the Holy Spirit.

A Brother Liu from Jiangsu had never seen anything like this in his entire life. He just stood there dumbfounded. Later, he begged the brethren to come to Jiangsu.

So five brethren accompanied Brother Liu to Suzhou. They ministered for three days and many sick people were healed.

One who had been deaf and dumb for eight years began to speak. Many came to the Lord with weeping and repentance, and were baptized in the Holy Spirit. The whole church entered a new level of worship.

Then the sisters from Suzhou led them to 'H' district in Jiangsu and in several large villages preached the Gospel to unbelievers. Several sisters, through their singing and beautiful dancing, were able to lead many men, women, young and old people into praise.

The preachers truly had a great love for the Lord and for lost souls, so whenever they stood up to preach Jesus to the people, tears automatically flowed. Each evening scores of people believed in the Lord.

One evening, they arrived in a village and saw a middle-aged man sitting on a bench. He did not move. Then they noticed that he was listening intently to the preaching. When the meeting ended, he still did not move.

The brethren asked him what was wrong with him. Tearfully, he told them, 'For 13 years my legs have been bleeding without ceasing. I have spent much money, but it's no use. I also lost two fingers. This has brought much suffering to my family.'

The Christians asked him, 'Do you believe Jesus can heal you?'

With tears flowing down his cheeks, he replied with hope, 'I believe.'

The believers then laid hands on him and in the name of the Lord commanded the sickness to leave. The pain left instantly, the abscess on his leg immediately burst and he was healed.

Soon after his healing, it was harvest time and he refused to rest until he had harvested over 10 acres of rice paddy!

The evangelistic team remained in the area for more than 10 days and saw much fruit. They returned home as victorious soldiers returning from battle.

These events sent ripples through the counties neighbouring 'H' county and it caused great alarm among the leaders of the Three-Self Church, who were determined to report their activities to the PSB and have them arrested if they held any more meetings like these.

In July of the same year, at the request of the Zhejiang church, the church in 'C' district sent several brothers and sisters to Suzhou and 'H' district for a baptismal service. The Three-Self authorities found out about it and duly reported to the PSB. They later learnt of the venue where the meeting was to be held and they sent several armed cadres with electric cattle prods and handcuffs to 'H' county.

When the morning meeting ended, the people ate their meal and then left. Only several workers from 'C' county remained. The authorities checked everybody's identification and began to question their reason for coming to that meeting. They wanted to find out if they had been there the first half of the year, since that was when the ministry of these preachers had the greatest impact. They also wanted to know where else they had been, with whom they had contact, and what relationship they had with these people. Led by the Holy Spirit the brethren answered these questions but the authorities were unable to obtain any information.

As the weather was very hot and the authorities were all very hungry, they said, 'Since you don't understand the religious policy, and this is your first time here, we will let you off this time.

'But if you should come here again, we will not be as lenient. You must leave here immediately otherwise you will be arrested.'

The Christians all left.

After the PSB officials left, the co-workers who had gone to eat returned. In the evening, they continued their meeting with praise and prayer. They preached until the next morning.

In February of 1991 three brothers and two sisters went to Shanghai again. There they caught a bus to Hongze County in Jiangsu. At about four in the morning their bus went off the road into a ditch. The driver had been driving too fast in the rain and the road was not the best of roads.

The five believers, who were in the back seats, were jolted upwards and hit their heads hard on the ceiling of the bus and when they came down one brother smashed his ribs on the side of the seat. He turned pale instantly and broke into sweat.

The others called out, 'Stop the bus! Someone has been injured.'

The vehicle came to a stop, and the five of them got off quickly and sat on the roadside, praying and waiting for the dawn. At first, they were very discouraged. This was a ministry trip and the Lord should have protected them, and now they had had this accident.

Then they remembered the words of the Lord, *'It is not in man that walks to direct his steps* (Jeremiah 10:23); *My thoughts are higher than your thoughts and my ways higher than your ways.'*

Then they realized that the Lord did not want them to go to Shandong, for He wanted them to remain in Suzhou, and some great thing would happen there.

After daybreak they hired a rickshaw and took the injured brother to a hospital. An X-ray showed that the fifth and sixth ribs had been broken.

The brethren decided to take him to a neighbouring county to recover from his injury, for there were several believers there. The other four decided to return to Suzhou, but the injured brother did not want to be left behind and pleaded to go with them to Suzhou.

At his insistence they allowed him to accompany them to Suzhou, but first they telephoned the Zhejiang brothers to tell them what happened so they could arrange for other workers to go to Shandong.

What happened next was most amazing. As soon as the bus left the station the injured brother felt less pain. As they continued to praise the Lord on the journey, the pain disappeared completely by the time they reached their destination.

Still, they took him to the hospital and told the doctor what had happened. After careful examination of the X-ray and medical report from the other hospital in the countryside, he said grimly, 'This man is truly foolish. He should have been admitted to hospital immediately.

'He has two broken ribs but he has waited two whole days before seeking medical help. Furthermore, the long ride on the bus could very possibly have caused one of the broken ribs to puncture his lungs.

'I would say your friend is now in critical condition. But I will take another X-ray to see if there is anything more I can do.'

However, the second X-ray showed no fracture in the ribs, not even a hairline crack! The astonished doctor simply shook his head and said, 'A miracle, truly a miracle, a miracle unprecedented in medical history ... !'

The five brethren were filled with praise and thanksgiving to the Lord. They went joyfully to Brother Liu's home.

Now, Brother Liu's wife happened to look out of her front door when she saw them coming. With a squeal of delight, she jumped up and shouted, 'Hallelujah! Amazing! Hallelujah! Amazing!'

She excitedly ushered the bewildered five brothers into her home. They were nonplussed at her behaviour.

After they sat down, Mrs Liu said joyfully, 'For several days I have been expecting you to come and all day today I've been praying fervently for you, and now you have come!'

Puzzled, the men asked, 'What happened?'

It turned out that in a city 200 kilometers away from Suzhou there was a middle-aged woman who had liver cancer and was on the verge of death. Her family were hapless and wept daily. Her daughter, Xiuhong, could not sleep night or day and in desperation sought help everywhere, hoping to find someone to heal her mother.

One day, she went as far as Suzhou in search of her mother's uncle. She had hoped that he could locate a very famous doctor there. However, the doctor refused to see her.

For Xiuhong it was like the end of the road. She just wanted to die. She wandered down a street and stepped into a small shop. It so happened that the shopgirl was a Christian, who shared Jesus with her.

The Gospel of love caused Xiuhong to weep and without hesitation she indicated she would accept Jesus. She then had a request. Could she go home and bring her mother here so that the church could pray for her? This sister consulted with the other co-workers, and they agreed to the plan.

Xiuhong's family scraped together ¥400 RMB and hired a vehicle to transport her mother to a believer's home in Suzhou. The brothers and sisters gathered immediately to pray for the sick woman. Soon, their prayers turned into praises and they sang, danced and clapped their hands for more than two hours.

Afterward, Brother Liu laid hands on her and, in the name of Jesus, commanded the pain to leave her and cursed the cancer. The pain left immediately and Xiuhong's mother announced that she was hungry! Rejoicing, they prepared some food for her.

The driver of the vehicle returned to his home county, full of amazement as he had never seen anything like this in his life!

Xiuhong's family was full of thanksgiving and they invited the Suzhou brethren to preach in their county. Now the people in that district had never heard the Gospel and there were idols of Guanyin (the goddess of mercy) and other idols in every home, for the villagers were a very superstitious people.

However, the Christians in Suzhou did not know what to say. The churches have only just begun to accept the work of the Holy Spirit in Suzhou and there were only a few co-workers. Besides, Brother Liu was not able to go at this time to preach. Therefore, they were fervently praying that the Lord would send His servants from Zhejiang instead. God heard their prayers, therefore He had allowed this bus accident to take place and force the five brothers to change course and head for Suzhou.

Mrs Liu then took her visitors to Xiuhong's home, and they once again prayed for her mother and gave God an offering of praise for the great miracle of healing.

The five co-workers then moved on, and went to another county. They held a meeting in a house church in Suzhou. Among the congregation was a 21-year-old man who had a severe spinal disease and an abnormal bone marrow count. He had spent over ¥20,000 RMB on medical expenses, but was still unable to walk and was bedfast.

That day, the believers carried him to the meeting, where he listened to the preaching from morning until four o'clock in the afternoon. The Word of the Lord was like a healing balm, full of power, and the young man was healed as he received God's Word! The next day, he danced in the meeting giving glory to the Lord.

On the third day, the five Zhejiang brothers, together with six brothers and sisters from Suzhou, Xiuhong and her mother – altogether 14 people – went to Xiuhong's home county.

It was pouring with rain the day they set out. But they all prayed that by the time they reached their destination, the rain would stop. True enough, as soon as they opened the bus door, the rain immediately stopped. By the time all of them got out of the vehicle the sun was already shining!

At the bus station there were also many private vehicles, and standing among them was the driver who had driven Xiuhong's mother to Suzhou. When he saw that Xiuhong's mother had completely recovered, he jumped to his feet and, pointing to her, loudly exclaimed before the crowd, 'This is an amazing miracle, this is an amazing miracle, come and see ...'

Then he proceeded to tell the curious folk who had gathered around him what had happened. The people gave Jesus the thumbs up and said, 'Jesus is amazing. Jesus is truly great.' Soon the drivers from all over the entire province were spreading word of this miracle everywhere.

The driver who shared then insisted that the Christians come to his house that evening to preach Jesus to his family and all the villagers.

But the brethren said, 'Four days ago, we had already sent a telegram to Xiuhong's family. They are now waiting for us. If you really want Jesus come tonight with your whole family to Xiuhong's house.'

The driver promised to come. The 14 of them arrived at Xiuhong's house where a large crowd had already gathered to see her mother come home. Seeing the great change in the old lady's physical state, they were all greatly touched and, weeping, said, 'Jesus is truly great. Thanks be to Jesus. Thanks to you eleven Jesus's from Suzhou.'

The brethren quickly corrected them.

'Countrymen, we are not Jesus. Jesus is in heaven, and we are his servants.'

The crowd then shouted, 'Thanks be to Jesus in heaven and thanks be to the eleven servants of Jesus.'

That evening, Xiuhong's house was packed to the gills with people. The Zhejiang sisters began by leading them in singing choruses, and each and every one sang with gusto and in unison, clapping their hands. When they heard how Jesus loved mankind, they were so moved they all wept.

The driver brought his whole family, and they all repented and believed. The brethren then laid hands and prayed for everyone who had a need. More then 100 people received Christ that night and many were healed. The sound of rejoicing could be heard everywhere.

From that day, many people would come to Xiuhong's house from surrounding villages and even distant counties. They all begged the brethren to go to their villages to preach the Gospel.

However, there were not enough co-workers to meet the needs of so many villages and districts.

But God was at work! An amazing fact was that many people had already removed the idols from their homes, even before hearing the Christians preach. Now, in that area there were idols in almost every household!

The revival was earth-shaking for the authorities, who were greatly alarmed at the 'spiritual upheaval' in many counties throughout Jiangsu Province. Christians and their activities were reported to the authorities. And even up to now, many house churches throughout Jiangsu are facing great persecution.

3. Missionaries from Henan

After the Church received the teaching on the baptism of the Holy Spirit the believers, especially the co-workers, were endued with power from on high. Over the past two years, they have conducted several training conferences. Thus, the believers grew in the knowledge of the Word and became even more eager to take the Gospel to the rest of China. Many testimonies are being reported from many provinces.

(a) The Work in Shaanxi

In 1986, a Sister Liu went to work in a factory in 'A' city in Shaanxi Province. She asked around if there were any Christians. Then she heard that there were some Christians in a village about 60 kilometers from the city. The next day, she started out very early in the morning and headed for that village.

When she got there, she continued asking the villagers where the believers were. To her dismay, she found only three old ladies who were Christians. Nevertheless, she was very excited.

So, together with these three sisters, Sister Liu started a home group. Soon they had more than ten believers. Sister Liu felt she could do with some help, so she wrote to the Henan brethren to send co-workers. A sister was sent to assist her.

The two of them spent much time in prayer for the lost souls in 'A' city. The Lord was with them, even right at the beginning of their ministry, there were signs and wonders following.

A man who had been blind for years received his sight. Many people came from far and near because of this miracle. Some walked up to 19 kilometers at night over mountain trails with their lanterns. Many were sick and the Lord healed them. Thus, the church grew daily.

There was a very beautiful middle-aged woman who had been confined to bed for seven and a half years because of a ligation operation. One day, her mother heard that a woman in the next village who had been ill with tuberculosis for many years had been healed because of her faith in Jesus. So she told her daughter about it.

When her daughter heard the story, she began to call on the Name of the Lord. She began to feel better and was able to get out of bed and walk the next day.

On Sunday, she went to Sister Liu's meeting place where they prayed for her and she was completely healed. She then asked Sister Liu to preach in her village. She accepted the invitation and took her co-worker with her.

As a result of Sister Liu's preaching, many turned to the Lord. A woman who had been blind for eight years received her sight and a widow was set free. The Lord was with them and many were added to their number daily.

When the PSB found out about their activities, they tried to stop the Christians.

Sister Liu and her co-worker then went to a certain county to minister. The people there were very superstitious; they worshipped all kinds of idols. They were really to be pitied!

'These are not gods that you are worshipping,' Sister Liu began. 'They are just idols and they are dead. They cannot save you. I now introduce a true and living God to you. He is the only true God. He is full of love and compassion and only He can save you from sorrow and suffering.' Many responded.

One day, it was raining heavily but Sister Liu preached as usual. Despite the rain, many villagers came to listen, standing in their straw raincoats. After the sermon, Sister Liu prayed for the sick and many people received healing, among them the crippled, who simply stood up and walked.

A fortune-teller in his forties also accepted the Lord after listening to Sister Liu's sermon. He returned home and burned all his books on fortune-telling. He had a tremendous experience in the Lord and the Lord gave him a great burden for souls. Within a year, he led more than 300 people to the Lord. He suffered much persecution, but the Lord helped him to overcome time and time again.

In 1990, the churches around 'A' city in Shaanxi received the baptism in the Holy Spirit. Believers there reached a new depth in praise and worship, and even the older brothers and sisters danced in worship to the Lord. Numerous people were healed while worshipping.

The Gospel flame spread quickly to other counties and many were added to the church daily. In a village in 'X' county, 90 kilometers from 'A' city, there were no Christians two years ago. Today, 60 per cent of the villagers are believers, a fact which made the village head absolutely furious. He would always interrupt the meetings and reprimand them. This made the brethren pray even more fervently for him.

A few months later, the village chief's only son fell ill and the doctor had no diagnosis. Desperate and helpless, he went to the church and sought help. The believers prayed for him and he accepted the Lord. They also prayed for his son and he was healed! The village head became a very zealous Christian and eventually opened his home to the believers.

Four years ago, there were only a few believers in 'A' city but within that time the church there mushroomed. Satan, of course, was not happy so he used all kinds of tactics to attack the church.

First, he worked through cults. Its members would twist the Word of God and cause confusion in the church. Next, Satan used persecution. The government authorities were bent on attacking the church and its members. In May, 1991, six co-workers were arrested. And in the following month, nine more were picked up. At the time of writing (November, 1991) they were still in prison.

Sister Lan's testimony

Shaanxi Province is a big harvest field. The believers prayed that the Lord of the harvest send more labourers. Thus, in December, 1990, Sister Lan from Henan Province arrived with another co-worker in Xian (a major city in Shaanxi).

They came to a certain village where once there were only a few Christians. But because of the fruit of the labour of a brother from Henan a year ago, the church had increased to more than 30 people. Naturally, they faced a lot of pressure from the Three-Self Church. So Sister Lan and her co-worker did not dare to hold public meetings. Instead, they met in small groups with the believers, and encouraged them to be bold and courageous.

Eight of them fasted and prayed for 24 hours, and then they went out to invite people to the meeting that night. Many people came.

Although Sister Lan had only three years of formal schooling, she could preach with boldness and clarity. The meeting went on until eleven o'clock; many people repented and the sick were healed. Lan and her co-worker remained there for ten more days.

Among those who came to listen to Lan's preaching were three sisters from the Three-Self Church. After a few days of the Truth, their eyes were opened. They began to see the light. The three later led other believers out of the Three-Self Church. There were no less than a few hundred people altogether!

A sister from 'X' city in north Shaanxi Province was touched by Lan's preaching too. Her spirit was revived. She beseeched Lan to go to 'X' city with her. After seeking the Lord about it, Lan parted with her co-worker and went with her.

'X' city was a desolate, poverty-stricken place. Lan's heart was moved with compassion. She thought to herself: these people are not just poor materially but they are also poor in their spirits.

One day, a sister came to see Lan with a request for prayer for her brother who had been paralysed for eight years.

Her brother's house was not much of a house. They had barely anything. In the middle of the room was a broken bed with a man lying on it. By the bedside were four bedraggled children, the oldest one only a teenager.

Lan's eyes brimmed with tears and she began to sob, moved by compassion. 'Lord,' she cried, 'You became poor for our sakes so that we may become rich. Have mercy upon this man and his family!'

Then Lan began to witness to him but he was very resistant and stubborn. His sister beseeched him, 'You have absolutely no hope at all! Jesus is your only hope and He can heal you ...'

Lan then decided to tell a true story which took place in Luoyang. There was a young girl who was her parents' only daughter. She left home and went to live with a man in a city. Before long, the man left her for another woman. She was heartbroken and wanted to end her life. So she headed for the river.

On her way, she passed by a crowd gathered around a lamp-post and heard someone reading out loud a notice posted on it: 'My daughter, where are you? Since you left home, we could neither eat nor sleep. We miss you. Your mother's eyes have become swollen from crying. If you still have a heart, please come home as soon as you see this notice. I hope to see you before I die. Come home, my daughter! Come home soon!'

She pressed through the crowd and read the notice herself. It was her father's handwriting and her photograph stared back at her. She began to make her way home.

When she arrived in her hometown, she waited till the evening because she was afraid to be seen. When evening came, she returned home. Her parents were overjoyed to see her. All three wept with joy.

Lan used this to illustrate our heavenly Father's love for us. The man wept and repented. Lan laid hands on him and prayed, and he was healed instantly. He got out of bed, leaping and crying and praising God. He jumped all over the house and then went out to tell his neighbours. Soon, the house was full of curious folk who came to stare at Lan.

Lan lost no time in preaching. 'Dear friends,' she addressed the crowd that had crammed into the house, 'your neighbour who had been paralysed for eight years has been healed and he can walk again. You have seen it with your own eyes.

'This is not sorcery or any kind of gimmick. It is in the Name of Jesus that this man was healed.'

Lan went on to tell them about God's plan of salvation. They all repented and accepted the Lord. The meeting went on until four o'clock in the morning and everybody went home rejoicing!

Even though Lan did not sleep a wink all night, she did not feel sleepy at all. Buoyed with excitement, she kept praising the Lord.

But Lan was stretching herself thin. Overworked and often going without food or sleep, she became very weak. Once she fainted when she arrived at a meeting place. The sisters carried her into a room. When she regained consciousness, they gave her some soup.

Another sister came in and said to Lan, 'Many people have come, are you ready?'

Lan, newly recovered and still very weak, knew that that night's meeting was very important because the Three-Self Church was very influential in that area. The believers did not know the Truth, and even the Three-Self elders and deacons were deceived. She must not miss this opportunity.

She prayed, 'Lord, thank you for bringing so many people here tonight. Strengthen me, anoint me and use me.'

Then she went to the meeting place with a sister. The whole house, including the courtyard, was packed with people. There were four men drinking and smoking in the sitting room.

A sister whispered in Lan's ears, 'You see those four men? One of them is from the PSB, one from the United Front Department, and the other two are pastors of the Three-Self Church.'

Lan thought to herself, 'Lord, I commit myself to You tonight.' All of a sudden, she felt a surge of strength inside her.

The meeting started. The man from the United Front stood up and talked about law and order and religious policies.

'Although there is freedom of belief, you still have to join the Three-Self Church,' he began. 'Otherwise, there is no freedom. Without the permission of the Three-Self Church, nobody is allowed to preach. We will not permit anybody from outside to come here and preach. We will deal with such people severely.'

Afterward, Pastor Chan stood up.

'Tonight, Pastor Wang will preach first. Then we'll ask a sister from Henan to share with us. I've heard that she can cause the paralysed to walk.'

There was a hint of sarcasm. Lan knew that they were hinting at her. So she prayed to the Lord and asked Him to help her.

Then Pastor Wang read John 10:7–8: '*He who does not enter through the gate (he meant the Three-Self Church) are wolves, thieves and robbers; they are the false prophets.*' He spoke for only 20 minutes. Pastor Chan then introduced Lan. 'Now we'll have the sister from Henan who can perform miracles to share with us.'

Sister Lan walked over to the platform. All eyes were on her. 'Is this the woman who caused a paralysed man to walk? What's so special about her?' went the whispers.

Lan preached on Matthew Chapter Two: the Magi looking for Jesus. The Holy Spirit gave her utterance and she spoke with authority.

'Jesus is not in the palace, you can't find Him there. Where is Jesus then? He is in a manger, in a cold stable.

'If you want to find Him, go to Golgotha, to Gethsemane, to Calvary …' She preached for three hours and brought the congregation to Gethsemane, to Golgotha and to Calvary. Their hearts were stirred and many repented and wept.

The two Three-Self pastors wept even more bitterly. They said to the officials from the PSB and the United Front, 'This sister here is a nice woman; she only came here to visit her relatives. We assure you that she did not cause any trouble at all.' So the officials left.

Then the two pastors said to Lan, 'We thank the Lord for sending you to us. He opened our eyes to see the truth and granted us repentance. It was we who reported you to the PSB. They have left now but they may come back tomorrow. We suggest that you leave early tomorrow morning.'

Lan heeded their advice and she boarded a bus early the next morning. As the bus began to move it took Lan a long time to calm down. She thought about the believers there, for they were like sheep without a shepherd. And there were many who had not heard the Gospel yet. Now she is leaving. When would she be back again?

(b) The Work in Sichuan

When one thinks of Sichuan one thinks of people and pandas. This vast province in central China is its most populous, with more than 100 million people or one-tenth of China's total population. With an area of 560,000 square kilometers it boasts more than two hundred counties and cities.

Until recently, there were few believers in this populous province. All the churches were to be found only in the big cities and were controlled by the Three-Self Church. As far as the countryside is concerned, most of the people have never heard of the Gospel. In many places the seed of the Gospel had never been sown and countless numbers die there daily.

The Henan church has a special burden for the work in Sichuan. For many years, they have sent workers to this field that is ripe for harvest. Most of the co-workers are village girls between 16 and 30 years old. There are many difficulties the co-workers face in Sichuan.

1. *Difficult living.* Due to the large population and near famine conditions in certain parts of Sichuan, it is very difficult for the co-workers to have sufficient food. Therefore, most of them always go hungry.

2. *Poor environment.* Persecution and imprisonment are commonplace to the ministers of the Gospel.

3. *Poor transportation.* Mountainous terrain make travelling a challenge since there are no good transportation routes. Therefore, the Christian brothers and sisters have to climb up and down the mountains, and walk a whole day sometimes before reaching a village.

4. *Hindrances from evil men.* Satan hates the sisters who dare to bring the Gospel to Sichuan. They are often harassed by gangsters who threaten, hinder, and even try to rape them. On many occasions these wicked men have even followed them.

Without the protection of the Lord, it is frightening to imagine what could have happened.

5. *Difficult to do pioneer work*. The preachers have to dress up like Sichuan natives before they enter the rural areas. They develop relationships with the people by helping to clean dishes, baby-sit, cut grass or cultivate the field for the villagers.

In spite of the above obstacles, these preachers have overcome the difficulties and dangers with amazing fortitude and faithfulness. They have 'sown with tears and reaped with joy.'

The first Henan preacher to begin an active ministry in Sichuan was Brother Enchuan. The first time he went to Sichuan in 1988, 'X' county was experiencing a famine. He saw many victims and had a great burden to save their souls.

He prayed to the Lord to strengthen him as he preached and ministered for 20 days. Then he baptized those who had repented. There were seventy the first day and 170 the second day. The Lord greatly blessed the work.

He returned to Sichuan during the winter of 1989 and stayed till the spring of 1990. During these three months he spread the Gospel from 'X' county to all the surrounding counties.

Then the following winter, he visited 'X' county for the third time. The congregation had grown larger and larger. Many native women carried their children in baskets and walked 60 kilometers up mountainous roads to the meetings in order to hear the word of God.

The numbers attending the meetings increased so much so that soon the meeting place was inadequate. Then the Lord touched the heart of a primary school teacher who allowed them to use the schoolhouse.

Enchuan led the people in praise and worship and they experienced an explosion of worship. Many sick people were healed, and many repented and believed in Jesus every day.

Later, God raised up many preachers from this village. The Lord's power came upon them and miracles, signs and wonders followed. An old man who had been dead for half a day came back to life when a young sister prayed for him. This miracle caused hundreds to repent and believe in Jesus.

The testimony of Lingmei

In February, 1990, a middle-aged sister who lived in 'B' county in Sichuan brought a Henan sister named Lingmei back to her home. She introduced young Lingmei, who was only 20, to her family as her husband's niece. They all welcomed her.

At meal times, Lingmei would use the opportunity to speak to them about creation and how it was all made by the Almighty God. They loved to hear this message.

However, a brother of the Sichuanese sister was a government cadre who was hoping to be promoted to a higher rank.

'The situation here has been very tense and the government is especially on the lookout for you people from Henan,' he told Lingmei. 'Therefore, you must remain in our home, but do not even consider going out to preach to the neighbours.'

So Lingmei prayed that the Lord would make a way for her. She began to visit neighbouring villages secretly to preach the Gospel. Many believed and knelt down to pray.

Her activities did not go unnoticed, however. The cadre in the family soon found out and he sternly rebuked her and asked her to leave immediately.

Reluctantly, Lingmei agreed but only after asking the Sichuanese sister to take her to other relatives. She decided to bring Lingmei to her sister's house. To get there they had to walk 80 kilometers up the winding mountain roads. This was hard for Lingmei as she was raised on the plain.

They set off early one morning and walked without stopping till they reached their destination that night. Their legs were swollen by then. But God gave Lingmei great love for the people. Even though she was exhausted she preached to eight people and they accepted the Lord.

However, the next day the younger brother of this Sichuan sister sent his mother to speak to Lingmei. The family was greatly opposed to Lingmei openly speaking about Jesus and said that by doing so the future of her son would be destroyed. She told her daughter not to receive Lingmei anymore.

Lingmei began to feel really helpless. The sister who brought her to Sichuan was herself a new believer and could do nothing to help. Unable to hold back the tears, she left the young lambs and this harvest field of multitudes to return to 'X' city in Shanxi with a heavy heart.

Although it seemed like Lingmei lost the first battle, she had already ploughed the ground and sown the seed.

Every time she thought of the young baby Christians she had left behind in those two villages, tears would well up in her eyes. How could she not have a burden for the more than 100 million souls in the poverty-stricken, undeveloped province that is Sichuan?

After attending a co-workers' meeting her faith rose once again and she was revived in the power of the Holy Spirit. Thus encouraged in the Lord, she took a 17-year-old sister with her this time and returned to Sichuan.

They had planned to go to 'B' county to visit the new believers, but due to rampant cases of kidnapping in the area it was difficult for outsiders to be granted permission to enter. So, they went to 'J' county instead.

The first night, several dozen villagers came to listen to the Gospel. They were very hungry for the Word and all accepted Christ. The two sisters remained there for three days teaching and preaching Jesus, and the whole village stopped work to come and listen to them.

Eventually, the entire village of more than 80 people knelt in prayer. Among them was a 16-year-old girl who was so touched by the Spirit that she left school and dedicated herself to the Lord. She begged the two sisters to take her along so that she could learn how to preach the Gospel.

From there, they went to a village in 'E' county. They told the story of Noah and the ark and how the last days would be as the days of Noah. Weeping, they pleaded with the people to repent of their sins and idolatry and to turn to almighty God.

After the message, all the villagers wept and accepted Jesus. The evangelists ministered for seven days. Not one who heard the Gospel rejected it. In the end, more than one hundred people knelt down to pray.

The sisters then selected a group of people who fervently loved the Lord and who were educated. These were taught how to conduct Bible studies, lead prayer and a Sunday worship service, build up the church and conduct different types of meetings.

Once a church was planted there the Gospel quickly spread to the neighbouring villages.

One night at 11 o'clock, Lingmei and her co-worker were kneeling in prayer together when six to seven rough-looking men burst into the house.

They were taken by force and brought before the village officials who interrogated them.

'Where are you from?

'What are you doing here?

'Do you have identity cards?

'Do you have relatives here?'

But the Lord strengthened His servants and gave them the right words and courage to answer in such a way that the officials had no charge to pin on them.

The next morning, many of the villagers gathered at the local government to seek the release of the two sisters. One of them was a well-known gangster in that area. He had caused no end of trouble with his drinking, gambling and fighting. Even the cadres could not handle him.

But that was all history now. A few days before, this thug had heard the Gospel, repented and accepted the Lord. That morning, he spoke up boldly.

'Why is it you were not able to control me when I used to get drunk, fight and gamble? Now these two nieces have come to urge me to repent and teach me to be a new man. I have done so. Now what kind of perverted justice is this that you would arrest these two?'

All the villagers chorused in agreement.

The cadres had nothing to say but to release the two sisters.

This trial increased the faith of the believers, and strengthened the church. They lifted their praises to the Lord.

Lingmei and her co-worker proceeded to 'K' county to contact the relatives of the brethren. An old lady who saw them coming began to prostrate on the ground, thinking they were goddesses from heaven.

Lingmei pulled her to her feet and rebuked her. 'Mother, you must not do this. I am not a goddess, but an ordinary person. Goddesses are false gods and cheats and you must never worship them again.

'I came especially to introduce you to the God who created heaven and earth, all things, the merciful true God. Only He can save you and give you eternal life.'

A crowd soon gathered. The sisters took turns to explain to the people about creation, the fall of Man, God's way of salvation and the coming of the Lord, the resurrection, judgment and so on.

These simple country folk who were afflicted, poverty stricken and without hope in the world had never heard such good news. They hungered and thirsted for the Truth. Listening intently, they could not take their eyes off the sisters and were not interested in returning home for their evening meal.

The Holy Spirit was in their midst and wooed the tender hearted. The two sisters rejoiced and praised His Name, giving Him the glory.

The sisters covered several dozen villages in several months, preaching the Gospel to thousands of people. When they left Sichuan they left more than ten new meeting points, some large and some small.

They remembered how the first Protestant missionary to China, Robert Morrison, preached for seven years and won only one convert.

They said, 'We are two very insignificant, simple, unlearned farmer's daughters. But within three short months so many people have repented and believed in Jesus.

'This is totally due to the work of the Holy Spirit and the amazing provision of the Lord. This proves that we are near to the Lord's return, for He wants to add to the numbers of those who are to be saved. He has already prepared the hearts of the people. All we need is to send forth more labourers to sow the seed and reap the harvest.'

The sisters left Sichuan to prepare for a new ministry.

The church in Henan realized that there were more than two hundred major cities and counties in Sichuan, all teeming with people. Even if a few persons spent their entire lives preaching the Gospel there, they would probably be able to reach only a small area of these districts, let alone the whole province. Therefore, the Henan church sent out many missionaries, most of them women.

There was a remote village in 'N' county which was steeped in superstition. Every household boasts not one but many idols. Each villager even carried an idol on his body.

About 500 families lived in this village, which had a population of more than 2,000. The village folk were very much
against Christianity as they were told, 'If anyone here believes
in Jesus, he can be put to death and nobody will be held
responsible.'

It had been reported that several preachers had previously
'disappeared' in this area.

In 1987, when several Henan preachers went there to preach
they were beaten half to death. Even so, they were not discouraged. The Henan co-workers had an even greater burden
for this area and felt a tremendous responsibility for the many
souls here.

The following year, several young brothers and sisters went
to this village and God performed many wonders and miracles
through them. God opened blind eyes and deaf ears. A villager
was healed of liver cancer. These were just a few of the many
miracles.

God used His Mighty hand to destroy Satan's stronghold of
many years. Almost the entire village eventually repented and
accepted Jesus as Saviour and Lord. After coming to the Lord,
they truly regretted rejecting the Gospel for so long. They
returned home and burnt and destroyed all their idols with a
vengeance.

It was fascinating to see how they conducted an 'open court'.
First, they collected all the idols from the temple, took those off
their necks and threw every one of them into a big pile in a
public square.

Many villagers then stood on the judgment bench and
accused the idols of crimes. Some of them screamed at the large
idols, 'You rotten thing! I was deceived by you for decades.
Half the money that my family earned through hard labour was
eaten by you in offerings.'

Others would hit the head of the idols violently and cry out
in tears, 'I had only one daughter and gave her to you to take
care of daily. I gave you incense and money. Why didn't you
take care of her? Now my daughter has died of sickness!'

Finally, they sentenced the idols to death and carried out the
sentence immediately:

Wooden idols were chopped up with an axe and burned.

Clay ones were taken to the river for a 'bath'. Idols made of metal were put in a furnace to be melted in high temperatures.

Stone idols were smashed to pieces and not one large stone was left behind, while other idols were taken care of in different ways.

At the end of the 'open trial,' the people were so joyful that they danced, shouted and sang. The sound of praise reverberated throughout the mountains and villages.

In 1989, Xiaolu and Xiaoping were sent to Sichuan. Before they embarked on their journey, they prayed that the Lord would give them sufficient faith as they knew they would face many trials and there were many ruffians.

When they arrived in 'F' county, they found it difficult to communicate with the local folk because they spoke a completely different dialect which they could not understand. Therefore, they went on a two-day fast.

Then they went on to another place and, along the way, they sang choruses without stopping. Their joyous singing first attracted a group of children. Later, other villagers swarmed around them, as though drawn by a magnet.

Xiaolu seized the opportunity to tell them how Jesus came to save sinners. They were all amazed at her eloquent speech since she, too, was a village girl.

When Xiaolu shared about the pain Jesus bore on the cross for all mankind, everyone wept. Then they all knelt down to pray and more than forty simple country folk were baptized in the name of Jesus.

The zealous evangelists preached anywhere and everywhere and to anything that moved! Whether they shared with individuals or to crowds they bore much fruit. Almost every person who heard them preach received Christ.

One day, they came by an old man at the roadside and began to share the Good News with him. Curious passersby would stop to listen in on the conversation. Before long, some thirty people believed in Jesus!

Xiaolu and Xiaoping determined to fast and pray for 24 hours once a week for the work of the Gospel in Sichuan. The Lord greatly blessed them and signs and miracles followed them.

Whether it was an issue of blood, a withered hand, heart disease or an inflamed gallbladder, the afflicted were all instantly healed and the name of the Lord was glorified.

During the winter of 1990, Xiaolu made a trip to 'G' county in Sichuan with two believers, a brother and a sister surnamed Yang, to visit their aged father who had been paralyzed for three years. He had spent much money on doctors, but his condition remained the same.

Xiaolu told the old father and the people who had come to visit him about the grace of Jesus.

'If you believe,' she said, 'not only will you be healed, but you can enter heaven and enjoy eternal joy.'

She laid hands on Old Yang, but due to his lack of faith nothing happened. Everyone simply shook their heads.

Xiaolu knew that this man's healing would be a key to the Gospel being preached in that village. She decided to fast and pray for four days on the mountain.

On the fourth night, she returned to the village and laid hands again on Old Yang. With the help of his daughter, they lifted him up from the bed and in the name of Jesus commanded him to start walking and to praise the Lord.

Suddenly, Old Yang felt power coursing through his body and he began to shout, 'Hallelujah!' without ceasing. He tossed his walking stick aside and pushed the two women away from him.

'Hallelujah! I can walk!' he cried excitedly.

Then he dashed out to the courtyard and ran around it twice. Overwhelmed with joy, he ran to the village and shouted emotionally, 'I can walk! All of you come and see!'

Villagers, young and old, spilled out of their homes upon hearing the commotion. Many old folk knelt before Xiaolu reverently.

'Great god, how amazing you are. We were previously deceived by false gods!' they cried.

But Xiaolu stopped them and told them it was Jesus who healed Old Yang. After this no one dared shake their heads in unbelief.

The news spread like wildfire. A day later, all the neighbouring villages heard about the miracle. Soon, all the village folk were streaming towards Yang's village, walking as fast as their legs could carry them. They were hoping to be the first to bring those who were demon-possessed and sick. Many were healed but the most precious gift they received was eternal life in Jesus Christ.

Another day went by, and the news reached some forty to fifty villages 100 kilometers away. People kept coming, crowding into Old Yang's house and spilling into the courtyard, overflowing the road to the village.

It was impossible to count how many people were saved. The sick were healed and the demon-possessed received deliverance. A villager who had leukemia was healed. A deaf and dumb boy spoke for the first time in his life as he and his mother were prayed for. Everywhere there was rejoicing as 'hallelujahs' echoed through the village.

There were so many miracles of healing that it caused panic among the doctors and pharmacy workers. The doctors brought a lawsuit against Xiaolu, charging her with deceiving many people and claiming that if no one stopped her there would be tragic consequences.

The county officials were also in a flurry of panic and they quickly despatched a group of PSB men and officials from the United Front Department to Old Yang's village.

Xiaolu was taken to the nearest district office for interrogation. Before long, Old Yang and all the villagers who had been healed by Jesus also descended on the district office. They testified before the officials about how God healed them from sickness and pain. The communists were stumped. Fearful of incurring the wrath of the people, they decided they had better free Xiaolu. But not before warning her to leave town by morning.

The next day, Xiaolu reluctantly left Old Yang's village. All the brethren wept bitterly, many of them swollen-eyed. As she boarded the bus the believers clung to her tightly.

(c) The Work in the North-East of China

For years, the Gospel has been preached in northeast China. In 1953, however, false teachers effectively destroyed the church that had been planted there and since then there has been little growth.

Then for a while things appeared to improve, that is, until the 'Three-Self' Patriotic Movement came into the picture. There has been no revival until fairly recently.

In 1988, an old Henan sister when to 'M' city in the northeast to visit her son. She planted the seed of the Gospel during that visit.

In October the following year, two brothers and one sister from Henan arrived in 'M' city, which is a newly developed, industrial city. Its residents were mostly labourers and they came from different provinces in China.

The Henan team had been sent there to take over the work that an older sister had started.

Believers in Jesus were as rare as phoenix feathers and unicorn horns, as one Chinese idiom goes. Although the city boasts a substantial population, the people worshipped 152 minks and wolves as gods, something that was hard to understand.

The Holy Spirit anointed the three co-workers and the Lord was with them. Many were saved. A deaf young man who could only hear faint sounds with a hearing aid, was prayed for and totally healed. There were countless miracles of healing.

One evening, many university students went to the meetings. They witnessed with their own eyes the supernatural power of God and were awe-struck. All the years of education they had received went out the window, as it were. They humbly knelt before the Lord to receive new life.

As news spread, the curious and inquisitive came by the numbers. Hallelujah! The Lord has found a people for Himself in this city. The Church was thus established.

It turned out to be a blessing that most of the city's residents were not native-born but come from all over the nation. So, after receiving God's grace they could hardly wait to return to their hometowns with the Gospel to share with their family, relatives and neighbours.

The Macedonian call was coming from every corner of the nation. The Henan churches have responded by sending workers to the field every year.

In September, 1990, two brethren went to 'M' city to conduct training sessions for the workers to teach them to lead their own churches. Through in-depth Bible study they clarified the differences between the work of the Holy Spirit and that of evil spirits.

The majority of the co-workers received the teaching on baptism of the Holy Spirit. Praise and worship was intense in all the meetings. Backslidden and lukewarm believers were revived and daily many were saved.

In January, 1990, two young sisters were called to do the work of training and equipping the workers. They went to several large cities and many villages.

But, unused to the cold weather up in the northeast, the girls soon had cold sores erupting all over their bodies. They went through howling sandstorms which stung their eyes. It was only because of their love for the Lord and their compassion for lost souls that they stuck it out for three months.

Empowered by the Holy Spirit, they dealt with hidden sin and division in the churches. The churches in several cities thus went through a period of cleansing and had unity of the Spirit once again. This brought great impetus to the Gospel work in northeast China.

How lovely were the feet of those who preached the Gospel in northeast China! When they left the church in 'M' city the brethren begged them to return soon.

(d) The Work in Hunan

We have seen thus far the superstition, utter poverty and backwardness in Shaanxi, Sichuan, and the northeastern provinces. Many Chinese are idol worshippers and Satan has broken up many families.

It was no different in Hunan Province. The multitude of idols that the Hunanese worshipped were more than one could count. Sin was rampant.

The Henan churches began to send labourers to Hunan. Their first candidate was Brother Chan, who ministered in a village for only a few days and saw more than 60 true believers baptized in water. Two sisters were sent to assist him. Their ministry there was rich with testimonies of miracles.

A man suffering from a brain tumour was given up for dead by the hospital authorities. They simply told him it was hopeless and that he would soon die. But neighbours and friends carried the man to one of the meetings conducted by the Henan brethren. He was in dreadful pain.

The two sisters simply laid hands on him and prayed, and he was immediately healed! Because of this miracle, many more people accepted Christ and 300 received water baptism in the next baptismal service.

A local believer later arranged for the two Henan sisters to preach at the local Three-Self church. The congregation was greatly inspired by the message but the person in charge of the church was fraught with fear. So he ordered the sisters to leave at once.

(e) The Work in Anhui

Anhui is one province that is saturated with Christians. This is especially true in the northern part where the number of believers in many districts has reached 100,000.

Previously, the church was hindered by lack of teaching and denominational differences. Then cults sprung up. Moreover, the majority of the believers were under the control of the Three-Self Church.

Anhui borders Zhejiang and Henan provinces. In 1988, co-workers from Shanghai city and Zhejiang went to Anhui to minister. However, the Henan missionaries had an established work in Anhui and there was already revival in the northern part of this province.

In the fall of 1990, a middle-aged Henan sister set off for north Anhui. It was her sixth trip there. She began preaching in 'P' district and one evening a believer was convicted by the presence of the Holy Spirit at the meeting. She began to weep bitterly and confess her sins.

The spirit of repentance was so great that several other co-workers also confessed their sins with much weeping.

The repentant sister had been very arrogant and had done great damage to the church, which was going through a difficult phase at that time with an impending split. But the Lord used the Henan sister to bring healing.

Next, she went to 'R' county and about 400 to 500 people attended the meetings. The Holy Spirit moved mightily. But envious Three-Self church leaders reported to the PSB.

Thus, in the middle of a Saturday afternoon meeting, more than a dozen PSB men rushed into the meeting place. A 17-year-old sister who was leading the worship was taken away together with the Henan evangelist. They were both interrogated and beaten. But the worship leader infuriated her interrogators by answering all their questions with praise choruses.

The Henan sister was locked up in a detention centre. She cast her eyes over her fellow inmates and saw women with dishevelled hair, in pain and without hope, and her heart was greatly burdened.

'These people are not only suffering in the flesh, but they will be judged one day and they shall receive everlasting punishment,' she told herself.

She began her work behind bars by teaching them some songs. These singing sessions were like shafts of light in their filthy, dark hearts. Eyes full of pain and despair began to shine with life. They heard about God's love and seven of them repented.

But there were obstacles. One of the inmates, a bad-tempered kidnapper, hindered the prisoners from accepting the Gospel. She was the supervisor of the cell and made reports to the authorities about their activities.

The Henan sister fasted and prayed for her. Three days later, the supervisor developed such a terrible headache that she began to hit her head on the floor in desperation. Finally, she asked the Henan sister to pray for her.

She asked the supervisor, 'Do you believe?'

'From now I will firmly believe.'

The sister laid hands on her and she was set free in less than three minutes. She was so happy that she began to dance and praise the Lord. Within two weeks, 14 more prisoners became Christians.

After her release from prison, the Henan missionary returned again to north Anhui and met with the co-workers from three counties. They were greatly encouraged.

It had been a while since the churches in north Anhui had a baptismal service. Due to the revival, however, there were numerous requests for water baptism.

But the local pastor smoked, drank and was a bad witness.

The brethren certainly did not want him to be responsible for this sacred work, so they invited Brother Jian from Henan to baptize the new converts.

When he learnt of this, the local pastor became jealous and caused trouble. He tried to interfere by telling Brother Jian, 'If you are to baptize here, you must submit to these three conditions:

1. 'You must write a guarantee that if anyone is made sick through baptism, you will be held totally responsible.

2. 'You must have an introductory letter from the Three-Self Church.

3. 'It is winter and the weather is freezing cold. You absolutely are not allowed to baptize in the river. You can only baptize in warm water in the bath house.'

The brethren, however, were of one heart. They summoned up courage and told the pastor, 'We will be responsible for everything. This has nothing to do with the Henan brother.'

The Christians made their way to the riverside. Many believers, fearing persecution and the freezing water, were afraid to step into the river. Only 20 brave believers received baptism that night.

Among them was a sister who, due to a sickness she had contracted after childbirth, was very fearful of the cold water. But she came out of the waters of baptism completely healed which greatly amazed her husband.

The next day he, too, wanted to be baptized along with 40 others. The third day more than 100 were baptized.

The most dramatic testimony was that of a crippled man who was carried into the river but after baptism ran out from the water! Even more came to be baptized the fourth day.

There was more work for Brother Jian in another county so he went there to baptize more believers. It was snowing heavily then. When the PSB heard that there was to be a baptism in the icy river, it sent its agents to look for the Christians. But the Lord's hand was upon them and more than 100 people were baptized without incident.

There was a mute who came out of the water praising the Lord.

There have been countless miracles and wonders that have

taken place in the waters of baptism in Anhui and other parts of China we cannot record them all! We simply shared two examples here to show how God has being doing marvelous things during these several years in China.

In China in the 90s more and more believers are coming out of the Three-Self Church, and the house churches in over 10 counties have a close network with more than 1,000 meeting points. The majority of the believers and co-workers have experienced the baptism of the Holy Spirit and there is a strong emphasis on praise and worship in their meetings.

4. A Beautiful Plan

In the Spring of 1991, a faithful servant who had been greatly used by God entered Henan to conduct a one-week training seminar for co-workers. At the close of the seminar he laid hands on every co-worker and blessed them.

Several scores of co-workers were thus thrust out into the harvest field to preach the Gospel of Jesus Christ in the different provinces and continue to sow seed.

They began in Henan and branched out to the different provinces pioneering churches. This included Sichuan, distant Xinjiang, Tibet and Beijing.

The path before them is rough and stony, with many difficulties, the way of the cross. But they know the Lord is with them. As they sow in tears they will reap with joy, bringing their sheaves with them (Psalm 126:5–6).

Once, a co-worker was spreading out a map of China when he saw a clear vision: The ministry of Henan will not only extend into Hunan, Hubei, Anhui, Hebei, Beijing, Manchuria, Shanxi, Shaanxi, Sichuan but will also penetrate Gansu, Xinjiang and areas bordering Afghanistan.

There will be missionaries from China crossing the western frontier into Afghanistan, Iran, Iraq, Syria and, eventually, Israel!

The other part of the vision showed another mission force moving from Zhejiang into Shandong, Jiangsu, Fujian and other coastal provinces and taking the Gospel across the seas to achieve the same goal.

The vision lies before the Chinese believers. What a beautiful blueprint!

God's love is so wide and deep. He will not forget the 1.2 billion Chinese people. His purposes for China will be fulfilled through his unlimited wisdom and power. He will complete His work that He began!

> *O the depth of the riches both of the wisdom and knowledge of God! How unsearchable are his judgments, and his ways past finding out!*   Romans 11:33